D1527987

Practical Rationality and Preference

What are preferences? Are they reasons for action? Is it rational to cooperate with others even when that means acting against one's preferences?

A prominent position in philosophy on the topic of practical rationality is that it is rational to act so as to maximize the satisfaction of one's preferences. This view is closely associated with the work of David Gauthier, and in this new collection of essays some of the most innovative philosophers currently working in this field explore the controversies surrounding Gauthier's position. Several essays argue against influential conceptions of preference, while others suggest that received conceptions of rational action misidentify the normative significance of rules and practices.

This collection will be of particular interest to moral philosophers, social theorists, and reflective social scientists in such fields as economics, political science, and psychology.

Christopher W. Morris is Professor of Philosophy at Bowling Green State University.

Arthur Ripstein is Professor of Law and Philosophy at the University of Toronto.

Practical Rationality and Preference

Essays for David Gauthier

Edited by

CHRISTOPHER W. MORRIS
Bowling Green State University

ARTHUR RIPSTEIN
University of Toronto

CAMBRIDGE
UNIVERSITY PRESS

PUBLISHED BY THE PRESS SYNDICATE OF THE UNIVERSITY OF CAMBRIDGE
The Pitt Building, Trumpington Street, Cambridge, United Kingdom

CAMBRIDGE UNIVERSITY PRESS
The Edinburgh Building, Cambridge CB2 2RU, UK
40 West 20th Street, New York, NY 10011-4211, USA
10 Stamford Road, Oakleigh, VIC 3166, Australia
Ruiz de Alarcón 13, 28014 Madrid, Spain
Dock House, The Waterfront, Cape Town 8001, South Africa

http://www.cambridge.org

© Cambridge University Press 2001

First published 2001

Printed in the United States of America

Typeface Times Roman 10/12 pt.   *System* DeskTopPro$_{/UX}$ [BV]

A catalog record for this book is available from the British Library.

Library of Congress Cataloging in Publication Data

Practical rationality and preference : essays for David Gauthier / edited by Christopher
W. Morris, Arthur Ripstein.
    p. cm.
Includes bibliographical references.
ISBN 0-521-78184-1
    1. Practical reason. 2. Preferences (Philosophy). 3. Gauthier, David P.
I. Morris, Christopher W. II. Ripstein, Arthur.

BC177.P734 2001
128'.33–dc21   2001025036

ISBN 0 521 78184 1 hardback

Contents

Contributors

Robert Brandom, Distinguished Service Professor, University of Pittsburgh

John Broome, White's Professor of Moral Philosophy, Oxford University

Peter Danielson, Mary and Maurice Young Professor of Applied Ethics, University of British Columbia

Claire Finkelstein, Professor of Law, University of Pennsylvania Law School

Edward F. McClennen, Centennial Professor of Philosophy, London School of Economics and Political Science

Christopher W. Morris, Professor of Philosophy, Bowling Green State University

Adam Morton, Professor of Philosophy, University of Bristol

Derek Parfit, Fellow of All Souls, Oxford University

Arthur Ripstein, Professor of Law and Philosophy, University of Toronto

Michael Thompson, Associate Professor of Philosophy, University of Pittsburgh

Candace Vogler, Associate Professor of Philosophy, University of Chicago

Practical Reason and Preference

CHRISTOPHER W. MORRIS AND ARTHUR RIPSTEIN

The traditional theory of rational choice begins with a series of simple and compelling ideas. One acts rationally insofar as one acts effectively to achieve one's ends given one's beliefs. In order to do so, those ends and beliefs must satisfy certain simple and intuitively plausible conditions: For instance, the rational agent's ends must be ordered in a ranking that is both complete and transitive, and his or her beliefs must assign probabilities to states of affairs relevant to the achievement of those ends. The requirement of completeness ensures that all alternatives will be comparable; the transitivity condition ensures that at least one alternative will be ranked ahead of the others in each situation. If the completeness condition is violated, the agent will not always be able to compare alternatives and consequently to make a choice. If transitivity is violated, a situation may arise in which the agent will be unable to achieve his or her ends because for any alternative there will be another that will be preferred to it. On the belief side, there are similar requirements of completeness and consistency: An incomplete ordering of beliefs might recommend no action at all, and inconsistent beliefs might recommend incompatible courses of action. Provided that the constraints are satisfied, whenever the opportunity to make a decision presents itself, the rational agent will choose the course of action that will be most likely to achieve his or her ends. Preferences and beliefs both enter into that evaluation: A highly valued outcome whose probability of achievement is low may be ranked lower than a less valued outcome that enjoys a higher probability of success. Once preferences and probabilities are fixed, the rational agent acts in the way that will directly maximize his or her expected payoff.

The theory treats reason as an instrument for achieving one's ends, whatever those ends may be, or so it is usually interpreted. Formal treatments often work with monetary examples, sometimes creating the impression that the theory is committed to some conception of self-interest or, worse, that it must put monetary values on alternatives. But although the interests with which the theory works are always the interests *of* a self, they need not be interest *in* oneself. Persons concerned to promote the interests of others or to set up just and equitable social institutions also have reasons to pursue those ends based on their estimates of their importance and the probabilities for various means of achieving them.

The forward-looking nature of the theory requires that it judge possible courses of action on the basis of their expected consequences. Past actions may provide grounds for expectations about what others will do in the future, but they cannot provide grounds for preferring one alternative to another, as the past cannot be changed. Importantly, this forward-looking focus seems to require one to treat all commitments as irrational or empty. Commitments are backward-looking and also require one to make decisions on the basis of general rules or principles, thus ignoring the specific consequences of particular acts. From the standpoint of the traditional theory, any such commitments either will be redundant, recommending the same course of action that forward-looking rationality recommends, or else will be contrary to reason, recommending a different one.

The hostility of the traditional theory to commitment gives rise to two distinct sets of problems. One set is internal to the theory itself: In a variety of familiar situations involving a plurality of interacting persons, the direct pursuit of one's ends makes cooperation impossible and thus seems in some sense self-defeating. The best-known example is the infamous prisoner's dilemma. In the original tale, two prisoners have been caught committing a crime, and each faces a short jail term, but each is offered a chance to further reduce his or her sentence by testifying against the other. If both remain silent, both will face the short jail term, but each can see that whatever the other does, he or she will do better by confessing. If the other remains silent, confessing will lead to no prison sentence; if the other confesses, doing the same will be the best option. Each thus has an incentive to confess, and the result will be that if both confess, both will spend more time in prison. The example supposes that each is concerned only to minimize his or her own prison time, but the underlying problem is structural, rather than one of selfishness as such. For example, parents concerned to provide for their children, or to protect them from automobile accidents, may find themselves facing a similar structure of incentives. A number of parents might choose to buy larger and larger cars in anticipation of other parents, equally concerned for the welfare of their children, driving larger cars. Each can see the advantages of driving a larger car, whatever others do, so all choose to drive larger cars, thus providing their children with protection from an increasing peril that is itself simply the result of each parent's attempt to protect his or her children. All would be better off if all could commit to small cars. But none can commit. Economic exchange often has the structure, at least on the surface, of a prisoner's dilemma.

The obvious solution in these situations is for agents to make some sort of agreement in anticipation of the situation. The difficulty, of course, is that the keeping of the agreement is subject to the same incentives, and so although all parties can see the clear advantages of making such an agreement, they will have incentives to defect from it, and consequently the agreement will be unstable. Thus all will end up worse off because of their inability to honour commitments or to abide by mutually beneficial agreements. Another possible solution for similar problems is the recognition of an authoritative decision-maker, someone whose directives are reasons for action and who could thus enable agents to cooperate on mutually beneficial outcomes. But again the problem reappears: Agents have incentives to disregard the allegedly authoritative directives and directly to select the individually most advantageous course of action.

The other obvious solution is coercive: to empower some person or agency to intervene so as to change the incentive structure (for instance, by imposing sanctions for defection), so that all will act in ways that will not be collectively self-defeating after all. In the context of the prisoner's dilemma, members of a criminal group might execute those of their number who testify for the state; in the parent's dilemma, the escalation might be halted by taxing larger vehicles. The difficulty with the coercive solution is not that it is impossible – as the examples suggest, such solutions are used all the time – but that it is wasteful, because it requires the expenditure of additional resources to get people to do what it is in their own interest to do anyway.

The second problem is related, but is, strictly speaking, external to the theory. This time the problem is that the making and keeping of commitments appear to be rational processes, not, perhaps, in the sense that is required by the traditional theory, but in the sense that it makes sense to stand back from particular agreements and evaluate them. In our earlier examples, the commitments that proved impossible to keep involved cooperation with others, but the external problem arises for a broader range of commitments. It is not uncommon to have the thought that one should not have agreed to something, or should have sought more favourable terms for something to which one did agree. Nor is it uncommon to regret one's failure to stick by a commitment one has made, even if one does not doubt that acting contrary to it was, at the time, the best way to secure one's ends. The straightforward or direct maximizer of orthodox rational choice theory cannot have such thoughts, for such an agent does not regard any commitments as binding. Yet the familiarity of such thoughts, and the way in which they are disciplined by considerations about the consequences of competing courses of action, should give us pause, for the traditional theory treats all commitments as alike, and none of them as rational, in ways that ordinary reasoning about them suggests they are not.

Among his many contributions to moral and political philosophy, David Gauthier has made two signal contributions to the debate about practical rationality and to the concerns we have raised. First, he has clarified the

concept of a preference, thus giving further specificity to the idea that preferences should be well ordered. The traditional theory of rational choice
developed both as an explanatory theory and as a normative theory. The
explanatory theory, at the heart of neoclassical economics, showed that the
assumption of individual rationality could be used to model a wide range of
economic behaviours. By viewing agents as maximizing their own utility,
their behaviours in markets and the behaviour of those markets can be rendered orderly and, to some extent, predictable. Such modelling makes it
possible to read a person's preferences off of his or her choice behaviour. As
a normative theory, rational choice involves advising people about their best
courses of action, given their beliefs and preferences. The two roles for a
single theory lead to a tension between them: The explanatory model reads
preferences off of behaviour by assuming that agents are rational, while the
normative theory takes preferences as its starting point and asks what reason
demands, without supposing that the agent will live up to those demands. To
render them consistent, preferences must be defined independently of choice
behaviour, but must remain subjective in an appropriate sense. For Gauthier,
to behave rationally is not just to do what one is disposed to do. Nor is it to
possess a well-ordered set of preferences. Instead, rational action maximizes
the expected satisfaction of expressed and revealed preferences. To the extent
that these two dimensions of preference diverge, rationality cannot give consistent advice. Gauthier's key idea is that reason demands the satisfaction of
preferences for which attitudinal and behavioural dispositions converge.

Gauthier's revisionist account of the nature of preference provides the first
piece in his well-known account of the rationality of commitment. Separating
rationality from choice behaviour makes room for a distinction between cases
in which an agent has behaved contrary to reason and those in which his
rationality has remained intact but his preferences have changed. Reason is
demanding enough to require a choice contrary to the disposition to choose
differently. Rational commitment requires that reason be unyielding in the
face of temptation.

Gauthier's central contribution to the theory of rational choice comes with
his account of the rationality of commitment. The central idea is straightforward and elegant: The formal theory of rational choice can operate not only
on the choice of action but also on the consideration of dispositions or
principles of action. The rational agent thus has reasons, traceable ultimately
to his or her own preferences, to adopt a disposition or principle to behave
cooperatively and to keep the commitments he or she has reason to undertake.
The agent has those reasons because, as the prisoner's dilemma illustrates,
the ability to undertake and to keep commitments has advantages in terms of
whatever ends an agent might have. The advantages are available only to
beings who are able to disregard competing incentives and so to honour the

commitments they have undertaken. The rational agent can appreciate the advantages of being that kind of agent and, in light of them, decide to adopt the appropriate disposition or principle. The decision to adopt a particular disposition affects a broader range of future behaviours than, for example, the decision whether or not to confess to a crime or the decision to purchase a particular automobile. But the choice is forced in the same way that other decisions are: Once a rational agent is aware of the structures of interaction in which commitment is advantageous, that agent cannot decide to forgo the choice of dispositions or principles. To do so would be irrational, for it would be to adopt a course of action with a lower expected payoff than another course that is available.

At the same time, as the dilemmas of parents and prisoners also show, the disposition to cooperate is not always advantageous. It is only when cooperating with others who have similar dispositions or principles that advantage can be had. Otherwise, those who keep agreements open themselves up to exploitation. Gauthier's solution to this problem rests on an idea that is familiar from ordinary life, though difficult to reconstruct in the traditional vocabulary of rational choice: People are capable of discriminating between fellow cooperators and potential exploiters, and they are also quite good at deciding which other people to trust.[1] (Con-artists provide only an apparent exception. They often can exploit trusting people, but their opportunities arise only because most people are trustworthy, and so most people do well by being trusting.) Indeed, Gauthier's account shows the rationality of developing and exercising those discriminating abilities. The capacity to distinguish cooperators from exploiters is useful to the extent that one is capable of entering into mutually advantageous cooperative relations with others; mutually advantageous cooperation is possible for rational agents only if they have that ability. It seems, then, that people can make and keep commitments without external incentives to compliance. The question is how to understand this capacity.

This disposition to cooperate is not a generic disposition to commit to any course of action that offers some advantages as against non-cooperation. Instead, according to Gauthier, it is a narrower disposition to cooperate only on terms that are fair. The basic idea is, again, simple and elegant: The rational agent choosing which disposition or principle to adopt will enter into all and only those cooperative arrangements that will yield fair and mutually advantageous outcomes. Any broader disposition would open one up to exploitation by those with narrower dispositions, and any narrower disposition would turn one into an identifiable exploiter, and so preclude participation in advantageous cooperation.

The status of Gauthier's project is analogous to that of the Hobbesian project of showing the advantages of the authority or sovereignty of states.

Gauthier's solution is internal and dispositional, rather than external and coercive. But the two accounts are alike in their emphasis on the rationality of submitting one's conduct to mutually advantageous norms. There is also an analogy to the Hobbesian problem of leaving "the state of nature": There is generally no point to constraining one's actions by a cooperative disposition or principle unless others do so as well. Hobbes's solution to this problem about leaving the state of nature was to argue that the case for "instituting" a sovereign state carries over to what he called "sovereignty by acquisition." Gauthier's analogous solution is to offer a rational reconstruction of what we might call "morals by socialization" as morals by agreement. It is a reconstruction in the sense that it is meant to explain the rationality of abilities that ordinary people plainly have, rather than being an apologia that must somehow suffice to convince any rational agent to behave morally. Indeed, his solution is not applicable to all rational agents: Opaque beings would not derive the full benefits of constrained maximization, because they would hesitate to depend on each other. And a single opaque agent such as Gyges, the Lydian shepherd of Book II of Plato's *Republic*, might benefit by making commitments but would gain nothing by being able to keep them. For cooperation to be rational, agents must be at least partially transparent – "translucent," in Gauthier's phrase – to each other.

If the revised account of rationality – constrained maximization or, to borrow Edward McClennen's term, "resolute choice" – explains the capacity for commitment presupposed by morality, its theoretical and practical interest is far broader. In particular, threats require the same kind of commitment as morality does, but they need not make cooperation or fair terms their subject matter. In order for a threat to induce others to behave as one wishes, it must be credible. Yet carrying out threats is usually costly, and once a threat has failed to induce the desired behaviour, there is, from the standpoint of the straightforward maximizer, no further point in carrying it out, because no further benefit can be expected from doing so. (Assuming, for the moment, that punishing in this case does not provide a significant signal about one's practice in future cases.) But just as this course of reasoning is available to the threatener, so too is it available to the person threatened, who may conclude that the threat is empty. Thus the sole concern with the future leaves the straightforward maximizer incapable of threatening convincingly. Constrained maximization or resolute choice provides a way of explaining how threats can be rational, and thus how they can be possible.[2]

Gauthier's account thus responds to the two objections to the traditional theory of rational choice. It addresses the internal objection by showing that commitment is rationally defensible in the situations in which it is advantageous. It addresses the external objection by providing a standpoint from which the rationality of commitments can be understood and assessed. Provided the commitment is rationally defensible, so too is the action that follows from it. Although rationality is itself always forward looking, it can provide reasons for taking account of the past.

The essays in this volume respond to and develop some of these themes in David Gauthier's thought. Robert Brandom's essay "What Do Expressions of Preference Express?" casts doubt on the concept of preference that is shared by the traditional theory of rational choice and Gauthier's important modifications of it. As we have seen, the traditional theory takes that concept as primitive and as having its authority primitively, while Gauthier's account limits its claim to authority to those cases in which the behavioural dimensions of an agent's preferences match the attitudinal ones. Drawing on Gauthier's distinction between these two dimensions of preference, Brandom opens up the question of what is expressed when someone expresses a preference. He argues that expressions of preference differ from the dispositions to choose that are behavioural preferences, because expressions of preference have propositional content. Brandom makes two claims about this content. He argues first that propositional content is necessary if preference sets are to be assessed for their rationality (or irrationality), because unless they have such content, sets of preferences do not stand in the relations of incompatibility that are presupposed by any evaluation. Second, he argues that the content must be understood in terms of the idea of a commitment to choose, rather than a mere disposition to do so. Drawing out the implications of this idea leads him to defend what he calls "minimal Kantianism" about normativity – the idea that values or norms are reasons only insofar as they are acknowledged as such by agents. On this view, reasons are not reducible to facts about agents. Brandom concludes that the concept of preference that is of interest to practical philosophy presupposes the idea of a reason, rather than explaining that idea.

Arthur Ripstein's essay "Preference" examines parallels between the role of preference in much recent moral philosophy and the role of preference in classical empiricism. Empiricist epistemology and utilitarian and contractarian moral philosophy have a common origin, and, so Ripstein would have it, a common weakness. Each seeks to account for a problematic concept – physical objects and knowledge in one case, a person's good or what one has reason to do in another – in terms of what is taken to be an unproblematic concept – sensation in the former case, preference in the latter. Each thus retreats to what appears to be a subjective account of the concept in question. The difficulties with empiricist accounts of perception are by now widely acknowledged; Ripstein seeks to show how the same problems undermine preference-based accounts of practical reason and goodness. The basic strategy of the essay is to show how the uncontroversial role of one's tastes in evaluating and justifying one's choices presupposes an independent account of what one has reason to do, in much the same way that the uncontroversial role of perception in evaluating and justifying beliefs presupposes an independent account of the reliability of the agent's perceptual apparatus, and so an account of what the world is like. In a new concluding section of the essay, he shows that the difficulties of empiricist accounts do not lend support to the rationalist view that is often thought to be the only alternative. Instead, the failures of empiricist accounts of practical reason reveal the sense in which normative concepts cannot be reduced to factual concepts of any sort.

In her contribution, "Rational Temptation," Claire Finkelstein explores certain tensions she finds in Gauthier's preference-based instrumentalism about practical rationality. She argues that he cannot free himself as easily as he wants from certain properties of the economist's or decision theorist's notion of preference. Accepting the economic understanding of choice as constrained by preference commits one, she argues, to regarding counter-preferential choice as irrational. Thus she contends that although Gauthier's account offers an explanation of the rationality of undertaking commitments, it must always regard acting on commitments, and so acting counter to one's preferences, as irrational. That is, although theorists like Gauthier seek to make room for plans and intentions in order to enable agents to better satisfy their preferences, they may be unable to do so given their acceptance of the received view that preferences constrain rational choice. In the end, Finkelstein urges a view that relaxes the constraints imposed by preference on practical deliberation.

In "Bombs and Coconuts, or Rational Irrationality," Derek Parfit develops some of his critical reactions to Gauthier's revisionist account of practical rationality. Exploring a series of examples of rationally motivated irrationality, Parfit tries to show that rather than supporting the claim that morality is rational, Gauthier's arguments show only that it is sometimes advantageous to believe that it is. While it may be in our interest to have a certain disposition to act against our interests, and while it may be rational to bring ourselves to have this disposition, acting on it will still be irrational.

John Broome asks whether intentions are reasons and argues that they are not. He endorses what has come to be known as "the bootstrapping objection," due to Michael Bratman: If something is not a reason, it does not become one simply because an agent takes it to be one (and if it is a reason, the fact that an agent has formed an intention to act on it does not provide a further reason to do so). Reasons cannot be created out of nothing, as it were. Broome addresses some intuitive objections to his account and at the same time defends his account of the normative relationship between intending and acting. Intentions are, he thinks, normative requirements of some sort. But they are unusual requirements, not least because it is often permissible to change one's mind. Then, Broome argues, the original intention must be *repudiated*. He argues that if one intends to do something and one does not repudiate this intention, the intention normatively requires one to do what one intended. His concluding discussion shows how his account addresses the problem of reasoning about incommensurate alternatives.

Michael Thompson's long and probing essay, "Two Forms of Practical Generality," explores the role of generality in normative practice. He displays a common logical structure in three kinds of examples: the idea, familiar from discussions of rule-utilitarianism, that an act can be justified by showing it to be an instance of a more general practice that is itself justified in some other way; Gauthier's idea that it can be rational to dispose oneself to act in certain ways; and the idea, familiar from discussions of promising, that having made a promise, one must put aside considerations that ordinarily would be sufficient to justify acting differently. In particular cases, the demands of the practice may come into conflict with the demands of the considerations that serve to justify the practice. Thompson explores the logical structure common to rules, practices, and dispositions that enables them to justify particulars. He shows that although they are not themselves substantive principles of morality or rationality, the "transfer" principles that allow an act to inherit its justification from a practice apply only to practices that have a certain sort of generality that cannot be characterized either sociologically or psychologically. Instead, they have a specific logical structure that is itself an expression of a fundamental feature of practical reason.

Adam Morton wishes to put aside questions of "rationality" for a moment and inquire about the *psychology* that is needed by maximizing agents whose interests lie in cooperation. Psychologies, in the sense that is of concern to Morton, are learned early in life as we pick up the doctrines, habits, and cognitive tricks of our culture. There is reason to think that these are connected to the patterns of interaction and cooperation in a culture. Morton asks what it would mean for a psychology in this sense to fit well with cooperative practices. The results, he conjectures, not only are instructive for agents such as ourselves but also allow us to avoid some of the counsels of despair of abstract decision theory.

Contemporary game theory has revealed the striking complexity of strategic human interactions. In earlier work, Peter Danielson has argued that many moral constructivists like Gauthier oversimplify the strategic choices facing rational agents who are choosing principles or dispositions to guide their actions. In this work, he deploys evolutionary game theory and computer simulations ("evolutionary artificial morality") to test which of several competing principles might prove most efficient for agents seeking to maximize utility. Modelling the interactions of sophisticated rational agents – capable of constraining their actions in complex ways – turns out to be even more daunting when one makes the choice of a principle or disposition part of the game itself. In his contribution "Which Games Should Constrained Maximizers Play?" Danielson considers a number of ways of representing the interactions of different kinds of cooperative or principles agents. He raises a number of considerations about different information conditions and suggests that it may be rational for agents to reveal less about themselves than many theorists have argued.

In "The Strategy of Cooperation," Edward McClennen argues that social theory has mischaracterized ideally rational and knowledgeable agents. He thinks that rather than choosing how to act strategically in all situations, such agents can come to view their interactions with others as defining a practice calling for principled or rule-governed choice. He takes seriously some mid-twentieth-century remarks by Thomas Schelling about reorienting game theory and argues that rational agents in many situations should seek to coordinate on mutually beneficial outcomes rather than sub-optimal or inefficient equilibria. Agents who are able to make rule-governed choices should do better in many contexts than should the straightforward maximizers of orthodox social theory.

This volume concludes with "We Were Never in Paradise," a critical essay by Candace Vogler, which examines the place of practical reason in moral life by considering whether or not selves are sufficiently unified for talk about rationality and commitment to apply to their lives. This theme, prominent in much "postmodern" thought, is developed by Vogler in ways that make it accessible to, and reveal its fundamental importance for, philosophers working in the analytic tradition of Anglophone philosophy. Through an engagement with Rousseau's writings on the self, she seeks to undermine confidence in the rationalist and liberal conception of the person that is prominent in contemporary philosophy. In its place she articulates a Rousseauian idea of a self lacking in unity, yet still subject to moral demands.

Notes

1. See Robert H. Frank, *Passions Within Reason: The Strategic Role of the Emotions* (New York: Norton, 1988), ch. 5–7.
2. See especially David Gauthier, "Assure and Threaten," *Ethics* 104 (4): 690–721, 1994.

What Do Expressions of Preference Express?

ROBERT BRANDOM

1. Actions, Reasons, and Preferences

Some, but not all, of our behavior deserves to be called 'action'. We distinguish, among *our doings* in a broad sense, a special class of performances that are both *doings* and (therefore) *ours* in a richer and more demanding sense. Action is behavior that is rational, in the sense that the question of what *reasons* can be given for actions is always, at least in principle, in order. Actions are performances that are caught up in our practices of giving and asking for reasons as moves for which reasons can be proffered and sought. Although there may be much more to the concept of action than is captured in this characterization, the connection between action and reasons is sufficiently tight that one cannot count as understanding the concept of *action* (as even minimally mastering the use of that and cognate words) unless one also counts as in the same sense understanding the concept of *reasons* (for action).

One specifies a potential reason for an action by associating with the performance a goal or an end: a kind of state of affairs at which one understands it as *aiming*, in the sense that its *success* or *failure* is to be assessed accordingly as it does or does not bring about a state of affairs of that kind. Because this is the form of reasons for action, actions, as essentially performances for which reasons can be offered or demanded, are also essentially performances whose success or failure can be assessed.[1] Talk of there being *better reasons* for one action than for another among some set of alternatives is convertible into talk of relative *values* associated with the ends, goals, or aims of those actions.

Enlightenment philosophers faced the problem of integrating this constellation of concepts of agency with the concepts of the new physics, inaugurated by Galileo, pursued by Descartes, and in many ways perfected by Newton. Described in the language of the physics they developed, the world does not come with *values* – or, equivalently, with *reasons for action* – in it. In this specific sense, the mathematized language of the new physics *practically disenchants* the world it describes.[2]

The characteristic response of Enlightenment philosophers to this challenge

was to seek to understand values and reasons for action as themselves products of human activity – as introduced into the physical world by our practices
and attitudes. Talk of values is talk of reasons for action; talk of reasons for
action comes into play only in the context of the behavior of rational creatures. We institute values and reasons by doing what we do, including reasoning about what we do. Our rationality consists, in the end, in properly taking
account of the values and reasons for action we ourselves have introduced
into the world.

This master-thought of Enlightenment theories of practical rationality can
be developed in different ways. My concerns in this essay are oriented by
one great divide among them: the distinction between theories that take it
that our reason-and-value-instituting activities can be adequately specified as
such in a resolutely *non-normative* vocabulary, by focusing on what agents
do in fact choose to do, and those theories that insist to the contrary that only
a normatively rich vocabulary – one making irreducible appeals to what
agents *ought* to choose – will do to ground talk of reasons for action.

The first approach is animated by the thought that the only theoretical grip
we have on what is valuable is the activity of valuing or treating as valuable.
Agents sort possible ends or goals into more and less valued ones (take them
to be more and less valuable) by pursuing some at the expense of others. We
discover their reasons for action by discovering what they actually take as
their ends. One cardinal culmination of the development of this tradition is
the contemporary economic theory of rational choice. Pursuing one end at
the expense of another is making a *choice*. Where the choices an agent is
disposed to make hang together in the right way, they can be understood as
revealing *preferences* for some kinds of ends (features of outcomes) over
others. For choices to "hang together in the right way" to be understood as
revealing preferences is for them to admit a measure, *utility*, such that in any
particular situation one is disposed to choose whatever end will *maximize* that
measure of preference. To be practically rational – not merely to *make*
choices, but to have *reasons* for them – can then be understood as having
dispositions to choose that admit of such a maximizing interpretation. Where
such an interpretation – the conditions for which can be made quite precise –
is available, value can be identified with utility, the measure of preference
that is maximized in choice.[3]

The second approach takes as its starting point the idea that there is an
important distinction between what *causes* actions and choices and what
justifies or provides *reasons* for them. Neither mere inclinations or dispositions to choose nor the preferences that under favorable circumstances can be
seen to be revealed by them can by themselves provide reasons for those
choices – though of course they can cause such choices. (As Anscombe
reminds us, to explain one's action by saying "I just wanted to, that's all," is

not to offer a reason for it.) Reasons for actions should be understood in terms of values that are in principle intelligible apart from consideration of what the agent in fact would choose to do. The wellsprings of rational action are found not in raw behaviorally revealed preferences but in a richer notion of an agent's *endorsement* of an end. For an agent to endorse an end (and so indirectly certain actions or choices) is to take it to be one she *ought* to pursue, to treat it as one she is *committed* or *obliged* to pursue, one that is *worthy* of being pursued. To be practically rational is to act according to the values one recognizes, the commitments, obligations, or duties one acknowledges as binding. This is the point Kant was making in defining a rational will as the capacity to derive acts from conceptions of *laws*.

The second sort of approach may be called "minimal kantianism" about reasons for action. Kantians in this sense may accept the Enlightenment insight by insisting, as Kant himself did, that no norms (values, obligations, commitments, duties, etc.) bind agents apart from the endorsement or acknowledgment of those norms by the agents themselves – that the normative statuses in question are not intelligible apart from reference to the normative attitudes of those who recognize them.[4] But they are committed to a construal of such endorsement or acknowledgment of the bindingness of norms that goes beyond mere dispositions to act in a certain way, as described in a vocabulary that eschews reference to values, obligations, commitments, or duties. The minimal kantian understands having a reason as acknowledging something that is there independently of the agent's acknowledgment of it, and accordingly he understands choices as answering to norms that are not instituted by an agent's dispositions to choose. Being rational is being sensitive, in one's practical reasoning, to the normative statuses (commitments, obligations) that, when acknowledged, provide the only real reasons for action.

The differences between the two approaches can be subtle, but they are real. The main divide is over whether or not reasons for action are grounded justificatorily – not causally – ultimately in normative statuses (for instance, duties), so that only such statuses can serve as the sources of reasons. On the minimal kantian view, relative value, codifying reasons for action, provides not only a *measure* of preference but also a *standard* of preference.[5] That is, choices can legitimately be assessed as better or worse, depending on whether or not they express the acknowledgment of commitments, obligations, and so on that actually bind the individual. This is to accept a view of practical reasoning as essentially involving concern with what ends of action *ought* to be recognized.

In drawing this distinction, I want to put to one side the issue of what reasons we could have to commit ourselves or to acknowledge one obligation rather than another – something with which Kant himself was much concerned. One might be inclined to insist that only commitments that were themselves rationally undertaken could serve as reasons for action. But it is instructive to consider things at the level of abstraction at which the minimal kantian *need* no more insist on the antecedent rationality of the individual reason-grounding normative statuses taken as the ultimate source of reasons for action than the orthodox economic rational choice theorist *need* insist on the antecedent rationality of the individual preferences or dispositions to choose taken as the ultimate source of reasons for action. I am suggesting that we think about that economic theory in relation to a view (picking up, to be sure, only one element of Kant's) according to which the not-necessarily-themselves-rational grounds of reasons for action are *commitments, endorsements,* or *obligations*. Like preferences construed as exhaustively manifested by dispositions to choice behavior, these can be treated as rationally (= inferentially) *articulated*, without being treated as, as a group, *grounded*. In each case, some of them may be something with which agents just find themselves.

2. Preference: Behavioral versus Attitudinal, and Raw versus Considered

In *Morals by Agreement*, David Gauthier develops the most powerful and significant variant of the classical economic account of rationality, within the broad outlines of the rational choice approach. His account agrees with that approach in identifying rationality with the maximization of a measure of preference, thereby, he says, disclaiming all concern with the ends of action.[6] He accordingly disavows the minimal kantian approach to reasons for action distinguished earlier. But he insists as well that however useful it may be in economics, the classical theory – according to which preferences are simply read off of choices – is not adequate as an understanding of practical rationality in general.[7]

Gauthier begins his reconstructive enterprise at the very bottom: "To move from the economist's account to a view of rational choice adequate to understand rational behavior, we must begin by reconsidering the conception of preference."[8] The notion of preference he introduces in order to create the space for his sophisticated variant of the master idea of rationality as maximizing (acknowledged) value is broader than the one that figures in classical theories in two ways. First, he thinks of preferences not only as *revealed* in *choice behavior* but also as *expressed verbally*. Second, he distinguishes the *raw* preferences that are manifested in these two ways from the *considered* preferences, stable under experience and reflection, to which they can give rise. Only the latter are understood as providing genuine reasons for action. These two moves are introduced in a few pages at the very beginning of the book. My main concern in this essay is to look more closely at the under-standing of preference that is implicit in them. My overall thesis will be that there is a significant unacknowledged tension between this reconstrual of preferences and Gauthier's rejection of minimal kantianism in favor of ap-proaches to practical reasoning that restrict it to a merely instrumental role. Since I think the reasons he advances for his rethinking of the concept of preference are compelling, this tension may require us to reassess Gauthier's own classification of the view he builds on that basis.

By distinguishing (merely) *behavioral* manifestations of preferences in dispositions to choice behavior from *attitudinal* manifestations of preference in (merely) verbal behavior – expressing what one wants by *saying* what one prefers – Gauthier drives a wedge between preference and choice, both conceptually and operationally.[9] Doing that is the first step in distinguishing *value* from *utility*, which is what makes possible his eventual identification of practical rationality with the maximization of value (the measure of consid-ered preference) rather than utility (the measure of raw, behavioral prefer-ence). These distinctions are needed to make room for Gauthier's notion of practical rationality as *constrained* maximization. If value is definitionally identified with utility, utility is definitionally identified as the measure that is maximized in choice behavior, and preference as what utility is the measure of – as classical economic rational choice theories do – then Gauthier's approach is ruled out conceptually: It cannot then even be coherently formu-lated.

The intra-theoretic need for taking seriously manifestations of preference not just in (dispositions to) choice behavior but also in (dispositions to) verbal behavior is significant as well in the context of Gauthier's second move, for the process of consideration, by which one's raw preferences are transformed into final preferences, stable under experience and reflection, requires prefer-ences to be expressible in a form in which they can serve as premises in reasoning about hypothetical situations. Only so can their interactions be gauged and calibrated, some rejected or modified in the light of others. An example would be reasoning of this form: "If I prefer outcome A to outcome B, and prefer outcome B to outcome C, then I ought not to prefer outcome C to outcome A." Only what is propositionally contentful, in the sense of verbally expressible in declarative sentences, can figure as antecedents of conditionals (codifying premises of inferences) such as these. So the second move requires at least that preferences be verbally expressible.

The basic idea is to "accept the general explanatory schema: choice maxi-mizes preference fulfillment given belief," while rejecting "the trivialization of this schema that results from denying independent evidential access to each of its terms – to choice, preference, and belief."[10] And this idea has good and sufficient pre-theoretic motivation. It is not simply an *ad hoc* device to clear the way for the theory of rational interaction to follow. For one thing, the role played by preferences and the role played by beliefs in practical reasoning about preferences are in many ways symmetrical. But beliefs are manifested both in what we *do* and in what we *say*. Though these two sources of evidence concerning belief often are consilient, they can come apart (and when they do, they may lead to action that is irrational, and not merely hypocritical). Construing preference on the model of belief would dictate admitting two sources of evidence concerning the former, as well as the latter.[11]

Another pre-systematic reason to move in the direction Gauthier urges is this. If we think it is irrational in a basic sense to have preferences that do not permit the definition of a utility measure – for instance, because of dispositions to cyclical, intransitive choices of the sort ruled out by the conditional forwarded earlier – but want to treat individual preferences themselves as data that are neither rational nor irrational, we need to take account of a process of assessing a whole *set* of preferences, each element in the light of its fellows, and all in the light of collateral beliefs about the relations among the outcomes over which those preferences are defined. We want to be able to criticize those disposed to choose A over B, B over C, and C over A as *irrational*. Yet if we define preference as that whose measure (utility) is maximized in choice behavior, we are obliged to deny that there can be cyclic preferences. The agent in question must be characterized as simply not having any preferences in the vicinity of these choices, and it is not irrational not to have preferences. We are thus debarred on the classical economic theory from satisfying what would seem to be a cardinal criterion of explanatory adequacy for any theory of rationality.

Another such criterion of adequacy on theories of practical rationality, besides that of addressing what appear to be formally defective structures of preference, is dealing with cases of *akrasia*, or weakness of the will. Sometimes it seems right to describe agents as acting against their own preferences: choosing to smoke, while insisting that they prefer health to illness and believe that smoking leads to illness and so on balance prefer not smoking to smoking. Definitionally tying preference to choice behavior obliges the theorist to explain these appearances away: Weakness of the will cannot coherently be described as a form of irrationality and so cannot pose problems for a theory of practical rationality. Acknowledging the category of verbally expressed preferences that may not be manifested also in dispositions to choice behavior is surely better than this Procrustean response. Then the akratic can coherently be described as having genuinely conflicting preferences and is potentially assessable as acting irrationally. These are the sorts of considerations Gauthier has in mind when he says that however adequate the classical account of preference exclusively in terms of choice may be for the purposes of economic theory, it will not do as an idiom in which to formulate a more general theory of practical rationality.

3. What Do Expressions of Preference Express?

For the acknowledgment of attitudinal preferences, manifested in dispositions to verbal behavior, to do this sort of work in a general theory of practical reasoning, the notion of preference cannot be limited to what is *also* revealed in dispositions to choice behavior. That is, the move must not be limited simply to adding one more way that preferences in that sense can be manifested. Both Gauthier's systematic aspirations and each of the three pre-systematic reasons for admitting expressions of preference in verbal as well as choice behavior canvassed earlier require that in at least some cases we can identify genuine preferences, even in the absence of dispositions to choice behavior, solely on the basis of dispositions to verbal expressions of them. This is what is meant by saying that verbal expressions of preference can give us evidence about preferences that in principle is independent of (even dispositions regarding) choice behavior. Nor will it do to make a purely formal assimilation of the latter to the former, on the basis that verbal behavior *is* choice behavior, namely, the choice of words to utter, for what matters is the *content* of the words – that they be expressions of preferences relating, in some cases (think of the akratic), to the same outcomes to which (merely) behaviorally revealed preferences are addressed. As Gauthier says, in some contexts "the two dimensions of preference are distinct, and may be in conflict."[12]

At this point, however, a question arises: What *are* verbal expressions of preference? If we had an independent grip on the notion of preference, we could leave this question to the semantic theorist – the one who tells us what verbal expressions of *anything* are. Thus if we start with dispositions to choice behavior and define preference exclusively by appeal to such behavior (taking preference to be what is measured by utility, which is taken to be what is maximized in choice), we can then go on to specify the truth conditions of (third-person) attributions and (first-person) expressions or avowals of preferences in those terms. Similarly, if we thought, as William James sometimes seems to have, that we could define belief behaviorally in terms of what agents are disposed to do, independently of what they are disposed to say, then we could go on to give truth conditions for verbal expressions of belief – claims – in those terms. Classical rational choice theory is the conative analogue of this sort of cognitive pragmatism. As classical pragmatism had to assume that the preferences on which one acted could be held fixed, or at least independently determined, so classical rational choice theory has to assume that the beliefs on which one acts can be held fixed, or at least independently determined – presumably, in each case, verbally.[13] Once one relinquishes this division of labor, as Gauthier does on the conative side, the explanatory strategy that depends on it must be forgone as well. Preferences must now be understood as what can be expressed either in choice behavior or in verbal expressions of preference. Choice behavior, we may assume, is no worse off from an explanatory point of view than it was for the classical economic rational choice theorists. But now we need an independent grip on the notion of expressions of preference, in order to understand what preferences themselves are.

We cannot just say that expressions of preference are first-person avowals whose main verb is a term like 'prefer', 'want', 'desire', or 'value'. The hard question is what these terms *mean*, and (so) what must be true of a verb for it to be *like* them in the relevant sense. The main clue that we have is that the locutions we are after, while they sometimes express preferences that are not also manifested in choice behavior, in the central and predominant cases express preferences that are *also* manifested in choice behavior. As Gauthier says: "We assume the coincidence of revealed and expressed preference unless we have clear evidence of divergence."[14] Thus in common, central, and favored cases, expressions of preference will be true, if true, because of their relation to preferences intelligible also in terms of dispositions to choice behavior. But what we want to understand is Gauthier's innovation: the purely attitudinal preferences that are manifested *only* in dispositions to verbal expression, and *not* also in dispositions to choice behavior. To understand the surplus of expressed over revealed preferences, we need to know what can make it correct to utter an expression of preference that does *not* correspond to a preference that is also behaviorally revealed.

To focus the question, suppose that in some language (perhaps our own) we find two locutions, each of which can correctly be used to report the presence in oneself of preferences corresponding to dispositions to choose, but each of which can also be used properly under other circumstances. Suppose further that they differ in what those other circumstances are. What, then, would make (at most) one of them a genuine preference-expressing locution, and (at least) the other a merely disjunctive locution, expressing preferring or Φing A to B (where Φing might be, say, admiring more, or finding more dramatic)? If an alien language had only one comparative verb properly used to report dispositions to choice behavior, but one that was also sometimes properly applied in their absence, what would settle the question (not epistemically, but in the sense of "make it the case that") whether or not *all* its uses expressed genuine preferences, some behavioral and some merely attitudinal?

I don't think Gauthier answers this question. But if he does not – if he does not tell us what verbal expressions of preference are – then he does not tell us what preferences are either. His abandonment of the classical definition of preference in terms of choice behavior means that for him, in the crucial surplus cases where attitudinal preferences outrun behavioral ones, preferences simply are whatever verbal expressions of preference are expressions of. Gauthier should be thought of as introducing a new primitive – verbal expressions of preference – and extending the classical choice-behavior concept of preference to include states picked out by their relation to this sort of locution. The challenge I am highlighting is to say more about the speech acts or linguistic expressions invoked by the new primitive whose introduction is mandated by Gauthier's explanatory strategy.

4. Verbal Expressions of Preference Express *Commitments* to Choice Behavior

The thing to do with such a challenge is not simply to contemplate it, but to take it up – to answer the question it asks. I have a hypothesis about what verbal expressions of preference are expressions of, and so how merely attitudinal preferences are related to behavioral ones. Here it is: The distance Gauthier opens up between choice and preference, by acknowledging merely attitudinal preferences as the things that are expressed by verbal expressions of preference, is a *normative* distance. The relationship between behavioral preference and attitudinal preference is the difference between *dispositions* to choose and *commitments* to choose. What verbal expressions of preference express are commitments to patterns of choice behavior.[15]

The idea is that when things go right, when attitudinal and behavioral preferences coincide, the commitments to choose that agents verbally undertake are accompanied by dispositions to make just the choices they have committed themselves to make. In saying I prefer listening to Bach to listening to Brahms, I am committing myself, *ceteris paribus*, to choosing to listen to Bach rather than to Brahms, should such a choice arise. When all goes well, I am disposed to act in the way I have committed myself to acting. On the other hand, I can acknowledge commitments to do things that I am not in fact disposed to do – just as I can promise to do things I am not in fact disposed to do. Attitudinal preferences, construed as commitments to choose, can outrun or even conflict with behavioral ones. Collisions of attitudinal and behavioral preferences, of the sort epitomized by the akratic, are collisions of a familiar sort: collisions between commitments (or obligations) and dispositions.

So construed – as commitments to patterns of choice behavior – the attitudinal preferences that are expressed by verbal expressions of preference (and so, indirectly, those expressions themselves) inherit a structure of entailments and incompatibilities from the outcomes over which those choices are defined. Thus if outcome A entails outcome C, then just as choosing A for that reason entails (will one nill one) choosing C, so *committing* oneself to choose A for that reason entails (will one nill one) *committing* oneself to choose C. And if outcome A is incompatible with outcome B, then just as choosing A is for that reason incompatible with choosing B, so *commitment* to choosing A is for that reason incompatible with *commitment* to choosing B. This is the relation, queried earlier, between the outcomes over which behavioral choices are defined, on the one hand, and the contents of the words used in verbal expressions of preference, on the other.

What makes a word *mean* 'prefer' (or 'desire', 'want', etc.), on this account, is its use as a primary verb to form a declarative sentence whose assertion acknowledges (in the first-person case) or attributes (in the second- or third-person case) a commitment to a pattern of choice behavior. What pattern, exactly? With an eye to the second stage in the process Gauthier envisages, the one at which preferences take the form of *reasons* for action, final or considered preferences, it will turn out to be best to think of the patterns involved in the first instance as patterns of *practical reasoning*. Since endorsements of plans of action, including choice, are the conclusions of bits of practical reasoning, patterns of this sort will entail patterns of choice behavior.

The motivating thought could be put this way. In saying "I prefer A to B," – that is, in expressing a *prima facie* attitudinal preference for A over B – I commit myself to a pattern of practical reasoning of this form: If doing X is necessary and sufficient for producing outcome A, and doing Y is necessary and sufficient for producing outcome B, and one cannot do both X and Y, then (in the absence of competing commitments) do X. This is a *pattern*, because the commitment I am undertaking or acknowledging by avowing my (attitudinal) preference is indifferent as to what the actions X and Y are. It is a pattern of *practical reasoning* because the commitment in question inferentially links doxastic premises (expressed by assertions) to a practical conclusion.[16] That is what was codified earlier in the conditional inferential structure of antecedent and consequent. Commitments to such patterns of practical reasoning include commitments to patterns of choice behavior, for to reason practically according to any instance of the pattern one commits oneself to by an assertion of the relevant sort *is* to choose one way rather than the other in the circumstances described by the antecedent of the conditional that propositionally codifies the practical inference in question.

One further observation must be registered in order to pick out the patterns of practical reasoning expressing "commitment to" which is necessary and sufficient for a linguistic locution to qualify as a verbal expression of preference. The patterns of practical reasoning, commitment to which is acknowledged or attributed by first- and third-person uses of verbal expressions of preference, are *agent-specific*. In acknowledging *my* commitment to reason practically (and so to choose) according to the schema of the preceding paragraph, I say nothing at all about what anyone *else* is committed to. And if you attribute to me that same commitment, you likewise say nothing about what anyone else is committed to. This fact is the formal reflection of the claim that preference is a subjective matter.

Understanding verbal expressions of preference as that which has the characteristic expressive role of putting into the form of assertions any acknowledgments and attributions of commitments to agent-specific patterns of practical reasoning of the structure schematically indicated earlier – and so understanding attitudinal preferences as the commitments such assertions acknowledge or attribute – answers the challenge put forward at the end of the preceding section. It explains the sense in which attitudinal preferences can be decoupled from, outrun, or conflict with behavioral preferences, as required by a general theory of practical rationality that wants to consider akratic choice (or cyclical preferences) as at least intelligibly describable. And it explains the tight connection between attitudinal preference and behavioral preference in virtue of which they deserve to be seen as species of one genus. Thus it allows us to say what must be true of a locution – whether in our own language or in another – for it to mean 'prefers'. Furthermore, as we shall see, the account of verbal expressions of preference as expressing commitments to patterns of practical reasoning and hence of choice behavior meshes nicely with the deliberative process invoked by Gauthier's second distinction among kinds of preferences, the distinction between *raw* preferences (whether merely attitudinal, or also behavioral), which agents may simply find themselves with, and *final* or *considered* preferences, which alone can serve as genuine *reasons* for action.

5. Preferences as Candidate Reasons for Action

The hypothesis just presented introduces a notion of *commitment* not to be found in Gauthier's text. Even if it is acknowledged that the questions put to Gauthier ("What are verbal expressions of preference?" "How is what is expressed by them related to behaviorally revealed preferences?") are genuine and important, we ought to be sure that the resources he does provide for answering them have been exhausted before we explore the consequences of supplementing his account in this way. And it may well seem that those explanatory resources have not been exhausted, for Gauthier's second move – introducing the process by which raw preferences are transformed into reasons for action – offers a further, potentially telling characterization of the role played by attitudinal preferences, beyond that considered thus far. Gauthier needs verbal expressions of preference available to express even behavioral preferences, so that the latter can play a suitable role as inputs in the process of forming *considered* preferences. (And, we recall, he needs attitudinal preferences expressed by verbal expressions of preference but not revealed in dispositions to choice behavior in order to treat as intelligible – albeit irrational – such prime elements of the subject matter of sophisticated theories of practical rationality as the phenomena of weakness of the will and cyclical preferences.)

This observation suggests that the notion of verbal expressions of preference might be explained by appeal not to what lies upstream – that is, by invoking an antecedent understanding of what is avowed or attributed by their use – but by appeal to what lies downstream: the role they play in the formation of *considered* preferences. That role is as potential reasons for action, for given his account of the process of consideration, nothing could count for Gauthier as a verbal expression of preference (the explicit verbal formulation of a raw preference) unless it also counted as formulating at least a candidate reason for action – a consideration that, if it is determined to be stable under experience and reflection in the light of other such considerations, provides a genuine reason to act. So when we ask what the merely attitudinal preferences that are manifested only in verbal expressions of preference have in common with behavioral preferences that are also revealed in dispositions to choice behavior, in virtue of which they deserve to be classed as species of a genus recognizable as *preferences*, one available answer is that they are alike in the roles they play as inputs into the process of consideration, whose outputs are reasons for action. According to this line of thought, 'raw preference' just means *non-doxastic input to the process of consideration whose product is reasons for action.*

The idea would be to understand preferences just as whatever needs to be added to beliefs to yield potential reasons for action. Davidson, for instance, would insist that the belief that it is raining, even together with the belief that only opening my umbrella will keep me dry, does not yet provide a reason for me to open my umbrella. To have a complete (candidate) reason to do that, we need to supplement those beliefs with a preference for staying dry. The verbal expressions of belief (claims), together with verbal expressions of preference ("I desire, or prefer,[17] to stay dry."), serve as premises in a potentially good piece of practical reasoning whose conclusion is the verbal expression of an intention to act: "So, I shall open my umbrella." (The practical inference is only "potentially" good, because collateral premises in the form of *other* complete reasons for incompatible actions may, upon consideration, turn out to override the preference in question.) The thought being considered is that one might *define* verbal expressions of preference in terms of the role they play in this process.

This thought is compatible with the suggested construal of attitudinal preferences as commitments to patterns of practical reasoning, and hence to patterns of choice behavior. But neither entails the other. So why not adopt this understanding of raw preferences, in terms of their role in the sort of practical reasoning characteristic of the formation of the considered preferences that provide an agent with genuine reasons for action? The short answer is that this response is not available to Gauthier, for two related reasons. First, it gets the order of explanation the wrong way around. Second, the notion it defines is far too broad to be recognizable as a notion of preference at all. A weaker way of putting the second point is that if one could justify characterizing the outputs of the process of consideration as considered *preferences*, rather than just reasons for action, then one would indeed have a warrant for also calling the inputs to the process 'preferences'. But if *all* we know about those outputs is that they are the acknowledgments of the *values* maximization of which is the essence of practical rationality (to which the bulk of Gauthier's story is addressed), then, as we shall see later, we cannot distinguish between preference-based approaches to practical rationality and the more committive minimal kantian ones, for in that case, "one might suppose that the quantity to be maximized was not a measure of but a standard for preference."[18]

The first point is that adopting the definition of raw preferences in terms of their role as fodder for transformation into reasons for action means that the notion of *reason for action* is not explained in terms of an antecedently specified notion of *preference*. Rather, the idea is to christen as 'preference' whatever provides a reason for action. That requires a conceptual grip on the notion of reasons for action that is antecedent to our understanding of preferences. Providing an account of this shape is the essence of minimal kantian approaches to action: Having a reason for action is acknowledging a value; being rational is choosing (revealing behavioral preferences for) acknowledged values. Refusing to recognize anything as a genuine reason for action for an agent that is not grounded in the preferences of the agent is the essence of purely instrumental, rational choice approaches to action and practical reason. The broadly humean approach to practical reason that Gauthier identifies with is the analogue on the conative side of the empiricist cognitive principle that there are no reasons for belief that do not originate in the senses: *nihil in intellectus est sed fuit prius in sensu.*[19] It is the claim that there are no reasons for action that do not originate in inclinations. Minimal kantianism opposes to this a view that makes reasons for action (acknowledgments of value – or obligation) codify, as Gauthier puts it in the passage quoted earlier, not *measures* of inclination or preference, but *standards* for it.[20] Gauthier shares with the more orthodox rational choice tradition commitment to an order of explanation that requires that the concept *reason for action* be explained in terms of the concept of *preference*, which accordingly

must be intelligible antecedently. So Gauthier cannot define the species "attitudinal preference," and therefore the genus "preference," in terms of the
concept *reason for action.*

The second point is just that there is nothing in this approach to rule out
as candidate reasons for action – inputs playing the role of 'raw preferences'
– considerations that do not have the right shape or significance to be called
'preferences'. To see this, we need to look a little more closely at the process
of forming 'considered preferences'. What is the process of consideration?
One important element is assessing the consequences of acting on one's
preferences and of securing the preferred outcome. Assessing those consequences involves inferentially bringing to bear both one's collateral beliefs
and one's other preferences, as auxiliary premises in extracting consequences
from the outcomes valued in the preferences being assessed. The core element
in forming considered preferences from raw ones is inferentially extracting
consequences from the rawly preferred outcomes, on the basis of one's
collateral beliefs, and assessing those consequential outcomes on the basis of
collateral raw (or, recursively, considered) preferences. I may be inclined (or
committed) to choose outcome A over outcome B, but if, in the context of
my other beliefs,[21] A entails C, then raw preferences concerning C bear on
my endorsement of A. After all, C might be incompatible with the obtaining
of the even more preferred outcome of some other choice. This is to say that,
in the context of an agent's other beliefs, some raw preferences can provide
reasons either to adopt or to relinquish other preferences. The reasons for
action that emerge from the process of considering each candidate reason in
the light of others, and in the context of concomitant beliefs, are preferences
endorsed after consideration of the rest of the agent's attitudes, both cognitive
and conative. We need to think of all the preferences involved in this process
as propositionally contentful, which is to say *attitudinal* preferences (some of
which perhaps correspond to behavioral preferences that are also revealed by
dispositions to choice behavior), manifestable in verbal expressions of preference, because it is a process of practical *reasoning* – and what can play the
role of premise in such reasoning (when explicitly codified, the role of
antecedent of a conditional) is propositionally contentful and can be expressed by a declarative sentence.

This process is readily intelligible in terms of the suggested model of
attitudinal preferences as commitments to patterns of practical reasoning, and
hence choice behavior. Considered preferences will be construed as attitudinal
preferences whose endorsement survives competition with other candidate
commitments through the exploration of their inferential relations and incompatibilities in the light of beliefs about how things are and how they might
evolve under various hypothetical circumstances. But what matters in the
present context is that there is nothing about the process of consideration
whereby tentative or *prima facie* practical commitments develop into genuine

reasons for action that restricts the practical commitments serving as its inputs to those with a structure that makes them recognizable as preferences (raw or not). For all that has been said so far, inputs to this process could include practical commitments in the form of promises, or obligations incurred because of one's institutional role, or the existence of rules or laws.[22] Nothing rules out acknowledged commitments or obligations of these sorts from operating as considerations in the process of coming to acknowledge reasons for action, even where pre-systematically we want to say that there are no corresponding preferences: where the agent does not care about fulfilling promises, keeping her job, or obeying the law. Such a situation, of course, is just the one envisaged and endorsed by the minimal kantian.

Why not take a hard stipulative line and insist that even what are apparently expressions of obligations or commitments are, when playing this role in practical reasoning, implicitly expressions of preferences? Because their role in practical reasoning is different. "I prefer to stay dry," which genuinely is an expression of preference, at most provides *me* with a reason to open my umbrella (at least absent second-order preferences on the part of others, for instance to prefer doing what I prefer doing). Obligations linked to institutional status, such as that expressed by "bank employees are obliged to wear neckties at work," by contrast, insofar as they by themselves provide reasons at all (*vide infra*) provide reasons equally for anyone who is a bank employee. Other norms, such as that expressed by "it is wrong to (one ought not) amuse oneself by torturing helpless strangers," insofar as they provide reasons at all, do so in a way that swings free of parochial considerations of social status or institutional role. The procrustean strategy of stretching the notion of preference so as to encompass norms of these disparate sorts – perhaps by distinguishing individual preferences from various sorts of group preferences – relinquishes all continuity with the classical economic notion of behavioral preference and empties the concept of *preference* of its distinctive content.

Put another way, if we start our theorizing with a bare notion of nondoxastic inputs to the process of consideration whose product is reasons for action, the strategy of restricting those inputs to *individual preferences* – which is the essence of the instrumentalist, rational choice paradigm of practical reasoning – will be *ad hoc* and unmotivated. The minimal kantian claims that a good reason for wearing a necktie to work could take the form of this conjunction:

I am a bank employee, going to work.

&

Bank employees are obliged to wear neckties at work.

By contrast, the broadly humean line that traces all reasons for action to individual preferences insists that such a conjunction still falls short of formulating a reason for an agent to act. When fully stated, such a reason must include reference to the preferences or desires of the agent. What more is needed is something like this:

I prefer (or desire[23]) to fulfill my obligations as a bank employee.

Or if the obligation cited in the second conjunct is taken as partly constitutive of the status invoked by both premises, and so implicitly or by implication invokes a possible sanction for noncompliance, perhaps what is wanted is something like this:

I prefer to remain a bank employee.

Otherwise, the thought is, the invocation of an obligation consequent upon a social or institutional status does not yet engage with the motivational economy of the agent in the way required to be recognizable as functioning as a reason for that agent.

This is an important, indeed fundamental, dispute – about whether or not, in what sense, and for exactly what explanatory purposes internal reasons must be discerned behind external reasons (in one sense of those elastic terms). But it cannot sensibly be conducted without some theoretical grip on the notion of preference that is independent of understanding reasons for action – the concept at the heart of the disagreement – for the order of explanation being considered seeks either simply to *define* expressions of preference as whatever is needed to supplement beliefs in order to yield reasons or to *stipulate* that the reasons in question are to be understood as having to have the form favored by the preference theorist.

6. Merely Attitudinal Preferences Provide Only Motivationally External Reasons

So it is not open to Gauthier to respond to the question raised here about his first broadening of the classical economic paradigm – including merely attitudinal as well as behavioral preferences in the raw materials of a theory of practical rationality – by invoking his second broadening – treating raw preferences, whether behavioral or attitudinal, as input to a process of consideration of preferences whose outputs alone are *prima facie* reasons for action. The issue of how to understand attitudinal preferences – some of which are expressed only in dispositions to verbal behavior, not also in dispositions to nonverbal choice behavior – is not settled by looking at the process of consideration by which preferences are turned into reasons.

The discussion of that issue pointed to an important motivation for preference-based theories of practical reasoning: the thought that whatever we treat as fundamental reasons for action should play a certain kind of role in the behavioral economy of the agent. In particular, they should be intrinsically motivating; what reasons for action an agent possesses should make a difference to what the agent is disposed or inclined to go on to do. This is one of the main points of contrast between broadly humean (empiricist) and broadly kantian (rationalist) approaches to practical reasoning: The kantian insists that something, say a commitment or obligation, can genuinely provide an agent with a reason for action even though the agent is not in the least inclined to act according to it. It is worth noticing that the minimal kantian need not follow Kant himself in denying that an agent's behavioral preferences, dispositions, or inclinations – Kant's "sinnliche Neigungen" – can be the basis of any genuine *reasons* for action. Where the minimal kantian differs from the humean is in insisting that such inclinations do not *exhaust* the reasons for action an agent may have.

If we draw the lines in this way, however, Gauthier's first move already marks his departure from the humean camp and his enlistment with the minimal kantians. For that move consists in allowing the possibility that merely attitudinal preferences, not accompanied by corresponding behavioral preferences, can provide (the raw material for) genuine reasons for action. Preferences of this sort are distinguished precisely by not engaging with the agent's behavioral economy so as to be intrinsically motivating. Attitudinal preferences may line up with dispositions to nonverbal choice behavior, but then again, they may not. When they do not, they function as motivationally external reasons. Calling them 'preferences' and pointing to their subjectivity (in the sense that distinguishes them from transpersonal obligations such as those associated with institutional roles such as being a bank employee) does not alter that fact.

It should not be thought that a concession to the minimal kantian along these lines is an optional or idiosyncratic feature of Gauthier's understanding of preference. *Any* account of preference or practical reasoning that can acknowledge *akrasia* as an intelligible form of practical irrationality must make this concession concerning motivationally external reasons for action. The possibility of decoupling what an agent has reason to do (indeed, *acknowledges* having reason to do) from what the agent in fact is disposed to do is the very essence of the phenomenon of weakness of the will. Of course, the decoupling is not complete: When things go right, attitudinal and behavioral preferences track each other. But the decoupling is not complete for those who would include motivationally external norms as first-class reasons for action either, for such theorists would insist that to be a properly trained agent is to be disposed, *ceteris paribus*, to respond to the acknowledgment of a commitment or obligation by fulfilling it. Gauthier is with the minimal kantian in claiming that genuine reasons for action are not restricted to motivationally internal ones and that those surplus external reasons need not for that reason be understood as motivationally inert. Both explore the important middle ground between requiring reasons for action to be *intrinsically* (because definitionally) motivating and being forced to see reasons that fail of that status as therefore motivationally *inert*.

Thus, consideration of the dispute about whether or not motivationally external reasons ought to be included along with motivationally internal ones as basic inputs to the process of practical reasoning underscores the urgency of answering the basic question raised by Gauthier's first move: How should we understand the relation between behavioral and attitudinal preferences, and hence the genus *preference* itself? With the formulation of the preceding paragraph in mind, we may ask how we should understand the notions of 'tracking' and 'going right', such that when things go right, attitudinal and behavioral preferences track each other. We may grant that allowing room for slippage – besides being true to the phenomena – need not rule out linkage. But what sort of linkage, and how should we understand the difference between things going right and things going wrong?

My suggestion, recall, is that this relationship is a *normative* one – just as talk of "things going *right* (as they *ought*)" suggests. An attitudinal preference is the acknowledgment of a *commitment* to act (choose) in a certain way (according to a specifiable pattern). Attitudinal preferences 'track' or correspond properly to behavioral preferences when those attitudes are explicit expressions of the behavioral preferences one implicitly commits oneself to by being disposed to act (choose) in those ways. Behavioral preferences 'track' or correspond properly to attitudinal preferences when one is in fact disposed to act (choose) as one acknowledges oneself to be committed to do. The sort of propriety involved – what is invoked by talk of "things going right" – is in the one direction that of acknowledging one's implicit commitments, and in the other direction that of fulfilling commitments or obligations one explicitly acknowledges.

Attitudinal preferences without corresponding behavioral preferences are commitments to patterns of choice behavior in which one is not in fact disposed to engage – a situation intelligible, indeed familiar, to us from the otherwise very different case of promises, which can coherently (if culpably) be undertaken even where the promiser is not disposed to fulfill the commitment made (in that case) to another. Behavioral preferences without corresponding attitudinal preferences are behavioral dispositions of which the agent is not discursively aware and cannot make explicit in the form of assertible (hence thinkable) expressions of preference. Since only such verbalizable expressions of preference can serve as premises in practical reasoning, and so are available as inputs to the process of consideration that will yield genuine reasons for action, such *merely* behavioral preferences are *rationally* inert.

7. Considered Preferences Are *Endorsed* Preferences

Gauthier's second innovation is to distinguish *considered* preferences from *raw* preferences (whether the latter are behavioral or attitudinal). I think that looking at the process of consideration, whereby raw preferences are transformed into genuine reasons for action, offers some confirmation of the normative reading of the relation between attitudinal and behavioral raw preferences, for I think that process should be understood as one in which raw preferences acquire a further sort of *normative* force. The force of *reasons* for action is a matter of considerations serving as premises in practical inferences that can *justify* or *entitle* the agent to various practical commitments (commitments to act).

Gauthier understands the inputs to the process as attitudinal preferences (some of which do and some of which perhaps do not correspond to behavioral preferences), for only these verbally expressible preferences are explicit in the form of claims, and hence available to serve as *premises* in bits of practical reasoning. Accordingly, only what is in this form can be understood as a candidate *reason* for action – the status acquired by preferences that survive the process of consideration. Why might some of them not survive? Gauthier's discussion of considered preferences is subtle, and its nuances deserve more discussion than they can be given here. For our purposes it will suffice to consider two of the major dimensions along which preferences can, upon consideration, be found wanting, and hence relegated to the status of not providing reasons for action. First, preferences that would provide reasons for action in isolation may fail to do so if they occur as part of a set that includes incompatible preferences. Second, preferences that would provide reasons for action if they were stable and persistent may fail to do so if upon consideration they are deemed to be transitory or short-lived, likely to be replaced, revised, or succeeded by contrary preferences – paradigmatically upon the receipt of further information. These two major ways in which raw preferences may fail to qualify as considered preferences play an important role downstream in Gauthier's subsequent argument for rationality as constrained maximization of the value that is a measure of considered preference. But each is independently motivated upstream by intuitions and considerations concerning the requirements of practical rationality.[24]

If we restrict ourselves to purely behavioral preferences, incompatibilities cannot arise, for those preferences are implicit in actual choices (or dispositions to make such choices), and those choices resolve any potential conflicts. But the addition of attitudinal preferences makes conflicts possible; indeed, this conceptual broadening is introduced in part in order to make intelligible such collisions of preferences as those exhibited by the akratic or the avower of cyclic preferences. What is irrational about agents who find themselves in these situations is that the reasons for action that otherwise would be provided by one preference are undercut by the presence of contrary preferences. Until and unless the conflict is resolved, the agent cannot be said to be acting for reasons at all. This situation makes perfect sense if, as I have suggested, we understand what such verbal expressions express as *commitments* to patterns of action (including choice behavior). I may undertake incompatible commitments to choice behavior, just as I may make incompatible promises – ones that cannot be jointly fulfilled. The akratic undertakes incompatible commitments: The commitments implicit in the pattern of choice behavior she is disposed to are incompatible with others she endorses verbally. The subject who finds herself with cyclic preferences also undertakes incompatible commitments. We want to say that these are two forms of irrationality. What is irrational about them is precisely that the commitments undertaken by the akratic and by the subject of cyclic preferences are jointly incompatible.

Two claims are incompatible just in case *commitment* to one precludes *entitlement* to the other. One is not precluded from undertaking the other commitment (making the other claim); there is nothing incoherent about undertaking incompatible commitments (think of promises). To say that a set of commitments is jointly incompatible is to say that one cannot be *entitled* to all of them.[25] Promising to take you to the airport tomorrow morning at ten does not make unintelligible or impossible my promising to take my son to his crew practice tomorrow morning at ten. But the distance between the airport and the river (along with other uncontroversial background facts) means that the one promise keeps me from being *entitled* to make the other promise. Practical reasoning is about *justification*, about the agent's *entitlement* to various commitments, and so choices or courses of action.[26] Reasons for action are practical commitments to which one is entitled and which can accordingly *justify* what one does. According to this way of thinking, the process of consideration is the process by which some of the raw preferences are *endorsed*, in the sense of taken as potentially justifying action (including choice). Endorsing incompatible commitments is structurally self-defeating. Just so, on Gauthier's view, one's *considered* preferences cannot be mutually incompatible.[27]

The requirement for stability of raw preference, in particular under increases in information, is also intelligible in these terms. The practical commitments expressed by verbal expressions of preference (desires) are like the doxastic commitments expressed by assertions (beliefs), and unlike the practical commitments (*to* someone) undertaken by promises, in that one is permitted to change one's mind – to alter or relinquish the commitment. Nonetheless, to take it that the candidate for endorsement (upon consideration) is a *commitment* involves taking what one is committed to by it to include a certain sort of stability over time and circumstance. What is expressed by a statement such as "I believe that neither the word 'problem' nor the word 'solution' occurs in the King James edition of the Bible, but if I looked into the matter further I probably would change my mind,"[28] is not a *belief*, for the attitude being evinced falls short of taking the contained claim to be true, of *committing* oneself to its truth. One is not treating the claim about the non-occurrence of those words as a premise whose inferential consequences ought to be endorsed. Just so with preferences. What is expressed by a statement such as "I prefer electing the city council by districts to doing so at large, but if I looked into the matter further I probably would change my mind," is not the endorsement of a preference. One is evincing one's offhand disposition to *say* something, but precisely with the proviso that one is not really endorsing that disposition. One is not putting that disposition forward as a *reason*, in the sense of a premise for practical reasoning whose consequences ought to be endorsed in the sense of enacted.

8. Conclusion

Gauthier does not talk this way about the process of turning raw preferences into considered preferences. He has good reasons to resist and reject the proffered transposition of his view into this normative idiom. For one thing, so translated, Gauthier's position would assume very much the shape considered – and rejected on his behalf – in Section 5. For if considered preferences are commitments to patterns of practical reasoning that the agent has endorsed as ones to which she is entitled, given her collateral commitments (both doxastic and practical-preferential, and including those concerning the likely evolution of her dispositions to undertake such commitments under the influence of extensions of her knowledge, assessment of the consequences of acting on those commitments, and so on), then it is hard to see a principled reason to restrict the inputs to the process of consideration to commitments that have the structure characteristic of individual preferences. In deciding which considerations to endorse as having the force of reasons for action, why should the agent not consider also commitments that do not have the shape of preferences, such as promises made, or obligations incumbent on social or institutional status – even when not accompanied by corresponding preferences? Although there is often confusion on this point, the fact that *if* the agent had *contrary* preferences (for instance, positively *wanted* to be fired from her job at the bank) these might well override acknowledged commitments does not entail that the commitments provide reasons for action only when combined with preferences for fulfilling those commitments. Nothing in this way of thinking about things entails Kant's own view that merely behavioral preferences are in principle not eligible for endorsement as reasons.[29] But if what one is doing in considering raw preferences is deciding which commitments to endorse, what rationale is there for restricting that consideration to commitments that have the special structure of individual preferences?

Of course, the only commitments that matter to the practical reasoning of an agent are commitments she *acknowledges*, or treats as in some sense binding on her. But to say that is not to say that they must be commitments she *prefers* to keep, for a preference is a commitment that binds only the one whose preference it is. In acknowledging that bank employees have an obligation to wear neckties at work, one is acknowledging an obligation that is part of playing a certain institutional role. What one acknowledges is something binding on anyone having that status *as* something binding on anyone having that status. Similarly, one might acknowledge an obligation or commitment not to amuse oneself by torturing helpless strangers as binding on agents in general. In doing that, one is acknowledging something whose bindingness is not taken to depend on anyone's acknowledgment of it – something that is not a matter of preference. Nothing in Gauthier's discussion of the process of consideration by which raw preferences acquire the status of reasons for action precludes, or even motivates precluding, other sorts of considerations besides *preferences* from serving as inputs to this process. His account is one the minimal kantian can endorse, adopt, and applaud.

In *Morals by Agreement*, Gauthier sees himself as continuing the broadly humean, empiricist tradition of classical economic theories, which understand rational choice in terms of maximization of utility, the measure of individual preference. He explicitly aligns himself with this camp, against those who would understand some source of reasons for action beyond the preferences of individual agents. But each of the dimensions along which he finds that the phenomena of practical reasoning oblige him at the outset of his enterprise to broaden the classical understanding of preference, I have argued, is best understood as implicitly introducing normative notions that move substantially beyond that picture. In fact, each of his basic moves – recognizing attitudinal preferences and not just behavioral preferences, and recognizing only considered preferences and not raw preferences, as constituting reasons for action – opens up the space it is characteristic of minimal kantianism to insist upon. Attitudinal preferences are what are expressed by verbal expressions of preference. I have argued that Gauthier does not tell us what they are. But I have suggested further that we should understand them as *commitments* to patterns of action or choice behavior. Considered preferences, further, should be understood as such commitments that are *endorsed* as *justifying* or *entitling* the agent to act.

Preferences constrain how action *ought* (in a distinctive sense) to go. The distance between behavioral and attitudinal preferences (so important for understanding the possibility of the distinctive form of irrationality that is weakness of the will) is a normative distance: the difference between dispositions or inclinations to act or choose and acknowledged commitments to do so. Acting according to this sort of commitment (made explicit by an 'ought') is being rational (having a rational will). But to see the distance that makes acting this way a task at which one could fail requires introducing the notion of a normative status, a kind of *commitment*, that is not intelligible in terms of the economist's – nor, indeed, of Gauthier's – notion of maximization, for it is *presupposed* by any notion of maximizing that starts with preferences understood in Gauthier's extended sense. Again, the notion of *endorsement*, and the corresponding sense of *entitlement* to a course of action that can be inherited from a commitment, which is what the notion of a reason for action comes to, is not one that can be understood in terms of maximization, for it, too, is part of the raw materials – the understanding of preference and value – in terms of which maximizing can then be introduced.

In the years since *Morals by Agreement* appeared, Gauthier has in many ways moved in a kantian direction. I think that if we press hard enough on the question of my title – if we ask what it is that is expressed by verbal expressions of preference – it becomes open to us to see that development not so much as an alteration of his views as the becoming more explicit of what was already implicit in the notion of preference with which he began his enterprise. But that possibility raises a final reason for the author of *Morals by Agreement* to reject the normative answer offered on his behalf to the question of my title, an answer that pushes his view substantially in the direction of minimal kantianism. For in this essay I have (possibly perversely) completely ignored the crucial third stage of Gauthier's story: I have said nothing whatsoever about constrained maximization. What we *finally* have reason to do, according his story, is not what is recommended by our considered preferences, but only what emerges from constrained maximization of those preferences. Put another way, Gauthier offers *three* stages in the grooming of reasons (raw preferences, considered preferences, and what maximizes considered preferences under the constraints it is his main task to argue for), while the account reconstructed here offers only *two* (commitments to act, and entitlements to those commitments). In effect, the minimal kantianism reconstructed here out of the raw materials Gauthier provides collapses the final two levels that he is concerned to distinguish. So the line of thought presented here, which begins with the question posed in the title of the essay, ends by posing a further question, which cannot be pursued here: How might the minimal kantian, for whom, I have been arguing, Gauthier makes room, understand the distinction between two sorts of entitlements to practical commitments that he urges on us in distinguishing considered preferences from final reasons for action?

Notes

1. Compare (and contrast) the relations hip between reasons for *judgments* and the liability of judgments to assessment as *true* or *false*.
2. Of course, a corresponding problem arises concerning the placement of reasons for *judgment* – and hence the pursuit of the new science itself – in the mathematized world described by physics. In a *tour de force* that brilliantly epitomized some of the deepest impulses of the Enlightenment, Spinoza, in his *Ethics*, sought to reduce the problem of practical reason to that of theoretical reason. What we have reason to *do*, in the end, is to give the reasons and make the judgments that improve science, to perfect our knowledge of the physical world, and thereby to become the mind of God.
3. In fact, what an agent chooses depends not only on what she wants (prefers, values) but also on what she *believes* – most importantly, about the outcomes consequent upon various candidate choices. Where the idealization that these can be held fixed is removed, one must introduce into the interpretation a further parameter: the agent's subjective (conditional) *probabilities*. Then we say that utility is what the agent is *attempting* to maximize and that rational agents maximize *expected* utility. Relaxing the idealization in this direction does not yet amount to making the transition from thinking about the sorts of parametric choice situations addressed by decision theory to thinking about the sorts of strategic choice situations addressed by game theory.
4. It is "minimal" kantianism because nothing in what has thus far been ascribed to the approach requires its completion by some analogue of a categorical imperative. Kant may be thought to have moved too quickly from consideration of the way in which endorsement can swing free of inclination to the conclusion that inclination is simply irrelevant to what we have reason to do. This move can usefully be compared to the classical rationalists' inference from the claim that awareness consists in the application of concepts to the claim that concepts must owe nothing to conscious experience save the occasions of their application.
5. David Gauthier, *Morals by Agreement* (hereafter, *MBA*) (Oxford University Press, 1986), p. 25.
6. *MBA* 26.
7. *MBA* 27.
8. *MBA* 27.
9. *MBA* 28.
10. *MBA* 30.
11. Davidsonian interpretation insists on doing this: Neither preference nor belief can be read off of nonverbal behavior, given their joint role in rationalizing that behavior. Not only must each be attributed as part of a story that includes an account of the other, but verbal behavior is crucial in attributing both.
12. *MBA* 28.
13. Of course, one can interpret agents by simultaneously assigning subjective probability functions and subjective preference functions, as David Lewis does. The present point concerns not the relation between attributions of preference and attributions of belief, but the division of labor between behavioral evidence and verbal evidence. The claim is that classical pragmatism about belief and classical rational choice theory about preference line these distinctions up.
14. *MBA* 28.
15. The remarks that follow are given a much fuller context and more careful expo-

sition in my *Making It Explicit* (Cambridge, MA: Harvard University Press, 1994), especially sections IV–VI of Chapter Four. In particular, the way I think we ought to understand the relevant sense of 'commitment' is laid out and defended there in a way precluded by the scope of the present essay.

16. I discuss this way of thinking about practical reasoning in more detail in "Action, Norms, and Practical Reasoning," in *Philosophical Perspectives*, vol. 12, 1998; reprinted in R. Brandom, *Articulating Reasons: An Introduction to Inferentialism* (Harvard University Press, 2000), Chapter 2, pp. 79–96.

17. The formal distance between preferences, which are comparative and therefore attach to ordered dyads, and desires, which are categorical and therefore attach to unary objects, can be bridged by understanding a desire to φ as a *ceteris paribus* preference to φ rather than not to φ.

18. *MBA* 25.

19. The claim that there is nothing in *action* that was not previously in *felt preference* is, like that of its analogue *cognitive empiricism,* crucially ambiguous between a *causal* reading of 'prius' (in the conative case, a *motivational* reading) and a *justificatory* one. One worry is that the pull of conative empiricism as a story about rationality is due precisely to this conflation. Minimal kantianism, as here described, explores a *conative rationalism. Cognitive rationalism* insists that one must already have concepts in order properly to perceive anything. The conative variety claims that one must already have principles and be able to *endorse* them in order to have inclinations (preferences) in a sense that suits them to serve as *reasons.*

20. A more full-blooded kantian view denies that inclinations provide even the raw materials for the practical commitments (endorsements of principles) that are the only genuine reasons for action. This point is discussed later in connection with the description of intermediate approaches.

21. cf. *MBA* 29.

22. See the discussion of different patterns of practical reasoning in *Making It Explicit*, Chapter Four, Section V, and in "Action, Norms, and Practical Reasoning."

23. For a way to fill in the implicit ellipsis, see note 17.

24. *MBA* 33–38.

25. I discuss this way of thinking about incompatibility in Chapter Three of *Making It Explicit*.

26. Of course, it is also about consequential commitments, for instance, how commitment to securing an end can commit the agent to a necessary means. But such committive consequences bring along relations concerning entitlements, for if commitment to bringing it about that *p* entails commitment to bringing it about that *q*, then one cannot be entitled to the first commitment if one is not entitled to the second.

27. One might object that satisficing considerations could make it rational not to resolve some residual incompatibilities, since the cost of doing so (given one's other preferences) is too high. But in fact, this need not be seen as an objection. Gauthier's aim is to say what we ultimately have reason to do. When rationality as satisficing dictates that we not resolve incompatible preferences, the situation might be understood as one where economic efficiency means it is not worth putting more effort into further refinements of one's idea of what one ultimately has reason to do – the current take is good enough for practical purposes. (Of course, taking this line would involve considerable work to entitle the theorist to the assumptions about approximation on which it relies.)

28. Those words do not in fact occur in that work. (I believe Raymond Williams was the first to point out this significant difference between our habits of mind and those of its time.)

29. There is an asymmetry in Kant, in that he allows that we can act morally, apart from all reference to inclination, but not that we can think apart from all reference to intuition. The view I am calling 'minimal kantianism' allows for intuition and inclination to play more parallel roles. I think Hegel has a view like this, which envisages a process of *conceptualizing inclinations* parallel to that of *conceptualizing intuitions*. These are mutually involving aspects of the other side of the process of *sensualizing concepts*, by which alone they acquire determinate content. But this is Hegel, not Kant.

Preference

ARTHUR RIPSTEIN

The concept of preference plays a central role in much recent moral and political philosophy. Partly because of its pedigree in such widely admired disciplines as economics and decision theory, its status seems secure. Preferences are taken by various philosophers to provide everything from a starting point for moral inquiry to the sole factor that elected officials should take into account.[1] My aim in this essay is to call that status into question. I shall argue that the concept of preference cannot bear the theoretical weight in normative inquiry that it has been asked to support. The argument has two parts. The first examines the place of actual or "revealed" preference in moral argument and shows how it fails to meet even minimal standards as an account of practical reason. The second part considers more sophisticated accounts of ideal or considered preferences, arguing that although they have enough structure to function in accounts of practical reason, their employment presupposes independent standards. This needn't be a damning criticism, except for the manner in which advocates of preference-based accounts maintain that those accounts do not incorporate any controversial normative claims. Much of the appeal of preference-based accounts of practical reason stems from their promise of providing a normative account of practical reason using minimal formal constraints of consistency and the prior motivations of the agent in question.

My strategy will be to establish and exploit parallels between the role of preference in contemporary moral philosophy and the role of perception in classical empiricism. Empiricist epistemology and utilitarian and contractarian moral philosophy have a common ancestry. They also share a common weakness. Each attempts to give an account of what is taken to be a problematic concept – physical objects and knowledge on the one hand, a person's good or what she has reason to do on the other – and explain it as a construct out of what is taken to be an unproblematic concept – sensation on the one

An earlier version of this essay appeared in *Value, Welfare, and Morality*, ed. R. G. Frey and C. W. Morris (Cambridge University Press, 1993), pp. 93–111. The critical portions of the argument have undergone only cosmetic changes, but the conclusion is different.

hand, preference on the other. Each retreats to what appears to be an individualistic and subjective account of the concept in question. Empiricist epistemology responds to skepticism about the existence of an external world by retreating to individual sensation as the building block of knowledge; empiricist ethics responds to controversy about practical reason and the good by retreating to subjective preference. The failures of classical empiricism are by now widely recognized. My aim is to extend anti-empiricist arguments to preference-based accounts of ethics. I shall argue that, like the empiricist retreat, either the retreat to preference is so thorough as to provide no account of practical reason or the good, or else the retreat is an illusion and presupposes an independent account of the concept it was supposed to analyze.

For the sake of clarity, I must put to one side two sets of distinctions that can be drawn among preference-based accounts of the sorts outlined earlier. First, the appeal to preference has been offered in two distinct guises. Sometimes it is presented as an account of an agent's good, on the supposition that an agent's good is to be identified with what he or she has chosen, or would choose. On other occasions, preferences figure in an account of what an agent has a reason to do. The two types of arguments are plainly distinct, for someone may well have reason to do things that are in no sense part of his or her well-being.[2] But these differences turn on an additional question that need not concern us here, regarding the relationship between a person's reasons for acting and his or her good. I shall focus on reasons for action, for it is here that preference-based accounts have both intuitive appeal and a distinguished pedigree.

In turn, on either construal, accounts of reason or the good have been offered as answering three different questions. First, they have been offered as conceptual accounts of the meaning of claims about what someone has reason to do. Second, they have been offered as ontological accounts of what it is for someone to have a reason to do something. Third, they have been offered as accounts of how claims about what someone has reason to do can be justified, and thereby used to underwrite specific claims. I shall speak of justification; those supposing that such accounts are conceptual or ontological will be addressed in passing.

The appeal of preference-based accounts of practical reason is easy to see. Preference is a concept with a well-established explanatory role – typically people behave as they do in order to get what they want. But preference can do more than allow views about practical reason to ride on the coattails of explanatory success. It is also possible to explain a person's action in light of what he or she had reason to do. A single concept provides the link between two disparate tasks.

1. Actual Preference

A standard view of rationality identifies it with the successful pursuit of one's preferences. Such an account, in turn, requires certain constraints on eligible preferences. Though some candidate constraints are debated, at a minimum there are two requirements of consistency. First, preferences must be transitively ordered: If I prefer A to B, and B to C, then I must also prefer A to C. Second, a preference ordering must be complete, in that any two outcomes must be comparable. Without satisfying these constraints, it is impossible for one to pursue one's preferences consistently, because there is no room for a contrasting concept of inconsistency. Further constraints make it possible to measure success in that pursuit, including the avoidance of strategies sure to lead to losses, and failures to take likelihoods into account.[3] In order for formal constraints on preference to do any work, the content of those preferences must be determined. Consistency must be applied to something systematically identifiable.

I begin by considering attempts to base accounts of practical reasoning on actual preferences. Such accounts, in turn, divide into two groups: those that look to the preferences revealed in a person's behavior and those that emphasize the preferences expressed by her.[4] Revealed preferences have recently been the subject of a considerable philosophical literature. Donald Davidson has argued that in order to make sense of an agent's behavior, one must suppose her to be rational, that is, to be acting in such a way as to optimally satisfy her preferences, given her beliefs about how to get what she wants. Davidson argues that without such an assumption of rationality, we have no hope of finding any sort of systematic relationship between the person and her situation. The argument is straightforward:

From a formal point of view, the situation is analogous to fundamental measurement in physics, say of length, temperature, or mass. The assignment of numbers to any of these measures assumes that a very tight set of conditions holds. And I think that we can treat the cases as parallel in the following respect. Just as the satisfaction conditions for measuring length or mass may be viewed as constitutive of the range of application of the sciences that employ these measures, so the satisfaction of the conditions of consistency and coherence must be viewed as constitutive of the range of application of such concepts as those of belief, desire, intention and action. . . . My point is that if we are to intelligibly attribute attitudes and beliefs, or usefully describe motions as behavior, then we are committed to finding, in the pattern of behavior, belief, and desire, a large degree of rationality and consistency.[5]

Some have supposed that this argument shows that a preference-based account of practical reason is inescapable.[6] We seem to have no choice but to view persons as, on the whole, doing what they have reason to do.

But if Davidson's argument is successful, it points in the opposite direction, showing that revealed preference is too weak to underwrite a normative account of practical reason. If rationality really is a constraint on interpretation, then the sense in which people do what they have reasons to do is different from the question that theories of practical reason look like they are trying to answer. An account of practical reason must, at a minimum, make possible the attribution of irrationality. Standard cases include throwing good money after bad – for example, replacing a muffler on an old car because one has just replaced the battery – overinsuring, and in general acting in ways that will be self-defeating in the long run. Other cases are more controversial, such as failing to use one's abilities, or indifference to the fate of others. But any account must make it possible for agents to succumb systematically to some of them. If a constraint on the attribution of preference is that the agent act systematically so as to get what she prefers, there is no further question of rationality to be asked. One cannot ask whether or not she is choosing her actions appropriately, because that very appropriateness is built into the notion of preference. If she appears irrational, or her behavior self-defeating, "charity" requires that we attribute a different set of preferences to her. Davidson's own (brief) career as an experimental psychologist illustrates this. Davidson sought to test whether or not people in general were capable of satisfying standard axioms of rational choice. He discovered that experimental subjects were very good – perhaps too good – at satisfying them, because in the long run they turned out always to act consistently toward satisfying *some* set of preferences.[7] The source of the difficulty here should be clear: The content of a person's preferences is fixed entirely by the need to find her rational. Plainly a more structured notion of preference is required.

Expressed preferences, which manifest themselves in what a person says she wants, seem like plausible candidates.[8] They have more structure than revealed preferences, because explicit avowals can depart from rational behavior. But when we focus on the agent's expressed preferences, supposing she has reason to do what she says she prefers to do, parallel difficulties arise. There does seem to be room for the criticism of behavior, since someone may fail to do what she claims to want to do. If Jane claims to prefer apples to oranges, yet chooses an orange on some occasion, she might seem to have failed to do what she has reason to do. But of course she can always claim either to have preferred an orange on this occasion or to have inadvertently picked up the wrong piece of fruit. That is, her expressed preferences, like her revealed preferences, can be reattributed in such a way as to make her come out rational. Now, one might suppose that to do so would be illegitimate, supposing that there is a fact of the matter about what Jane prefers, quite apart from any special pleading that she or some interpreter might do, that determines whether or not she is rational. But if there is such a fact, we need more than expressed preferences to work with. Like revealed preferences, expressed preferences are too easily adjusted to guarantee rationality. In order to make preferences more determinate, their content cannot be exhausted by an assumption of rationality. For such a determination, more structure is needed.

2. Corrected Preference

Both expressed and revealed preferences, taken at face value, fail to make sense of the extent to which rationality, and even consistency, must be thought of as an achievement, rather than something to be assumed. The appeal to actual choice or desire does not allow the minimal amount of structure needed to make sense of that achievement. The formal apparatus cannot be made to act as a constraint at all unless the circumstances of choice or declared preference are specified. Otherwise, some set of preferences will always be satisfied.

One possible strategy, recently suggested by S. L. Hurley and John Broome,[9] requires importing additional distinctions between eligible combinations of preferences. Hurley and Broome each argue that if preferences are to be attributed to an agent, the attributor must assume that the agent has some reason for preferring one outcome to another. Broome illustrates with the case of Maurice, who prefers going to Rome to going mountaineering, prefers staying home to going to Rome, and prefers going mountaineering to staying home. Maurice seems irrational; his preferences are intransitive, indeed cyclical. But Broome points out that Maurice can get himself off the hook if he has reasons for preferring one to the other. Thus he might hate climbing, because he fears it, and so prefer Rome. Yet he might also prefer home to Rome because he tires of sightseeing, but when given the choice between home and mountaineering, Maurice might well suppose that to stay home would be cowardly. Thus he is able to rationalize his preferences, and restore his own rationality. Broome points out that not just any rationale will do; had Maurice claimed that his preferences reflected the fact that it was Thursday, we would convict him of irrationality.

Whatever its other strengths and weaknesses, it is clear that this strategy will not save preference-based accounts of rationality. It imports an independent account of rationality in order to give preferences a job to do. If whether or not a particular distinction is "eligible" constrains possible preferences, then preference depends on an account of rationality, rather than providing one.

An alternative and more popular strategy is to let some specification of the choice situation constrain the agent's preferences. By holding the situation of choice fixed, we avoid the easy rationalization that caused problems for expressed and revealed preferences. An agent has reason to do not whatever she actually does, but what she would do in appropriately idealized circumstances.

The easiest way to see this is to focus on the parallel structure of accounts of practical reason in terms of hypothetical choice and empiricist accounts of color and shape in terms of hypothetical perception. Just as claims about what an agent has reason to do are supposed to be defended by appeal to what he or she would choose under appropriate circumstances, so classical empiricism sought to treat perceptual properties and physical objects as constructed out of (because justified in terms of) the way things would look to a person under normal perceptual circumstances. Just as fatigue, misinformation, or emotional agitation can interfere with choice, so too can bad lighting interfere with perception. In each case there is a need to correct for unusual circumstances, but both normal perception and undistorted choice are supposed to be essential components.

Claims about physical objects cannot be justified in terms of actual sense contents alone, for two reasons. First of all, counterfactual sense contents allow us to make sense of the possibility of error. If we want to claim that the world of medium-sized physical goods is constructed out of (i.e., justified in terms of) the world of sense, we need to be able to explain how the two can ever diverge. Non-standard lighting conditions can make a tie that normally looks red look orange; a round coin appears oval from most angles. The phenomenalist can say as much only by talking about how the tie would look under normal conditions. But this is just the tip of the much larger iceberg that provides the second reason: It won't do simply to talk about the tie having changed color, because to do so would leave no way of individuating and reidentifying the "constructed" physical objects.

The language of physical objects is a language of regularities involving enduring objects that retain some of their features. Although a dime may look round from one angle, elliptical from another, and flat from a third, it is essential to describing it as a single enduring coin to be able to relate those appearances to one another. Talk about actual sense contents provides only what Wilfrid Sellars calls "autobiographical regularities,"[10] with no basis for assigning priority to any particular configuration of objects. Blinks, head angles, the pattern of the wallpaper, and more substantial empirical regularities are all on a par, as are the various ways a coin looks from different angles. The obvious way around this problem is to specify sensations in terms of head angles, locations, and perceptual conditions. But to do so is transparently circular, because head angles, locations, and perceptual conditions must be specified in non-sensory terms. Thus non-sensory terms enter into their own definition and justification. Counterfactual sensations – how things would look – seem a more plausible solution to this problem because they make it possible to relate sense contents to one another by talking about how they *would* be related independent of accidental circumstances.[11]

The situation with hypothetical preference is strictly parallel. Actual choice is not sufficient, for a pair of reasons, strictly paralleling those that drove the epistemic phenomenalist to hypothetical perception. First is the possibility of error: An account of practical reason must allow for the possibility that a person has made an irrational choice. If we hope to construct the notion of rationality out of the notion of choice, we can't merely make them equivalent, on pain of being unable to say that something was a bad choice even relative to the agent's other ends. Yet people often do make choices under duress, when misinformed, when tired or upset, that can't plausibly be treated as providing authoritative reasons for action. Just as talk about physical objects must satisfy the requirement that a single object endure even if it is misidentified, so must the idea of what is rational for a person to do satisfy the requirement that it be rational even if it is not chosen in some particular case. To account for overall consistency while allowing for inconsistent particular choices, there must be some way of distinguishing those choices that are definitive from those that are not.

Once again, this is the tip of a much larger iceberg. Like perceptual episodes, choices cannot be merely serially arranged, on pain of losing the distinction between choosing something one didn't want and changing one's mind back and forth. In order to maintain that distinction, one must appeal to what the agent would choose under suitable conditions.

Hypothetical choice has an additional wrinkle. Unlike perception of a public world of enduring objects, the content of rational choice may well vary across similarly situated individuals, as may the choices that they would make. Thus hypothetical preference must always be relativized to a particular individual.

3. Two Kinds of Procedures

The difficulty with accounts of hypothetical preferences can be laid out in terms of John Rawls's distinction between pure and imperfect procedures. Both pure and imperfect procedures are supposed to justify their outcomes by showing that they were generated in an appropriate manner. But the appropriateness of the procedures differs considerably. The outcome of a pure procedure is justified entirely in terms of the procedure that generates it. Rawls gives the example of a fair lottery: The winner just is the person whose number is drawn. An imperfect procedure, in contrast, justifies its consequences because it is a reliable indicator of a result that can be specified independently, but cannot be identified. Rawls offers two examples. The first is the familiar practice of dividing a cake equally by having the person who cuts it get the last choice of pieces. The other is a criminal trial, which seeks to convict all and only those who are guilty. In each case, the desired result can be specified apart from the process, while the process is a reliable means of generating it. In contrast, the result of a pure procedure cannot be specified except by reference to the procedure itself.[12]

In Rawls's terms, the notion of hypothetical choice is ambiguous between a pure procedure and an imperfect one. If it is an imperfect procedure, then there must be some independent specification of the rationality, in which case choice is not definitive of rationality.

The suggestion that hypothetical choice is a pure procedure fares no better. Because the choice is never actually made, a sophisticated specification of the conditions of choice is needed in order for it to determine what a person has reason to do. But to do so in any detail is to rig the choice in favor of a specified outcome. Hypothetical choice becomes merely an expository device. But if the conditions of choice aren't specified, then the hypothetical choice ceases to be an expository device because it turns out to be no device at all.[13]

I examine these possibilities in turn.

4. Moral Phenomenalism

The parallel between hypothetical perception and hypothetical choice reveals the deep motivation for appealing to hypothetical rather than actual preferences. But it also reveals its fatal flaw – which is once again clear in the more familiar case of perception. Hypothetical perception is also ambiguous between a pure procedure and an imperfect one.

The difficulty with supposing that hypothetical perception constitutes an imperfect procedure should be clear: If physical objects exist whether or not they are perceived, and perception is merely a "reliable indicator" of their existence, they cannot be justified in terms of actual or hypothetical perception. At best, particular claims about what would be perceived depend on independently accepted claims about the way things are. Perception is ineliminable, but no longer constitutive.

But hypothetical perception cannot be a pure procedure either. The heart of the phenomenalist's claim is that the physical world is "constructed out of" actual and hypothetical sense contents, insofar as claims about it are justified solely in terms of them.[14] Phenomenalism runs into difficulty in providing a non-circular account of that construction. The appeal to hypothetical sense contents was introduced to make it possible to avoid the patently circular move of describing sense contents in terms of such physical features as head angles and the like. But this merely widens the circle without essentially changing it. Once we are committed to the existence of counterfactual sense contents, it turns out that they cannot be specified except by reference to the physical objects they are sensations of. The reason is simple: To talk about what something would look like under normal conditions is to appeal to an account of normal conditions. But "normal conditions" must be specified in terms of physical objects. To specify what is normal in terms of what would be perceived leads to a regress of hypothetical perception. The alternative is to recognize that some account of the veridicality of normal conditions is required in order for hypothetical perception to figure in an account of the physical world.

As Sellars puts it, "We thus see that

x is red $\equiv$ x looks red to standard observers in standard conditions

is a necessary truth *not* because the right hand side is a definition of 'x is red', but because 'standard conditions' means conditions in which things look what they are."[15]

Thus, Sellars suggests, talk about how things seem depends on how things (normally) are, rather than vice versa. Although it is couched in terms of meaning, Sellars's argument is best understood in terms of the role of hypothetical perception in justifying claims about how things are: Claims about how things would appear can justify claims about how things are only because they depend on yet other claims about how things are. The claim is not that sensory experience is not possible without public concepts and an account of normal conditions, but that perceptual judgments about the way things are depend on accepting the truth of claims about normal conditions. Unless some specification of normal conditions is accepted, the two sides of the "definition" are not related; talk about how things look cannot be used to justify claims about how things are. But to accept an account of normal conditions is to go *outside* the vocabulary of sense out of which claims about the physical world were supposed to be justified.

I want to suggest that the situation is parallel in the case of hypothetical choice: Insofar as it is illuminating at all, talk about what would be chosen in appropriate circumstances is parasitic on some prior account of what the agent in question has reason to choose.

Modifying the Sellarsian formula accordingly, we get

x is rational (for Y) $\equiv$ x would be chosen (by Y) in ideal conditions

is a necessary truth *not* because the right-hand side is a definition of 'x is rational (for Y)', but because 'ideal conditions' means conditions in which people choose what is rational for them.

Recast in terms of justification rather than meaning, the claim is that talk about what would be chosen can count as a justification only against a background of an account of conditions of choice. Why suppose that the parallel holds? A careful examination of the role of ideal conditions provides the key. Why do people choose what they do in ideal circumstances? Again, there are two possibilities. Either ideal choice serves as an imperfect procedure for determining a rational course of action, or else it is a pure procedure. The difficulty with claiming that it is an imperfect procedure should by now be clear: To claim it is an imperfect procedure is to require that some prior specification of the result it aims at be possible. To talk about a specified result in hypothetical terms is to add nothing to that prior specification.

What of the suggestion that it is a pure procedure? Phenomenalism about physical objects ran into difficulty because it turned out not to be a pure procedure. Can moral phenomenalism do any better?

The difficulty is to provide an account of the conditions under which a choice is to be made that is sufficiently determinate without begging any questions. Claims about what would ideally be chosen are empty unless some account of the ideal conditions is provided. Yet the idealization must be somehow justified. The trick is to do so without presupposing an account of what someone has reason to do.

If no account of the basis of choice is specified, the hypothetical choice is indeterminate. We are told only that such choices diverge from actual choices, without any account of which possible choices are authoritative. There are too many circumstances, and too many ways in which the agent might work his or her existing preferences into some coherent order. To identify what the person has reason to do with one of those choices, without saying which one, is to offer no account at all. The notion of rationality is tied to choice in the same way that truth is tied to inquiry in a caricature of Peirce's convergent realism: We know that truth is whatever an ideal community of inquirers would eventually agree on, while having no idea of which practices or communities count as ideal.

This indeterminacy is not simply a matter of not knowing in advance what the agent will choose. The problem goes deeper, because there must be some way of adjudicating between alternative idealizations. If some determinate account is provided, the question arises of how it in particular is to be justified, except by recourse to considerations about what the agent has reason to do. To do so, though, is to fall into the very sort of circularity that created problems for phenomenalism.[16]

5. A Way Out?

Perhaps the dilemma is too stark. Why not slip between the horns by limiting the degree of idealization? Bishop Butler spoke of a "cool hour" of choice, in which various influences recognized as disturbing proper choice were eliminated, thus clearing the mind and allowing choice to proceed. Thus anger, weakness of will, temptation, fatigue, and other forms of duress are readily discounted, just as legal contracts made under duress are thought to be void.

This apparent middle ground turns out not to be a middle ground at all. The dilemma recurs in a more acute form: How specific are normal circumstances? How are the circumstances of the cool hour themselves to be specified?

Consider the seemingly straightforward case of the requirement that an agent be well informed.[17] In deliberating about how best to satisfy my ends, extra information is always useful, subject only to time constraints. Yet if that is all that information is doing, it would seem that I must already know what is good for me and should be concerned only about how to get it. In contrast, if I am reflecting about what ends matter to me, the role of extra information is less clear. The problem is not that it would take too long to learn of the alternatives (for hypothetical time is no time at all), but that it is hard to see what role the information plays. If one is choosing means toward some end, the advantage of additional information is obvious. If information is not supposed to concern how to adapt means to ends, it is not obvious what role it plays, nor why decisions made in the presence of information count as well informed. Might one not be driven to despair by knowing too much?[18]

Similar difficulties multiply. Does it include the absence of all emotions, or only short-lived ones? To exclude all is to make emotional attachments irrelevant to rationality; yet to specify which are to be excluded is not a simple matter. Do moods count? Are choices made when one is bored, lonely, or elated significant? Does exposure to advertising linking beer with hard work, or chewing gum with sexuality, undermine choice? Does working at a tedious job or taking orders undermine the capacity to choose? What about attitudes toward risk, or general levels of insecurity? How many alternatives should the agent be familiar with?

I mention these examples not to belittle them, nor even to show that describing a "cool hour" is impossible. Indeed, most of them turn up in debates between defenders of ideal preference who disagree about which conditions are ideal. My aim is to show that to justify some particular description of ideal conditions requires a tacit appeal to some independently motivated account of what the agent has reason to do. That is what makes questions about the effects of various constraints seem appropriate. Otherwise we are left with no way of deciding between alternative ways in which an agent's preferences might be filtered. Unless such questions are answered, the notion of undistorted reason remains empty, and hypothetical choice remains entirely open-ended. But the only way to justify answering them in a specific way is to look at its probable results – in other words, to rig the choice, and render it impure.

Even if an uncontroversial account of distorting influences could be supplied, a further difficulty emerges when we consider what they are being
distorted *from*. It is often reasonable to talk about what would happen if
circumstances were normal – the canoe would ride better if there were less
weight in the bow, the soap would lather if the water were softer – because
the distorting influence is distorting what is taken to be a normal course of
events. Normally (i.e., when properly trimmed) canoes ride bow up; soap
normally lathers in water. Even in the case of perception, "normal" conditions
are specifiable, provided one has an independent account of veridical perception. Likewise, the concept of duress in contract law is parasitic on an
independent assumption that people are normally capable of making responsible choices. Talk about hypothetical choice has no such background to rely
on.

Once again, the parallel with phenomenalism is instructive. Phenomenalism
grows out of a set of reasonable assumptions about the circumstances in
which perception fails to be veridical: A rectangular tower looks round from
far away; a blue tie looks green under yellow light. Under such circumstances,
perceptual experience fails to be a reliable indicator of physical properties
and events. Suitably corrected, its reliability is restored. But the appropriate
corrections can be made only in terms of an independent specification of the
conditions of successful perception. A suitably corrected imperfect procedure
does not become a pure one.

By the same token, moral phenomenalism starts with plausible assumptions
about conditions that interfere with an agent choosing rationally. If someone
is tired, upset, or excited, she may choose badly. Under such circumstances,
choice fails to be a reliable procedure for determining what an agent has
reason to do. Suitably corrected, it is such a procedure. But once again, the
appropriate corrections can be justified only in light of an independent specification of what is rational. A suitably corrected imperfect procedure does
not become a pure one.

This is not to say that were a person to be in suitable circumstances, his or
her choices would not provide reasons for action, any more than the difficulties with phenomenalism show that looking at something in normal lighting
does not show its color. Rather, the point is that the connection between
preference and rationality depends on an independently established account
of the latter.[19]

6. Two Versions of Hypothetical Choice

Questions about what someone would do or want in hypothetical circumstances admit of two very different construals. These can be brought out by
considering second-person queries about a person's behavior in imaginary

situations. Such questions have the form "What would you do if . . . ?" If someone offered a bribe? If your best friend was being considered for a position for which you supposed there were better-qualified candidates? If you were caught arguing inconsistently? Such questions admit of two construals. One might be asking for something like a *prediction*: Based on what you know about yourself, how do you think you would react in such circumstances? Such questions are often asked in the context of a sort of unmasking: Don't be so critical, you probably wouldn't be able to act any differently. Alternatively, one might be asking for *advice*: What do you think someone ought to do in such circumstances? The two construals invite different answers: A person might deny that he would accept a bribe, while conceding that he might well be enticed; one might predict that she would favor a friend, while hoping for the strength not to; one might hope that he would change his views on the basis of a compelling argument, while suspecting, based on past experience, that he would be dogmatic. In each case, talk about what one would do is ambiguous between an appeal to any regular course of events and an opaque way of capturing what one ought to do.[20] To be sure, there are cases in which the two construals collapse into one: An instrumentally rational agent concerned only with advancing her ends will predictably do what she ought to do in order to advance those ends. But the two construals diverge in all those cases where what someone judges best is not what he or she will predictably do.[21]

7. Choice, Reflection, and Hypothetical Choice

The idea of basing practical reason on preference has two further sources of plausibility. The first is the view that a person's life is his to live in light of a conception of the good he has chosen. Not only is much political rhetoric couched in terms of choice, but also political culture more generally is informed by a presumption of a burden of proof according to which every issue must be treated as a matter of individual choice unless there is some reason to interfere with it. But this is a substantive political claim, and the concept of rationality cannot be rigged to presuppose it.

The second is the importance of reflection in such choices. A choice made in a cool hour is more likely to reflect one's deepest aspirations than one made in haste, under pressure, or in conformity with one's social situation. Moral reflection is also intimately connected to notions of autonomy and seems to make choices worthy of respect. But hypothetical reflection is no reflection at all; the importance of reflection is that it take place, not the particular result it achieves. That is, if reflection is a "pure procedure," it must take place to justify its outcome. Just as a fair lottery is fair because it has actually taken place, so too is a reflective choice legitimate because it has been made. To talk about what would have been chosen is like justifying some distribution of wealth by saying it could have been the outcome of a series of fair bets. Reflection that never actually takes place provides no justification at all, because the process itself carries the moral value. Hypothetical choices do not require constitutional protection.

Still, the difficulties with ideal-choice accounts of rationality do not depend entirely on the fact that the choices are non-actual. An account that applies only if the agent actually has gone through the process of reflective choice subject to some set of constraints[22] avoids the problems that result from the fact that the choice was never actually made. But it still faces the central problem: It collapses an imperfect procedure into a pure procedure. Whether or not the process of deliberation is actually carried out, some justification must be given for employing some particular set of constraints on that process. Given the multiplicity of possible constraints, there is no way to choose between them without taking into account the results they issue. To do so, though, involves an independent standard of practical reason.

8. Conclusion

I have argued that accounts of practical reason that take preference as their starting point fail for the same reason that empiricist models of perceptual knowledge fail: In each case, the apparent explanatory credentials of the concept in question that makes the account seem promising guarantee that the account will lack the resources to give an account of reasons, for either belief or action. To give an account of reasons, it must be possible for an agent to fail to do (or believe) what he or she has reason to. The explanatory power of the concept of revealed preference deprives it of the ability to *assess* the rationality of actions. Any attempt to repair this problem inevitably imports some independent account of what a person has reason to do.

The failure of empiricist accounts of perception is often thought to constitute an argument for a certain kind of realism about perceptual arguments. If perception provides reasons for belief only against the background of other beliefs about physical objects and the causal relations between them, perceptual knowledge presupposes an external world of enduring objects and cannot, on its own, provide a grounding for belief in such a world.

Does a similar conclusion about the objectivity of moral reasons – the existence of some set of independent moral facts – follow from the failures of empiricist accounts of practical reason? One might suppose, by strictly parallel reasoning, that it does. If preferences provide reasons for action only against the background of other beliefs about what some person has reason to do, then there must be facts about what persons have reason to do. Thus, in place of empiricism, we get a certain sort of rationalism about practical reason, one that appeals to novel facts of some mysterious sort. Such a conclusion will be thought by many to create more problems than it is able to solve.

I want to offer a different account: The failure of empiricist accounts of practical reason is rooted in the attempt to reduce the concept of a reason to purely factual concepts. To say that someone has reason to do something is to evaluate that person's conduct in light of a standard of conduct. Although we can ask, as a matter of fact, whether or not someone *accepts* a particular standard, no set of facts is sufficient to show that a person is *bound* by a standard. Only first-order normative argument can do that. Such normative argument always begins by accepting some things as reasons. Preferences are among the things that might be considered reasons. When it comes to choosing everything from flavors of ice cream to occupations, the mere fact that I happen to prefer one option to another is an important factor to consider. But in such cases, preferences enter into practical reasoning in the same way that any other first-order claim about reasons does. Considerations about whether or not something would be disloyal, or undignified, or humiliating enter in just the same way, and might enter into any of the same decisions. As a result, preferences enjoy no special priority, no privileged status as basic reasons. Like all other reasons, they are among the things to be considered in some cases, but not in others. And they might be assigned no weight at all in any particular case.

The situation is thus strictly parallel with the perceptual case. No set of facts is sufficient to determine what I ought to believe; I must accept some beliefs as justified in order to have reasons to accept other beliefs. How things appear to me will be among the potential reasons for accepting or rejecting particular beliefs, but they have no privileged status. But beliefs about ordinary background conditions do not enjoy a privileged status either; they too may be called into question on the basis of how things appear. Both are parts of ordinary first-order reasoning; no part provides a foundation for the other parts. Instead, each can support, or fail to support, the others.

In the same way, what I prefer, or what I would have chosen under different circumstances, is often important in deciding what to do – as I ask myself whether or not I am being rash in making some decision, I am asking myself whether or not I would have chosen differently under conditions that I take to be more conducive to choice. But beliefs about appropriate conditions of choice do not enjoy a privileged status either; they too are subject to revision, in part on the basis of choices in which they issue. Both are parts of ordinary first-order practical reasoning; no part provides a foundation for the other parts. Instead, each can support, or fail to support, the others.

In the first appendix to *An Enquiry concerning the Principles of Morals*, Hume says,

Ask a man why he uses exercise, he will answer, *because he desires to keep his health*. If you then enquire, *why he desires health*, he will readily reply *because sickness is painful*. If you push your enquiries further, and desire a reason *why he hates pain*, it is impossible that he can give any. This is an ultimate end, and is never referred to any other object. . . . Something must be [un]desireable on its own account, and this because of its immediate accord or agreement with human sentiment and affection.[23]

The view that Hume seems to be expressing here rests on a confusion. The reason that we take a person's dislike for pain as a final step in justification is not that "agreement with human sentiment" automatically provides reasons for action, any more than perception on its own provides reasons for belief.

Hume is concerned with the fact that the process of giving reasons seems to come to an end once a person appeals to his or her preferences. Hume's suggestion seems to be that preferences just *are* reasons. It seems to me that Hume's regress argument goes wrong in one way, but not another. Hume is right to note that in the context of deciding what to do, justifying our acts to others, or evaluating behavior we must simply *take* certain things to be reasons – in Hume's example, avoiding pain. But he abandons his insight when he goes on to try to explain their status as reasons in terms of their "agreement with human sentiment." The reasons we have need not fall into the sort of sequence that leads Hume to suppose that one must eventually come to a reason that requires no justification because it cannot be called into question. To the contrary, pointing to the extent to which a motivation is in "agreement with human sentiment" does not always lead one to suppose that it is a good reason. And it is only if one accepts Hume's sequenced account of justification that one would suppose that there is some *other,* deeper sentiment that leads us to refuse the invitation of a particular desire, to suppose, that is, that only a sentiment can defeat a reason. But such a view rests on a confusion. Perhaps only a sentiment can defeat a sentiment,[24] and perhaps only a reason can defeat a competing reason. But no theses about whether or not something can be defeated by something that is not of the same kind will serve to show that sentiments, motives, or any other psychological facts must be the bases of all reasons. Once we free ourselves of the idea that *something* must be the basis of any reason, we still need to decide what to do.

Notes

1. In connection with starting points for moral inquiry, see, for example, the following: Derek Parfit, *Reasons and Persons* (Oxford University Press, 1984); John Mackie, *Ethics: Inventing Right and Wrong* (Harmondsworth: Penguin, 1978); David Gauthier, *Morals by Agreement* (Oxford University Press, 1986); G. H. von Wright, *Varieties of Goodness* (London: Routledge & Kegan Paul, 1963); James

Griffin, *Well-Being* (Oxford University Press, 1986); John Rawls, *A Theory of Justice* (Cambridge, MA: Harvard University Press, 1971); John Harsanyi, *Essays on Ethics, Social Behavior, and Scientific Explanation* (Dordrecht: Reidel, 1976); Richard Brandt, *A Theory of the Good and Right* (Oxford University Press, 1978); David Lewis, "Dispositional Theories of Value," *Proceedings of the Aristotelian Society*, suppl. vol., 63:113–37, 1989.

    The entire "public-choice" literature presumes that preferences are the appropriate inputs to governmental decision-making. Seminal works include the following: James Buchanan and Gordon Tullock, *The Calculus of Consent* (Ann Arbor: University of Michigan Press, 1962); Kenneth Arrow, *Social Choice and Individual Values*, 2nd ed. (New Haven, CT: Yale University Press, 1963). For a critique, see Cass Sunstein, "Preferences and Politics," *Philosophy and Public Affairs*, 20(3):3–34, 1991.

2. The literature on this subject divides roughly equally between accounts of reason and accounts of the good. In their works cited in note 1, Derek Parfit, John Mackie, and David Gauthier seek to derive preference-based accounts of the requirements of practical reason. In their cited works, G. H. von Wright, James Griffin, and John Rawls all defend accounts of the good that appeal to choice. In the nineteenth century, accounts of good were offered by J. S. Mill in *Utilitarianism* and Henry Sidgwick in *The Methods of Ethics*. John Harsanyi (*Essays on Ethics*) defends choice-based accounts of both, in different places, as does Richard Brandt (*Theory of the Good and Right*). David Lewis ("Dispositional Theories of Value") offers a preference-based account of value that appears to be generic between the two.

3. Of course, the details of these constraints are controversial in ways that need not concern us here. For standard treatments, see the following: Richard Jeffrey, *The Logic of Decision*, 2nd ed. (University of Chicago Press, 1983); R. D. Luce and H. Raiffa, *Games and Decisions* (New York: Wiley, 1957); David Gauthier, *Morals by Agreement*.

4. A third possibility, though immediately tempting, quickly proves hopeless: the view that preferences are experienced conscious states. That view, associated both with traditional empiricism and, more recently, with "Austrian Economics," was put forward by Eugen von Böhm-Bawerk, *Karl Marx and the Close of His System* (New York: Augustus M. Kelley, 1949; translation of *Zum Abschluss des Marxchen Systems*, Berlin, 1896), and was developed by Ludwig von Mises in *Human Action* (University of Chicago Press, 1949). Its difficulty arises from its claim that preferences both are present to consciousness and apply to indefinitely many possible cases. For reasons made familiar by Wittgenstein, such an account works no better for preference than for rule following (see *Philosophical Investigations*, paragraph 70).

5. Donald Davidson, "Psychology as Philosophy," in his *Essays on Actions and Events* (Oxford University Press, 1980), p. 237.

6. Including Davidson: See "A New Basis for Decision Theory," *Theory and Decision*, 18:87–98, 1985.

7. Donald Davidson, "Psychology as Philosophy," in *Essays on Actions and Events*.

8. Davidson's view does not include a sharp line between expressed and revealed preferences. Speech behavior is treated as simply more behavior, on the basis of which preferences can be attributed, given an assumption of overall rationality.

9. See the following: S. L. Hurley, *Natural Reasons* (Oxford University Press, 1989); John Broome, "Rationality and the Sure Thing Principle," in *Thoughtful Eco-*

nomic Man, ed. Gay Meeks (Cambridge University Press, 1991); John Broome, *Weighing Choices* (Oxford: Basil Blackwell, 1991).

10. Wilfrid Sellars, "Phenomenalism," in *Science, Perception, and Reality* (London: Routledge & Kegan Paul, 1964).

11. Berkeley provides an alternative way out of this problem: He claims that to be is to be actually perceived by God. As a result, all things are always actually perceived, so no counterfactuals need to be introduced. Subsequent phenomenalists have been unwilling to embrace Berkeley's solution.

12. Rawls, *A Theory of Justice*, p. 85. It is not clear that there are any procedures that are entirely pure in Rawls's sense. Even a lottery produces a result specifiable as random. Still, it must actually take place in order for there to be a winner. The same may be true of cake cutting – there are infinitely many equal divisions, though cutting is required to produce a specific one.

13. Although it is hard to resist the temptation to say that an agent ought to do what she would decide to do if she knew everything, it is not at all obvious why this should be so. It may be that if I knew everything, I would offer people unsolicited advice; it does not follow that I should do so now.

14. Rudolf Carnap, *The Logical Structure of the World and Pseudo-problems in Philosophy*, translated by Rolf George (Berkeley: University of California Press, 1967), pp. 5–10, 148–51. See also J. S. Mill, *An Examination of Sir William Hamilton's Philosophy* (1865, appendix).

15. Wilfrid Sellars, "Empiricism and the Philosophy of Mind," in *Science, Perception, and Reality*, p. 147.

16. In *Well-Being*, James Griffin offers another (heroic) compromise, claiming that under ideal circumstances people will in fact choose just those goods that are independently known to be valuable. The role of choice in Griffin's account remains obscure, except insofar as it leaves room for a state to actively promote those goods without being coercive.

17. This construal is offered as an account of what is good for a person by, among others, Rawls, Brandt, and Sidgwick, and (with a minor modification incorporating "experience" rather than full information) by Lewis as an account of value.

18. This point has been made in various ways by the following: Mark Johnston, "Dispositional Theories of Value," *Proceedings of the Aristotelian Society*, suppl. vol. 63: 139–74, 1989; J. David Velleman, "Brandt's Definition of 'Good'," *Philosophical Review*, 97(3):353–71, 1988; Allan Gibbard, *Wise Choices, Apt Feelings* (Cambridge, MA: Harvard University Press, 1990).

19. Sellars's own account of color treats it as a feature of perceivers rather than of objects. Perhaps an account of choice can be constructed in parallel fashion. The account I have given of hypothetical choice need not take a stand on this question. Phenomenalism's parallel structure, like Sellars's account of it, applies to shapes as well as colors. The issue concerns the need for a nonperceptual account of perceivable properties, not their mind-independence.

20. Stanley Cavell makes a related point in discussing what he calls "projective imagination." See *The Claim of Reason* (Oxford University Press, 1979).

21. In experiments studying obedience to authority, Stanley Milgram found that most subjects were willing to inflict what they believed to be painful and even lethal electrical shocks when pressured to do so by experimenters. But of course most people, when asked what they would do, denied that they would be so obedient. Plainly the evaluative and predictive senses of "would" have come apart in these

cases. See Stanley Milgram, *Obedience to Authority* (New York: Harper & Row, 1974).

Annette Baier has proposed that the worthiness of a particular case of trust can be assessed by considering whether or not it would survive knowledge of its basis. Baier's suggestion employs the normative sense of "would" involved here. Psychological mechanisms of various sorts may reinforce bad trust as they reinforce bad faith. The test has content because it relies on assessing whether or not one could justify continuing the trust, rather than whether or not one could psychologically pull it off. See "Trust and Antitrust," *Ethics*, 96: 231–60, 1986.

22. See, for example, David Gauthier, *Morals by Agreement*, Chapter 2, which supposes that preferences are rational only if revealed and expressed preferences coincide.
23. David Hume, *An Enquiry concerning the Principles of Morals*, in *Enquiries concerning Human Understanding and concerning the Principles of Morals*, ed. L. A. Selby-Bigge (Oxford University Press, 1975), p. 293.
24. Heidegger offers this as an analysis of Kant's account of moral personality in the *Critique of Practical Reason*. See Heidegger, *Basic Problems of Phenomenology* (Bloomington: Indiana University Press, 1982), pp. 140–2.

Rational Temptation

CLAIRE FINKELSTEIN

1

"To characterize a person as rational is not to relate him to any order, or system, or framework, which would constrain his activities," writes David Gauthier.[1] Reason is free, he thinks, to develop its own path to any ends it takes as given. The suggestion appears in the earliest of Gauthier's essays in which he recognizes the freedom of reason from the strict constraints of maximization. And while Gauthier did not intend his words in this sense, he might have put his point about maximization in this form as well: To conceive of practical reason as subservient to a system of ends is to conceive its independence from any determinate path in the pursuit of those ends. The form of reasoning, as well as its content, must be instrumentally supplied. Gauthier's famous claim that instrumental reason sometimes demands the constraint of its own maximizing activity is thus dependent on the recognition of reason's freedom from constraint.

But to say that reason is free from constraint in *this* sense is to posit reason's constraint in another. Like many committed to understanding practical reason instrumentally, Gauthier accepts the economist's picture of the ends it is reason's purpose to pursue as established by the preferences of the agent whose ends they are. Reason's freedom, Gauthier thinks, is the freedom to serve the preferences of rational agents. Gauthier's recognition of reason's freedom from maximization thus depends on his willingness to accept the idea of reason's constraint, constraint by the preferences of the rational agents it serves.

As we shall see, a tension emerges in the attempt to treat reason both as

I wish to thank Kurt Baier, Michael Bratman, Donald Bruckner, Bob Cooter, Meir Dan-Cohen, Peter Detre, Logi Gunnarson, Ed Harcourt, John Searle, Scott Shapiro, and Michael Thompson, as well as members of Bob Cooter's and John Searle's seminars on rationality, for comments on various drafts of this essay. At the risk of saying what could go without saying, I am especially indebted to David Gauthier, whose generosity and patience have been my philosophical *terra firma* for the past dozen years.

constrained by preferences and as free to conduct itself in any manner necessary to serve the ends those preferences establish. Constrained maximization requires a rational agent to act at times against the weight of her current preferences in pursuit of reason's ends. But the economist's understanding of practical reason as preferential is imperialistic: Once it is accepted anywhere in an account of rational agency, it becomes difficult to reject that same restriction on a rational agent's choice of each and every action. It thus becomes difficult to reject the idea of preferential constraint as a pervasive feature of rational agency.

In this essay, I shall argue that making sense of preferential constraint as a standard feature of practical reasoning commits one to regarding counterpreferential agency as irrational across the board. I shall argue the point in reference to the problem of changing preferences over time. As we shall see, Gauthier and others who share the central features of his account lean heavily on a supposed asymmetry between the way a rational agent forms plans and the way she executes them: Plan-adoption is preferentially constrained, but the performance of actions in the execution of a plan is potentially counterpreferential. I shall argue that this asymmetry is not defensible and that proponents of this approach must choose between preferential constraint and freedom from preferences generally. I shall then make the further suggestion that the tension inherent in the sort of account Gauthier's theory exemplifies is best resolved by rejecting the idea that preferences *ever* function as an absolute constraint on practical deliberation for a rational agent. While I cannot argue for this rather bold claim in any detail, I can present some intuitive reasons for thinking it correct, reasons I hope will be of special interest to the rational choice theorist. My thought is that those who accept the broad picture of rational agency as self-interest ought to hesitate before articulating that view in terms of preference maximization.

2

I shall focus on a kind of change-of-preference case we might call *rational temptation*. A rational temptation is a temptation an agent faces due to a temporary shift in her preference ordering. By calling the temptation *rational*, I mean to distinguish it from another sort of familiar case. Sometimes agents are drawn to do things on the basis of appetites or urges, despite the fact that their overall preferences do not support doing them. A smoker trying desperately to quit might retain a preference that she not smoke, even while she finds herself drawn to take another cigarette. On all but the narrowest possible interpretation of "preference," we might describe this by saying the smoker is tempted to take another cigarette *against* the weight of her preferences.[2] In this way, we can distinguish an agent who yields to a rational temptation from an agent who yields to an appetite or urge. The former faces a problem in rational choice theory. What she requires is an argument to convince her of the rationality of resisting temptation. The latter faces a problem in action theory or psychology. She is convinced of the rationality of resisting the temptation; she simply cannot conform her behavior to what she knows it is rational to do.

As our case of rational temptation, let us take an example of Michael Bratman's.[3] A pianist performs nightly at a club, prior to which he eats dinner with a friend who fancies good wines. Each night the pianist is tempted to drink with dinner. He knows, however, that drinking wine will impair his evening performance, and thus prior to dinner he prefers that he refuse the wine. Nevertheless the pianist invariably finds himself tempted to sacrifice his performance for the sake of a good Cabernet.

The pianist's case is one of shifting preferences. Prior to and after dinner he prefers the option *drink no wine with dinner and play well tonight*. During dinner, however, the pianist has a reversal of preference. He temporarily prefers the sequence *drink wine with dinner and play less well tonight*. If he were to determine his behavior in accordance with deliberations conducted during dinner, he would maximize his preferences at that time by opting for the wine. Were he to do this, however, he would later regret his decision, since after dinner he would prefer to play well that evening and would wish he had forgone the wine. He is, moreover, *aware* that he will regret it if he drinks, for he knows that after dinner he will return to his prior preference ordering, which favors protecting his evening performance above all.

If the pianist is *myopic* with regard to his future preferences, he will go to dinner thinking it best to refuse the wine, but he will end up choosing to drink after all, since his preferences will have shifted by the time he must decide what to do. The myopic deliberator is hostage to his preferences at all times. The economist suggests a solution: The pianist should find a way of precommitting to the decision to resist wine with dinner before the change in preference occurs. The pianist might accomplish this, for example, by deciding not to go to dinner at all. This is the *sophisticated* solution to rational temptation cases. There is a sense in which it is an unfortunate solution, since it requires the pianist to deprive himself of dinner in order to avoid drinking. He most wishes he could go to dinner and not drink rather than having to avoid dinner entirely, but he knows he will drink if given the chance. He should therefore settle for eliminating the source of temptation altogether, by precommitting to a course of action that precludes drinking. The sophisticated solution is accordingly second-best, but it is a clear improvement over the myopic solution.

Drawing on reflections about interpersonal coordination in bargaining contexts, however, an alternative to the economist's solution has recently gained adherents, Gauthier among them. Thinking of the pianist ex ante (prior to dinner) as a different self from the pianist ex post (during dinner) suggests a way of conceiving the situation that makes going to dinner but not drinking an available solution. Call this the *resolute* solution.[4] The resolute solution is available, the argument runs, because it is a better solution for both the ex ante self and the ex post self than is the other available solution, namely, the sophisticated solution. It is better than the sophisticated solution because avoiding dinner altogether would give the ex ante pianist his second-best solution and the ex post self his worst solution. The resolute solution, on the other hand, would give the ex ante pianist his best solution and the ex post pianist his second-best solution.[5] And although the ex post pianist would prefer the myopic solution, that solution is unavailable, since the ex ante self has every incentive to avoid it by being sophisticated and skipping dinner altogether. Going to dinner and not drinking is thus optimal. Speaking of the pianist as divided into different time-slice selves is of course intended meta-phorically. The resolute solution does not depend on any particular account of personal identity. The point can be put just as well in terms of a unified self: The pianist should regard himself as faring best under the plan that involves choosing to go to dinner and not drinking, since he does better under that plan at each moment in his history than he would do under any alternative plan he might adopt.

It is not clear, however, that the foregoing argument can allay concerns about the resolute solution's availability.[6] At dinner, after all, the pianist will have nothing further to gain from refraining from drinking. The only reason he accepted the plan in the first place was to ensure he would be able to go to dinner. But here he is at dinner, so what is now to stop him from drinking? Unfortunately the pianist will realize prior to dinner that he might come to reason in this way, and this will make him think that the plan of going to dinner and not drinking is infeasible. Against the resolute solution, it might be argued generally that plans calling for actions contrary to an agent's preferences at the moment of execution are not available for a rational agent to adopt. Indeed, we might say that the resolute plan is either infeasible or unnecessary: It is feasible only where the actions it calls for are preferential, in which case it is unnecessary, since a rational agent would have acted in accordance with it even in the absence of a prior intention or plan.[7]

Gauthier and Bratman, who both endorse the resolute solution in this context,[8] account for its availability by specifying conditions under which it is rational for an agent to refrain from reconsidering a previously formed intention or plan. Bratman argues that it is rational to refrain from reconsidering a prior intention in cases that satisfy what he calls the "no-regret condition."[9] That condition asks whether the agent believes that at some time in the future she will be glad she stuck with her intention, and whether she believes she will wish she had stuck with it if she does not. In this case the pianist knows, even at dinner, that he would regret abandoning his plan to refrain from drinking and that he would be glad he had stuck with the plan if he does. Assuming that no new information emerges that would cast doubt on the original advisability of the prior intention, the pianist should think it rational to refrain from reconsidering his intention not to drink with dinner.

For Gauthier, it is rational to constrain one's deliberations in accordance with a prior plan when one can expect to do better under the plan than one would have done if one had never adopted the plan at all.[10] When this condition is met at a given time, Gauthier says the plan is "confirmed" for that agent at that time. "Full confirmation" is when a course of action is "confirmed in each possible situation in which it would require some particular action or decision."[11] Full confirmation constitutes a filter on eligible plans: "only courses of action that the agent expects would be fully confirmed are eligible for adoption."[12] Gauthier presumably would regard the pianist's plan to go to dinner and refrain from drinking as fully confirmed, since the pianist can think of himself as better off under it than he would have been without the plan both in the ex ante and in the ex post contexts, and thus he can regard himself as better off under the plan at each point at which he must make a decision – first when he must decide whether to go to dinner, and later when he must decide whether to drink with dinner.

One way to defend the resolute solution to cases of rational temptation is thus in terms of a two-tier story involving constraint by preferences in the selection of intentions or plans, on the one hand, and a relaxation of that constraint in the context of plan-execution, on the other. This is the defense of resolution Bratman and Gauthier favor.[13] Our question will be whether they can resist allowing counter-preferential deliberation outside of plans once they have accepted it in the execution of an existing plan. If, as I shall argue, they cannot resist the extension, they will have reason to rethink their use of a prior intention or plan in cases of rational temptation. If counter-preferential behavior cannot be ruled out by the theory of rationality outside the context of plan-execution, then the fact that the pianist does better in terms of his current preferences would not be sufficient to make his adoption of the plan required by the resolute solution rational. I shall suggest accordingly that the formation of the prior intention the resolute choice theorist advocates is an explanatory fifth wheel in rational temptation cases, since the benefit resolution is supposed to provide turns out to be available without it.

3

Rationality sometimes seems to require agents to reason counter-preferentially outside the context of a previously formed plan. A slightly modified version of our pianist case will illustrate the point. Suppose the temptation to drink wine with dinner is sprung on the pianist, such that he must decide whether to drink without the advantage of advance deliberation. This means he must decide whether to drink at the same moment that his preferences most strongly support drinking. What could possibly entitle the resolute choice theorist to say that the pianist should abstain from drinking in the modified case? Since the pianist has no opportunity to form an intention not to drink, a counter-preferential reason to refrain from drinking cannot be derived from a preferentially formed intention to do so, as it might be in the original case. The answer that is consistent with the solution Bratman and Gauthier favor, then, is to say that the pianist *should* drink with dinner in the modified case. It is not that he lacks the ability to resist wine with dinner, or at any rate, not *just* that he lacks the ability. It is rather that it would not be rational for him to refrain from drinking with dinner, since there is no reason in that case not to maximize the preferences he has at the moment of choice. In Gauthier's terms, the plan to refrain from drinking with dinner is not "fully confirmed" in the modified case. The rational choice theorist is thus apparently committed to saying that resisting drinking with dinner would be irrational for the pianist in the modified case.

Now I think this answer is likely to sit uncomfortably with anyone who is not already in the grip of a theory that endorses it. One is inclined to say that whether it is rational for the pianist to refrain from drinking with dinner should not be a function of whether he had advance warning he would be offered wine with dinner. That, at any rate, would be a curious principle for a theory of rational choice to endorse. Furthermore, the rationality of refusing wine with dinner in the modified case is suggested by the fact that the pianist knows he will regret it later if he drinks now. Should we really think it rational for a person to do something he knows he will regret? Bratman in particular might be concerned about a theory with such an outcome. Why, after all, should regret have significance for a rational agent inside a plan but none outside it? Let us then consider whether the resolute choice theorist can account for the rationality of not drinking with dinner in the modified case.

A recent suggestion of Gauthier's holds out some hope. In quite a different context, Gauthier distinguishes between an agent's "proximate" preferences, meaning the preferences he has at a given moment of choice, and his "vanishing-point" preferences, the preferences he acknowledges when choice is not imminent. Gauthier suggests that "at any given time, although a person may want to act on his now proximate preferences, he does not want to act at other times on what would be his then proximate preferences, where these are in conflict with the vanishing-point preferences that he now holds."[14] A rational agent will thus realize that he must not deliberate in a way that leads him always to act on his proximate preferences. He must instead adopt a policy of deciding in accordance with his vanishing-point preferences.

The example Gauthier gives is a person faced with a choice of chocolate or fruit on each of five occasions. Suppose that when the choice is imminent, the agent prefers chocolate, but at any other time he prefers fruit. Gauthier suggests that the agent can regard his choice between a chocolate and a fruit as a choice between two policies or modes of decision-making he might adopt: *choosing on the basis of proximate preferences*, on the one hand, or *choosing on the basis of vanishing-point preferences*, on the other. Although the agent prefers chocolate to fruit on each occasion on which he must choose, he does not prefer the mode of decision-making that involves choosing on the basis of proximate preferences, for then he would choose chocolate on all five occasions, and this is something he does not want to do. Indeed, he prefers a mode of decision-making that requires him to choose fruit on all occasions to a mode that requires him to choose chocolate on all occasions, even though he currently prefers a chocolate to a fruit. He should thus choose the mode of decision-making that requires him always to choose in accordance with his vanishing-point preferences, and this will result in his choosing a fruit on this occasion, despite his current preference for chocolate.[15]

Might the resolute choice theorist use the idea of choice over modes of decision-making to solve the modified pianist case?[16] The pianist does not want to choose on future occasions in accordance with his proximate preferences, since he does not want to drink every night prior to performing at the club. He prefers to drink wine with dinner tonight, but he does not now prefer that he drink wine with dinner on each successive evening on which he must face the same choice. He should therefore choose in accordance with his vanishing-point preferences now, and this will enable him to refrain from drinking on this and on all future occasions. Bratman suggests he might endorse this sort of solution as well. In "Planning and Temptation," he says that cases of temptation may be solved by the adoption of what George Ainslie calls "personal rules."[17] A personal rule applied to a series of choices means that an agent can think of himself as choosing "a whole series of rewards at once." Indeed, he claims it a virtue of a planning theory of agency, by contrast with standard utility theory's outcome-oriented assessment, that it is able to make sense of personal rules of this sort.[18]

While the appeal to personal policies is a natural one for the resolute choice theorist to make, it ultimately proves unsuccessful. The reason is that the pianist in the modified case will have no reason to select the series that requires him to refrain from drinking on all occasions. That would be irrational, given his current preferences. True, the pianist prefers that he not drink on all future occasions, but his preferences with respect to the present occasion support his drinking now. The rational series for the pianist to adopt would thus be *drink now and refrain from drinking on all future occasions*. The same is true of the choice between fruit and chocolate. I may have a strong preference for choosing fruit on all future occasions. But what is to supply the preference for choosing fruit on this occasion? After all, the sequence *chocolate now and fruit on future occasions* would satisfy my preferences better than any other available sequence. And if I worry that I would reason that way on each future occasion, and so choose chocolate each time, my fears should be allayed by the thought that on those occasions I will merely be implementing a plan that is already in place. I should therefore be able to resist the chocolate on those occasions. Since my present choice is a choice of which plan to adopt, by the resolute choice theorist's own lights it seems I cannot choose counter-preferentially, and thus I am constrained to choose the plan that involves chocolate now and fruit later.

What Gauthier seems to have in mind is that a choice over a series of choices is structurally different from a choice on a single occasion. Insofar as the former involves a choice of a mode of decision-making, he thinks there will be constraints on an agent's choice that there would not otherwise be. Thus Gauthier presumably would want to say that there is no mode of decision-making that corresponds to a choice of chocolate now and fruit on all future occasions. Such a choice would involve choosing on the basis of proximate preferences for this occasion and choosing on the basis of vanishing-point preferences for all future occasions. This does not represent a generalized pattern of decision-making. In this sense, Gauthier's theory is asymmetrical as between modes of decision-making and plans, since he apparently sees no comparable structural constraints on what can count as a feasible plan.

Two obvious questions present themselves. First, why is choice over a series of choices structurally different from choice on a single occasion? Why, in particular, does it involve a choice of a mode of decision-making? Second, what is Gauthier using to individuate modes of decision-making, and thus what is he using to rule out some potential 'modes' from consideration? If the test of the feasibility of a plan is its benefit to the agent who adopts it, as measured by his current preferences, why would we not use the same test for modes of decision-making? Presumably the feasibility of a choice of a mode of decision-making should be the product of a theory of rational choice (as it is in the case of plans) rather than a constraint on it. And since it would be preference-maximizing for an agent to adopt whatever mode allowed him to choose a chocolate now and a fruit on all future occasions, *that* mode should be feasible for a rational agent to adopt.

If the foregoing is correct, appeal to a series of choices can do no work in the modified pianist case, for it cannot enable the pianist to resist temptation on the present occasion. The only reason the pianist may be able to resist future temptation is that he knows about those occasions in advance. That is, with respect to each future member of the series, he is like the pianist in the original case prior to being tempted with the wine. If he knows in advance that he will be subject to temptation, he can form the intention to resist and then rely on some reasonable approach to reconsideration to avoid abandoning the intention once formed. But if he does not know about the temptation prior to being subject to it, he has no basis for resisting, and so he must choose to eat the chocolate or drink the wine, as the case may be.

Now I want to claim that its inability to deal with cases of rational temptation absent advance notice of the temptation is a major defect of the resolute approach. The rational response to temptation ought not depend on how an agent is situated temporally with respect to his exposure to it. The best that can be said in support of the asymmetric positions of the pianist with advance warning and the pianist without it is that the asymmetry may capture something of our experience in dealing with temptation: We may find it easier to resist temptation if exposed to it after having had an opportunity to prepare ourselves for its onslaught. But even if phenomenologically plausible, this surely does not suggest that an account of the rational response to temptation should enshrine this asymmetry as a virtue. The problem, then, with the resolute solution is that it must treat a rational agent as precluded from resisting some temptations to which she knows she will regret succumbing, temptations it would be rational for her to resist given advance notice. This seems a highly dubious feature of a theory of rationality.

The appeal to modes of deliberation, had it succeeded, would have given the resolute choice theorist a way of justifying decisions that currently are counter-preferential, consistent with the requirement of preferential constraint on plans. It would thus have made preferential constraint on plan-adoption a more plausible requirement, for that requirement would not then have stood in the way of the intuitive answer to the modified pianist case and its ilk. Absent some other solution to cases of this sort, the resolute choice theorist should feel himself under pressure to abandon preferential constraint on plan-adoption. And if he abandons that requirement, the prior intention becomes an unnecessary element of a solution to the original pianist case as well.

That is the intuitive case against the resolute solution to cases of rational temptation. But what if the resolute choice theorist is willing to bite the bullet in the modified case and accept that the pianist has no reason to refrain from drinking with dinner? I shall argue in the next section that he faces difficulties even if he is willing to make this move. The reason is that the resolute choice theorist's account of plan-execution commits him to the possibility that plan-adoption might fail to be preferential. This supplies a second reason to think he cannot have his solution to the original pianist case, since, if correct, the formation of the prior intention would once again turn out to be otiose. I shall further suggest that there are at least two reasons for the resolute choice theorist to favor his account of plan-execution over his account of plan-adoption, and to abandon the requirement of preferential constraint: First, the modified case is most sensibly dealt with by saying that the pianist should form an immediate, counter-preferential plan not to drink with dinner. Second, preferential constraint on plans can be defended only if one is prepared to accept preferential constraint on *both* practical judgment and decision. I shall suggest, however, that these are implausible requirements.

4

It seems natural to think the pianist would reason as follows when confronted with the choice whether to drink in the modified case: "If I drink now, I will regret it, and so I will refrain from drinking with dinner." That, at any rate, would be a Bratman-type thought to have. Alternatively, he might think, "I will fare better overall if I refrain from drinking with dinner," to frame matters as Gauthier suggests. The question is why Bratman and Gauthier think the pianist cannot reason in this way, and why, in particular, he is constrained to reason on the basis of his current preferences.

The explanation must lie in some principle or thesis they accept that rules out counter-preferential behavior outside the context of a previously adopted plan. What thesis might it be? First, they might subscribe to a thesis having to do with the nature of *judgment*. Suppose a rational agent lacked the capacity to judge that she had reason to do a thing if doing it would conflict with her preferences at the time of judgment. Then no rational agent could adopt a plan that was not supported by her current preferences at the time of plan-adoption, since presumably she would have to judge it favorably in order to incorporate it into a plan. Let us call this the *thesis of the dependence of judgment on preferences* (TDJ).

Second, they might think a rational agent lacked the capacity to *decide* to do what she judged she had most reason to do if her decision would conflict with her immediate preferences at the moment of decision. Although an agent could judge that she had reason to forgo a certain temptation, she might be unable to allow that judgment to determine her actions, because she would be unable to decide to act on the basis of a judgment that derogated from her preferences at the moment of action. Let us call this the *thesis of the dependence of decision on preferences* (TDD).

Third, a rational agent might simply be unable to perform actions that would derogate from her preferences at the time of action. That is, although she might be able to judge that she had reason to adopt a course of action that would be counter-preferential at the moment of execution, and although she might be able to decide in favor of such a course of action, she might be unable to translate judgment and decision into action in defiance of preference. Let us call this the *thesis of the dependence of action on preferences* (TDA). The question we shall ask is whether Bratman and Gauthier might subscribe to any of these principles to preclude counter-preferential plan-adoption. If any *one* of these principles is correct, they would have a basis for maintaining preferential constraint at the level of plan-adoption. I take it, furthermore, that there are no other plausible theses by which the rational choice theorist might seek to justify preferential constraint. So he must subscribe to one of these three if he is to defend his requirement that plan-adoption be preferential. The question will then be whether the relevant thesis can be adopted consistent with retaining counter-preferential plan-execution.

TDA can be summarily dismissed for present purposes, for clearly neither Bratman nor Gauthier can subscribe to it. This follows directly from a feature that is common to their solutions: They think an agent can act against the weight of his current preferences, as long as he has formed the intention to do so in advance. The resolute choice theorist thus assumes the falsity of TDA, since he is attempting to offer an account of the very phenomenon it declares impossible. Indeed, even the economist believes that rational agents can act against the weight of their preferences. He simply arranges matters so that the counter-preferential action does not depend on counter-preferential rational processes at the moment of execution. It is thus the resolute choice theorist's commitment to *deliberative* counter-preferential behavior that provides the thin edge of the wedge: Once he accounts for counter-preferential behavior by positing counter-preferential deliberative processes, he is hard-pressed to account for the necessity of *preferential* deliberation elsewhere.

Let us now consider whether the resolute choice theorist can explain his commitment to preferentially constrained plan-adoption in terms of either TDJ or TDD.

We might formulate TDJ as follows:

> *Thesis of the Dependence of Judgment* (TDJ): A rational agent cannot judge at a time *t* that it would be rational for her to perform an action *A* rather than another action *A'* if *A'* is better supported by the balance of her preferences at *t*.

It does not matter for TDJ what the agent believes her preferences at the time of action will be: TDJ requires only that the content of the agent's current preferences, whether preferences over present or future actions, determines the content of the judgment she forms about what she ought to do. Should the resolute choice theorist think of judgment as constrained by preferences in this way?

The thesis that judgment is constrained by preferences seems implausible on its face. After all, judgment is a cognitive faculty, "a faculty of thinking," as Kant says.[19] As such, it need make no essential reference to the preferences of the judging agent. Moreover, it would be patently absurd to think of judgment about theoretical matters as constrained by preferences. Why should practical judgment, namely judgment about what an agent ought to do, be any more constrained? While I think the idea that judgment is constrained by preferences as implausible in practical as in theoretical matters, we need not make the case against this view of judgment directly at present. As I shall argue, the resolute choice theorist's view of reconsideration within plans commits him to rejecting TDJ, and thus it is not open to *him* to adopt it.

Both Bratman's no-regret principle and Gauthier's account of plan-confirmation suggest that an agent can judge counter-preferentially in the context of the execution of an existing plan, since on both accounts an agent must judge that she should not reconsider in the face of current preferences that support reconsideration. The agent is to reach this determination by judging in accordance with the relevant principle that suggests when it is rational to reconsider. On one version, the agent judges that she should not reconsider on the grounds that she would regret not performing the action to which her prior intention committed her. On the other version, she judges that she should not reconsider on the grounds that she can see herself as better off having formed and executed her prior intention than she would be had she never formed the intention in the first place.

It is somewhat unclear whether the resolute choice theorist thinks of the relevant judgment as judgment in favor of the action called for by the prior intention or whether the judgment pertains solely to reconsideration, that is, whether it is a judgment by the agent that she ought not reconsider. But the difference between these formulations is irrelevant for our purposes, for either way the judgment must be counter-preferential. It is counter-preferential by hypothesis if it is a judgment in favor of the action called for by the plan. And it is presumably also counter-preferential if it is a judgment in favor of non-reconsideration, since the refusal to reconsider is what stands in the way of the agent's maximizing her preferences at the time of action. So both Bratman and Gauthier recognize counter-preferential judgment in at least one context. The burden is on them to explain why they would disallow it in others.

The resolute choice theorist may wish to argue that the relevant judgment is not counter-preferential, since it is only a judgment in favor of non-reconsideration, and the agent in fact has no preference in favor of reconsideration itself. What she has is a preference for the action she would take were she to reconsider. Since she does not know what she would do until she reconsiders, he may argue, she has no preference in favor of reconsideration *per se*. But this interpretation of the resolute choice theorist's account strikes me as implausible. For each principle suggests that the agent's decision about whether to reconsider is transparent with respect to the action she would take were she to reconsider. Transparency is presupposed both by the no-regret condition and by the confirmation condition, since whether the agent would regret reconsidering or would regard herself as better off under the prior plan is at least partly a function of the action she would perform after reconsidering, as compared with the action required by the plan. So I think it fair to regard the judgment in favor of non-reconsideration on the resolute choice theorist's view as counter-preferentially formed.

If this is correct, the resolute choice theorist appears to endorse counter-preferential judgment in the context of a plan at the same time that he denies its possibility in the context of plan-adoption. If he cannot account for the difference between these contexts, he must abandon one claim or the other. If he abandons preferential constraint on judgment in the context of plan-formation, that does not yet commit him to abandoning the idea that plan-formation must be preferential. For he might still accept preferential constraint on decision, and that would provide an independent ground for the restriction on plan-formation. So let us turn to TDD:

> *Thesis of the Dependence of Decision on Preferences* (TDD): A rational agent cannot deliberatively decide at a time t to perform an action A if another course of action A' is better supported by her preferences at t.

Commitment to TDD is essential if preferential constraint on plan-adoption is to be maintained, now that we have rejected TDJ, since otherwise an agent could judge a counter-preferential plan best and could decide in favor of it. Moreover, it should be clear even at this stage that TDD is essential for the claim that plan-formation is necessary for dealing with cases of rational temptation, even apart from the stance one takes on judgment. For it is only because an agent has no resources for deciding against the weight of her current preferences that she must resort to plan-formation, according to the resolute choice theorist. So the resolute choice theorist needs TDD. The question is whether he can have it.[20]

There are two reasons for thinking the resolute choice theorist cannot accept TDD. The first is that it is not compatible with rejecting TDJ. The second is that he is committed to accepting counter-preferential decision in the context of reconsideration within an existing plan, and once again he offers no basis for distinguishing the context of plan-adoption from the context of plan-execution.

First, suppose the pianist in the modified case formed a judgment of the sort *I ought not to drink with dinner*. If judgment is not constrained by preferences at the moment of judgment, then he could form such a judgment, despite the fact that he preferred to drink with dinner. Suppose we accept TDD. The pianist would then be incapable of deciding to adopt a plan that required him to refrain from drinking, a plan he himself judged best. So a commitment to TDD, without the analogous commitment to TDJ, would imply that a rational pianist could not adopt a course of action he thought it best for him to adopt. This sort of split between judgment and decision is generally thought to be the mark of akrasia, an irrational condition. An akratic agent intentionally decides to do something that her better judgment speaks against doing, or intentionally decides not to do a thing that her better judgment speaks in favor of doing.[21] TDD thus appears to endorse irrational behavior, unless the analogous restriction on judgment is assumed as well. But, as we have seen, there are independent reasons for thinking the restriction on judgment cannot be accepted.

Second, by both Bratman's and Gauthier's lights, a resolute agent will need to make a counter-preferential decision in the course of executing a plan that calls for counter-preferential action: He will need to decide in favor of carrying out the prior intention, and that decision arguably will be counter-preferential. Again, we have an ambiguity in this account between the decision to carry out the action called for by the plan and the decision to refrain from reconsideration. But again it looks as though the decision implemented in the context of a plan is counter-preferential either way. If the decision is a decision in favor of the course of action, it is counter-preferential by hypothesis. And if the decision is a decision to refrain from reconsideration, it is counter-preferential too, for we can suppose the agent wants to reconsider, so that he can decide to do what will maximize his preferences. Once again, we can treat reconsideration as transparent with respect to the action performed pursuant to reconsideration, since the agent knows that by reconsidering he would decide in accordance with his current preferences, and this entitles us to conclude that the agent would prefer to reconsider. The resolute choice theorist thus appears to affirm the possibility of counter-preferential decision in the context of a plan at the same time that he denies that possibility outside the context of plan-execution. And this creates pressure for him to choose between his account of decision at the level of plan-adoption and the account he offers at the level of plan-execution.

Now the resolute choice theorist can choose to side with his account of plan-adoption only if he is prepared to accept both TDD and TDJ, since he cannot have one without the other, as I have argued. The economist would certainly favor this solution. For him, judgment and decision cannot come apart from preference, since their connection is assumed in his articulation of the notion of revealed preference.[22] Unlike the resolute choice theorist, the economist is thus free to accept both TDJ and TDD, and in fact, their acceptance is fundamental to his account. This is why he rejects the resolute choice theorist's account of plan-execution, and also why he believes in the need for precommitment. My claim, then, is that the resolute choice theorist's account of plan-adoption requires him to accept the economist's position on preferential constraint, since it requires him to accept both TDJ and TDD. But, as I have also suggested, the view of judgment and decision that TDJ and TDD reflect is implausible. The resolute choice theorist should therefore distance himself from the economist and abandon the idea of preferential constraint.

The resolute choice theorist might consider two possible solutions to this difficulty, both of which are compatible with the idea of preferential constraint. First, there is a version of resolution that does not accept the asymmetry between plan-adoption and plan-execution. Ned McClennen, for example, has suggested that the adoption of a plan requiring counter-preferential action produces an endogenous preference change, such that the action called for by the plan will not be counter-preferential at the moment of execution.[23] The suggestion, in short, is that the preferences of a rational agent will support the actions she determines it is in her interest to take. It looks, however, as though endogenous preference change is itself a fifth wheel in an account of rational agency. For the change in preference is supposed to *follow* from the fact that the action is a rational one to perform. The preferences are not themselves the grounds for regarding the action as rational. The fact that the action is preferential can do no work in recommending it to a rational agent on McClennen's account, and the notion of preferential constraint has not itself been vindicated.[24]

Second, there is a strategy that would allow the resolute choice theorist to defend the asymmetry between plan-adoption and plan-execution. This would be to adopt a non-deliberative account of plan-execution, such as an account based on habit. Bratman himself seems once to have held such a view.[25] If the decision to reconsider were a matter of habit, instead of deliberation, then the resolute choice theorist would not need to assert the existence of counter-preferential judgment and decision, and thus the difficulty I have pointed to for the resolute choice theorist would not emerge. Notice that the appeal to habit is not far from the economist's sophisticated solution, which is also a non-deliberative account of plan-execution. And as we noted in our discussion of TDA, the device of precommitment allows for the possibility of counter-preferential behavior, without requiring counter-preferential deliberation.

Without fully exploring the defects of such non-deliberative accounts, it may suffice to point out a few of the reasons that weigh against them. First, precommitment, whether of the habitual or the economist's external variety, involves costs. That was the basis for thinking the resolute solution preferable to the sophisticated solution in the first place. It applies no less to those non-deliberative accounts that appeal to the notion of habit, for it may cost something to form a habit, and there may also be costs associated with the manifestation of a habit once formed.

Second, rationality seems to require that agents hold their intentions and plans open to reconsideration, and non-deliberative accounts of plan-execution have the effect of foreclosing reconsideration. The advocate of the habitual account might point out that the relevant habits pertain to patterns of reconsideration itself, and thus the habitual account leaves the possibility of reconsideration open. But the question is whether the account can make sense of an agent's performing a deliberatively based counter-preferential action pursuant to reconsideration. If not, then reconsideration will always lead to the abandonment of the prior intention anyway, and so accounting for it in a given case will not be compatible with accounting for counter-preferential behavior in the execution of a plan.

Finally, and I think most significantly, an account of rational plan-execution seems to require that the action performed in furtherance of a plan be deliberatively grounded. If not, it is hard to distinguish rational plan-execution from what some would think of as rationally induced irrationality. Performing an action called for by a plan through habits of non-reconsideration would be like getting oneself to perform an action by taking a pill. The fact that the action is beneficial to the agent does not suffice to make its performance an instance of rational behavior.[26] For these and other reasons, I do not think non-deliberative accounts of plan-execution will prove successful. But further exploration of these points would be necessary before definitively ruling out such accounts.

<h2 style="text-align:center">5</h2>

I have been arguing that the project of finding a middle way between the economist's full-blown preferential constraint and the conception of practical deliberation as entirely free from preferences is not tenable. The departure from preferential constraint in the context of plan-execution the resolute choice theorist proposes has a tendency to spread to other aspects of rational agency and cannot be contained in the way Gauthier and others have attempted to contain it. This is because freedom from preferences in the choice of actions within a plan establishes the possibility of counter-preferential practical judgment generally, which in turn carries counter-preferential decision in its train. Together, counter-preferential judgment and counter-preferential decision seem sufficient to establish the possibility of counter-preferential deliberation in any context.

Allowing for counter-preferential judgment, along with counter-preferential decision in accordance with that judgment, seems to capture our ordinary thinking about practical reasoning better than accepting thoroughgoing preferential constraint in deliberation. It also appears to capture the phenomenology of practical deliberation better than a theory premised on preferential constraint. It is common for a person to feel that she goes to the dentist, for example, because she thinks she should go, not because she has preferences in favor of going. It would be odd to think that a rational agent would cancel her trip if she were to reflect on whether to go in the middle of executing a plan to go, or that she would cancel her trip were it not for the fact that she was preventing herself from thinking about what she really wanted to do at the time. She plans to go because she knows she should go, and that is also why she carries out her plan.[27] In such cases, we are most inclined to think not only that judgment is not constrained by preferences but also that an agent's judging that she ought to do a thing can be sufficient to explain her doing it. These considerations tend naturally in the direction of a cognitive account of motivation.[28]

The rejection of preferential constraint on judgment tends in the direction of a purely cognitive account of motivation, but it does not lead inexorably to one. For the question still remains whether there might be a non-cognitive source of motivation *other* than preferences, and thus whether judgment, and hence decision, might not be thought of as constrained by *it*. I am inclined to think that the problems with conceiving of judgment as constrained by preferences would likely apply to a conception of judgment as constrained by any other non-cognitive item as well. But I cannot argue the point here, and I wish to suggest only that the cognitivist solution is an attractive way to think of practical judgment.

The strategy of trying to explain away the counter-preferential character of much of human behavior has a persistent and somewhat surprising allure. The resolute choice theorist's two-tier approach is only one among many accounts in this vein. The idea of preferences over preferences, or second-order preferences, has been another prominent variant. These accounts rest on a mistaken thought about what is of value for rational agents: The thought is that we must understand practical rationality as preferential if we also want to understand it in terms of the personal commitments of the deliberating agent. Tying practical reasoning to preferences thus seems the only way to avoid an objectivist account of the demands of rational agency. But if that is the basis for attempting to preserve preferential constraint, the motivation misses its mark. For a subjective account of the value of an action or state of affairs for an agent is compatible with a non-preference-based account of rational motivation. Instead of maximizing his preferences, an agent might reason on the basis of what we can call his *interests*, where these are distinguishable from any set of preferences he currently has. Granted, a person may regard it as in his interest to satisfy certain of his preferences. But others, he may think, are best ignored. The notion of an interest can remain thoroughly subjective, because we can still refuse to count as among an agent's interests any consideration the agent himself is not prepared to recognize as contributing to his life going as well as possible.[29] The reason it is rational for the pianist to refrain from drinking with dinner is that *he* recognizes it as in his interest to do so. This need not imply that the importance to the pianist's life of refusing wine with dinner is determined by his preferences with regard to such an action, even if "importance to his life" is entirely a matter of the importance *he* attaches.

It counts strongly in favor of resolving the tension in the resolute choice theorist's account, I have argued, that preferential constraint in plan-execution requires a general commitment to constraint on judgment and decision and that this seems inconsistent with any plausible account of ideal rationality. Worse, preferential constraint on both judgment and decision looks more like a symptom of deep irrationality than like a condition on rational agency. Rational agents should have the ability to act in accordance with their assessments of what they ought to do, assessments reached by considering what would be best for them overall, even in the face of their immediate preferences to the contrary. Moreover, as I have suggested, there is a perfectly plausible account of how practical reason can operate that makes no mention of preferences: A rational agent can reason practically on the basis of more general assessments he makes about what would increase his well-being across his life as a whole. He would then assess particular actions in terms of the contribution they would make to that well-being. And once agents are no longer restricted to the kind of local reflection that preferential reasoning seems to involve, the need for a prior intention drops out in many cases in which the resolute choice theorist posits its necessity, in particular in cases involving temporary shifts in what an agent is inclined to do on the basis of his more immediate concerns.

By contrast, I am prepared to allow that the prior intention or plan is not dispensable in the so-called autonomous-benefit cases, cases where an agent stands to benefit from forming the intention to do something that it will not benefit her to do. Turning to the notion of an interest from that of a preference does not seem to solve the difficulty there. The point is clearest in the toxin puzzle. Under no plausible account of what an interest is can the agent regard actually drinking the toxin as independently in his interest. What *is* in his interest is intending to drink, and so by hypothesis the prior intention is not dispensable in that case. Less obviously, a prior intention may be necessary in the reciprocation cases as well. Here, the move from preference to interest does not give the person who must perform second any additional reason to make good on his promise to perform. The special features of these cases, however, should not mislead us into thinking of rational agency as requiring an intention or plan every time an action contrary to preference is called for. The excessive focus on the peculiarities of rational agency in the more extraordinary cases perhaps explains why the resolute choice theorist has gotten off to the curious start he has in analyzing the more ordinary problems of rationality the change-in-preference cases raise.

6

There is an ambivalence in Gauthier's work about preferential constraint, an ambivalence manifested even in those parts of his account where he is at his most "preferential." In *Morals by Agreement*, for example, he specifies that rational agents maximize value only if they reason on the basis of their *considered* preferences.[30] Preferences are considered, Gauthier says, "if and only if there is no conflict between their behavioral and attitudinal dimensions and they are stable under experience and reflection."[31] A considered preference, unlike the raw desiderative item the economist favors as a source of motivation, is thus a partially normatively constructed item.[32]

In later writings, the distance between the economist's idea of preference as the source of value for rational agents and Gauthier's account of practical rationality increases. In a recent paper, for example, Gauthier acknowledges that there are cases in which a rational agent would recognize that it is better *not* to ensconce his current preferences in his future life by being resolute with respect to them. Some preference change is to be welcomed, and one would not want to stymie one's personal development by locking in any particular set of preferences for all future occasions. The example he gives is the boy who seeks to bind himself to a way of life in which he will be sure of avoiding the attractions of girls, since he now thinks girls are "yucky," and he is sadly aware that the day will come when he will not find them so. As Gauthier says: "Stepping back from any particular shift in preferences or change in concerns to the recognition that such shifts and changes are a normal and necessary part of human life, an agent may judge that it makes sense to deliberate about her future in a way that leaves herself open to their effects."[33] It is to solve this sort of case that he introduces the distinction between proximate and vanishing-point preferences, along with the claim that it is more rational to reason on the basis of the latter than the former.

That Gauthier has not entirely incorporated the implications of this recent departure from preferential constraint into the body of his account is clear from the fact that cases like that of the pianist could not be solved by resolution if we accepted the foregoing point, leaving aside the problems with resolution I have signaled. For the fact that the pianist can ensconce his ex ante preference for not drinking does not yet suggest that he should on this later thought of Gauthier's. It might turn out that the ex ante preference is one the agent would be better off living without. An effort to reconcile the idea of preferential constraint on plan-adoption with the idea that some preferences are not worth ensconcing in one's future life would require criteria for distinguishing those preferences it is rational for an agent to maximize from those he would do better ignoring entirely.

Now Gauthier does present something that might serve as such a criterion.

The agent who chooses in favor of his vanishing-point preferences (say, for fruit over chocolate), because he will otherwise be committed to choosing in accordance with proximate preferences on all future occasions, can expect to do better in terms of his "overall concerns," Gauthier says, since he will not choose on the basis of his proximate preferences on all future occasions. This explains why it is rational for him to choose against the weight of his proximate preferences now.[34] But a question about the relation between an agent's "overall concerns" and his preferences naturally arises at this point. If the notion of an overall concern is not limited to current preferences, Gauthier is assuming that practical deliberation can take place from a standpoint outside of preferences. It would accordingly be difficult to argue that preferences by themselves ever constrain our choices and hence that a preferentially formed intention would be required for us to act against them. On the other hand, if the notion of an overall concern is limited to current preferences, it is not clear that Gauthier can justify plans that call for current counter-preferential behavior, as he seems to want to do to accommodate cases of immature preferences. As we saw in the case of the series of choices between a chocolate and a fruit, it is not clear why an agent would ever settle on a plan that required current counter-preferential behavior, in view of the fact that there would always be some other plan he could adopt that would not call for it and so would satisfy his preferences better than one that would. The turn to the notion of an "overall concern" seems an implicit recognition on Gauthier's part that preferential constraint may not function in the way his official view treats it.

More recently still, Gauthier has come quite close to embracing the idea that rational deliberation takes place on the basis of something like an agent's view of what her interests require, where the notion of an interest need not be a preferential one. In the beginning of "Assure and Threaten," for example, he says that the aim of a rational life is *one's life going as well as possible*.[35] Although an agent must "fill in" what it means for her life to go as well as possible, choosing in a way that makes one's life go as well as possible is the maximizing activity in which an agent's rationality consists. Gauthier once again appears to miss the implications the suggestion has for his overall account. For presumably if an agent has a view of what would make her life go as well as possible, she can use *that* as a basis for evaluating courses of action directly, for settling on plans as well as on isolated actions outside of plans. And there is no reason to suppose that when an agent settles on a course of action she regards as maximally conducive to her life going as well as possible she will be maximizing her preferences at the level of plan-adoption, any more than there was to suppose that in settling on a plan on the basis of preferences the actions that fell under that plan would be preferential. Once one allows for a more global perspective from which an agent can ask questions about her life as a whole, apart from any particular set of preferences within that life, the local restriction that reasoning take place on the basis of preferences becomes difficult to sustain.

Gauthier himself has thus felt the tendency of counter-preferential deliberation to spread across an account of rational agency: The moves from considered preferences to vanishing-point preferences, to overall concerns, and finally to the aim of one's life going as well as possible suggest that he has felt the pressure on the idea that reason is constrained that one would expect the recognition of reason's freedom to provide. One is led to wonder whether the full recognition of this freedom will eventually cast doubt on the understanding of reason as instrumentally constrained itself.

Notes

1. David Gauthier, "Reason and Maximization," reprinted in *Moral Dealing* (Ithaca, NY: Cornell University Press, 1990), pp. 210–11.
2. The notion of a preference can be interpreted in a variety of ways. The common use of the term in the philosophical literature makes it a middle-sized object: It is larger than a mere appetite or urge, but smaller than everything an agent takes as valuable or worthwhile. For a general discussion of broad and narrow interpretations of the notion of a preference, see L. W. Sumner, "Welfare, Preference and Rationality," in *Value, Welfare, and Morality*, ed. R. G. Frey and C. W. Morris (Cambridge University Press, 1993).
3. The example is from Michael Bratman, "Planning and Temptation," in *Mind and Morals*, ed. L. May, M. Friedman, and A. Clark (Cambridge, MA: MIT Press, 1996). I use Bratman's example instead of the more familiar case of Ulysses and the sirens in the hope that it will help to focus attention on the problem of changing preferences. There is a tendency to see Ulysses' problem as one of weakness of will, and hence the case as one of 'irrational' rather than 'rational' temptation.
4. The term was originally Ned McClennen's. Edward F. McClennen, *Rationality and Dynamic Choice: Foundational Explorations* (Cambridge University Press, 1990).
5. Of course, if it turns out that the ex post self prefers missing dinner altogether to going to dinner and not drinking (he goes to dinner only to drink, let us say), he will not regard himself as better off under the ex ante self's most preferred solution. In this case he will have no reason to refrain from drinking with dinner, and so the ex ante self will have to choose his second-best option in order to avoid drinking. The optimal solution in this case is the solution that is second best for both, namely avoiding dinner altogether.
6. Economists would say that the solution is not in equilibrium, since the ex post undominated response to the ex ante decision to go to dinner is to drink. The availability of the resolute solution, they think, simply cannot be inferred from its optimality.
7. A plan calling for preferential action may still be necessary in a case in which an agent has insufficient time or resources to determine what the right decision is at the moment of action. A plan for dealing with an emergency, for example, may

be necessary if the agent expects to lack the emotional and material resources necessary to determine the correct course of action when the moment for action comes, even if her preferences support acting in the way called for by the plan.

8. Bratman, however, rejects it in other contexts, in particular in the so-called autonomous benefit cases. See Michael E. Bratman, "Toxin, Temptation, and the Stability of Intention," in *Rational Commitment and Social Justice: Essays in Honor of Gregory Kavka*, ed. J. L. Coleman and C. W. Morris (Cambridge University Press, 1998), pp. 59, 61–7. He thinks, for example, that it simply is not possible to win a million dollars if to do so one must form an intention to drink a toxin one will lack any reason actually to drink. And similarly he thinks it impossible to enter into a sincere agreement to assist someone later on the condition that he assist you now when his willingness to assist you depends on your intention to assist him, rather than on your actually assisting him. Bratman rejects the resolute solution for these cases, because he thinks it a basic fact about our rational agency that we reason about what to *do*, and not what to *intend*. So in a case in which the benefit to the agent arises from forming an intention, rather than from performing an action, an agent can plan in a way that will inure to his greatest benefit only if the action he must plan to take in order to equip himself with the desired intention is one it is independently to his benefit to take.

   It is not clear why Bratman thinks the change-of-preference cases are distinguishable from the autonomous-benefit cases on this point, for it might equally be said that the gains the ex post pianist enjoys – going to dinner rather than having to miss dinner altogether – are won simply by his intending ex ante not to drink with dinner. In this sense, the intention not to drink with dinner supplies an "autonomous benefit" as well, at least if one is inclined to view the necessary intention in the reciprocation cases as conferring an autonomous benefit.

9. Bratman, "Toxin, Temptation," p. 70. Following Bratman, I shall use "intention" and "plan" roughly interchangeably. As Bratman says, plans are intentions "writ large." Michael Bratman, *Intention, Plans, and Practical Reason* (Cambridge, MA: Harvard University Press, 1987).

10. David Gauthier, "Intention and Deliberation," in *Modeling Rationality, Morality, and Evolution*, ed. P. Danielson (Oxford University Press, 1998), pp. 41–54.

11. Gauthier, "Intention and Deliberation," p. 49.

12. Gauthier, "Intention and Deliberation," p. 49. Presumably Gauthier would also accept the converse, namely that every plan that satisfies full confirmation is eligible for adoption by a rational agent.

13. McClennen does not, but there are other problems with his account. *Vide infra*, part 4.

14. David Gauthier, "Resolute Choice and Rational Deliberation: A Critique and a Defence," *Noûs*, 31(1):20, 1997.

15. Gauthier allows that there are cases in which the agent's proximate preferences might overwhelm the value to her of avoiding choosing on the basis of her proximate preferences on all future occasions. These would be cases in which the agent's proximate preferences surpassed a certain threshold of strength. Above that threshold, the agent would regard no damage to her ability to satisfy her preferences regarding future decision-making as too high a price to pay to satisfy her current preferences. In what follows, however, I shall ignore this wrinkle, since it does not affect our present concerns.

16. Gauthier has indicated to me in conversation that he would favor this sort of approach to the modified pianist case.

17. Bratman, "Planning and Temptation," pp. 296–7.
18. It is beyond the scope of our present discussion to consider whether Bratman is correct that standard utility theory cannot make sense of personal rules of the sort Bratman has in mind, but I suspect that he may not have given the economists their due on this point.
19. Immanuel Kant, preface to *Critique of Judgement*, trans. J. C. Meredith (Oxford University Press, 1952).
20. There is a nice argument that shows that Bratman implicitly accepts TDD. Consider a principle we might call the *thesis of the dependence of intention on preferences* (TDI).

    Thesis of the dependence of intention (TDI): A rational agent cannot form the intention at a time *t* to perform an action *A* if another course of action *A'* is better supported by her preferences at that time.

    Bratman clearly accepts TDI outside the context of an existing plan: If an agent could form an intention that ran counter to her preferences at a given time, then the pianist could simply form the intention not to drink at the time of action, and this Bratman thinks he cannot do. In order to show that Bratman must accept TDD, I need only show that TDI commits him to TDD.

    For Bratman, an agent's formation of an intention to *A* is part of his choice of an overall scenario that has *A*-ing as a "by-chain" leading, in the relation of means to end, to the agent's goal in acting. In his book, Bratman presents the following principle: "If on the basis of practical reasoning I choose scenario S in the pursuit of intended end E, then I will intend at least one by-chain in S." Michael Bratman, *Intention, Plans, and Practical Reason*, p. 157. Suppose, then, it were possible for Bratman to be committed to TDI but not to TDD. This would mean that our modified pianist could decide, when he sees his friend in the restaurant, to have dinner with him but not to drink. That is, he could choose the following scenario: *not drink at dinner in order to play well tonight*. There is only one by-chain in this scenario. According to Bratman's principle relating intention and choice, the agent must intend that by-chain. But the agent cannot intend not to drink with dinner, according to Bratman, since Bratman accepts TDI. So Bratman cannot accept TDI and reject TDD, and since he accepts TDI, we must conclude that he is committed to TDD.
21. Davidson says "[a]n agent's will is weak if he acts, and acts intentionally, counter to his own best judgment. . . ." Donald Davidson, "How Is Weakness of the Will Possible?" in *Essays on Actions and Events* (Oxford University Press, 1980), p. 21.
22. Strictly speaking, the economist may not be able to think of preferences as constraining judgment and decision after all. This is because he treats an agent as preferring whatever it is that she judges and hence chooses as best for herself (i.e., "revealed choice"). If an agent can be said to prefer to do everything she does, then it looks as though there can be no independent item called a "preference" to do any constraining. True there are conditions on preferences themselves, such as transitivity, reflexivity, and completeness, and thus an agent's choices are constrained by conditions of rationality. But this is not itself preferential constraint.
23. See Edward F. McClennen, "Constrained Maximization and Resolute Choice," *Social Philosophy & Policy*, 5(2):95–118, 1988.
24. See David Gauthier, "Morality, Rational Choice, and Semantic Representation: A Reply to My Critics," *Social Philosophy & Policy*, 5(2):207–13, 1988. Mc-

Clennen has since partially recanted the idea of endogenous preference change, and he now professes to be agnostic on the question whether resolution involves coming to have a preference for the action the resolute solution recommends. Edward F. McClennen, "Pragmatic Rationality and Rules," *Philosophy and Public Affairs*, 26(3):210–58, 1997.

25. *See* Bratman, *Intention, Plans, and Practical Reason.*
26. This is a failing of other recent accounts of rational choice. Scott Shapiro, for example, argues for a version of resolution that eliminates reconsideration: "The Difference That Rules Make," in *Analyzing Law: New Essays in Legal Theory,* ed. Brian Bix (Oxford: Clarendon Press, 1998). He suggests, in effect, that an agent should execute intentions automatically, namely, without allowing herself to deliberate about their adequacy at the moment of action. But I would argue that Shapiro's account is not an account of rational agency per se, because he makes forming an intention or adopting a rule too much like swallowing a pill. It is in my view a *sine qua non* of an account of rational agency, as well as of rule-following, that the intention or the rule be executed deliberatively, namely pursuant to a rational decision at the moment of execution.
27. There might be many reasons why she requires a plan to go to the dentist, other than that she needs to overcome preferences at the time of action in favor of not going. For example, she must coordinate with other people, such as the dentist, not to mention with other aspects of her own life. Bratman's insight that plans constitute an important part of a rational human life is not at all dependent on thinking plans necessary as a bulwark against recalcitrant preferences.
28. A common objection to an account of this sort is that it rules out any sensible account of *akrasia.* Alfred Mele makes the point thus: "Resisting temptation, Mary A-s as she judged best. Mary's behavior cannot be explained simply by noting that she judged it best to A; for if judging A best (in conjunction with such standing conditions as having the ability to A) were sufficient for A-ing, we would never act akratically." *Springs of Action* (Oxford University Press, 1992), pp. 122–3. But Mele's criticism is unclear to me. If an agent is ideally rational, then her judgment that she must A *is* sufficient to explain her A-ing. The capacity to act on one's judgment of what it is best to do may be what is meant by calling an agent ideally rational. Akrasia is a phenomenon premised on insufficient rationality. Thus Mary's B-ing, instead of A-ing, when she judges it best to A, only serves to suggest that she is not ideally rational. It is not clear why Mele thinks that a theory of rational agency should have to explain Mary's behavior in this case.
29. There will be complications here. For example, what should we do about agents who are unaware that their current motivational makeup commits them to treating a certain state of affairs as desirable? Should we allow that it is in the agent's interest to bring about that state of affairs?
30. David Gauthier, *Morals by Agreement* (Oxford University Press, 1986), p. 23.
31. Gauthier, *Morals by Agreement,* pp. 32–3.
32. Once again, there is a difficulty in understanding the economist's position on this point. The economist seems committed both to the idea that preferences constrain deliberation and to the idea that there is nothing more to having a preference than an agent's willingness to choose in a certain way under certain conditions. The notion of "revealed preference" is in this sense misleading, because the economist does not appear to think that there is anything there to be revealed, and thus the notion of preference itself seems to collapse into a kind of choice, or into a way

of understanding choice. But if preference is really to constrain choice, it must be separately identifiable from it, and this would seem to require the economist to recognize the possibility that choices and preferences might, in a given case, come apart.

33. Gauthier, "Resolute Choice and Rational Deliberation: A Critique and a Defence," *Noûs*, 31(1):18, 1997.

34. I am again ignoring the modification of this thesis that Gauthier introduces having to do with a threshold beyond which it would be rational for one to choose in accordance with proximate preferences, since it does not affect the current discussion.

35. David Gauthier, "Assure and Threaten," *Ethics*, 104(4):690–721, 1994.

Bombs and Coconuts, or Rational Irrationality

DEREK PARFIT

In an early article, Gauthier argued that, to act rationally, we must act morally.[1] I tried to refute that argument.[2] Since Gauthier was not convinced, I shall try again.[3]

1

Gauthier assumes that, to be rational, we must maximize our own expected utility. Though he distinguishes between 'utility' and 'benefit', this distinction does not affect his main arguments. We can regard him as appealing to the *Self-interest Theory*.[4]

Many writers have argued that, in self-interested terms, it is always rational to act morally. According to most of these writers, morality and self-interest coincide. But that is not Gauthier's line. Gauthier concedes that acting morally may be, and be known to be, worse for us. He claims that, even in such cases, it is rational to act morally.

If we appeal to the Self-interest Theory, it may seem impossible to defend that claim. How can our acts be rational, in self-interested terms, if we know them to be worse for us? But Gauthier *revises* the Self-interest Theory. On the standard version of this theory, an act is rational if it will maximize our expected benefit – or be *expectably-best* for us.[5] On Gauthier's version, we should aim to benefit ourselves not with our *acts* but only with our *dispositions*. A disposition is rational if having it will be expectably-best for us. An act is rational if it results from such a disposition.

Besides revising the Self-interest Theory, Gauthier restricts the scope of morality. To act morally, Gauthier claims, we must honour our agreements. In the cases with which he is concerned, each of us promises that, at some cost to ourselves, we shall give a greater benefit to others. If we all kept such promises, we would all gain. The cost to each would be outweighed by the benefits received from others.

Though such agreements are mutually advantageous, it would often be better for each if she broke her promise. Either she could break it secretly, or the damage to her reputation would be outweighed by what she gains. We may think that, in self-interested terms, it is rational to break such promises. But Gauthier argues that, if we do, we are fools.

Gauthier's argument starts with a prediction. If we were straightforwardly self-interested – or, for short, *prudent* – we would intend to break such promises. Other people, knowing this, would exclude us from these advantageous agreements. That would be worse for us. It would be better for us if we were trustworthy, since we would then be admitted to these agreements.

It would be even better for us, as I remarked, if we appeared to be trustworthy but were really prudent. We would still be admitted to these agreements, but we would break our promises whenever we could expect to benefit.[6] Gauthier replied that we are too *translucent* to be capable of such deceit. When we were negotiating such agreements, we would sometimes be unable to conceal our true intentions. He therefore claimed that, on balance, it would be better for us if we were really trustworthy.[7]

Gauthier then appealed to his variant of the Self-interest Theory – which I shall call *Gauthier's view*. On this view, since it is in our interests to be trustworthy, it is rational for us to act upon this disposition. It is rational to keep our promises, even when we know that what we are doing will be worse for us.

Should we accept this argument? I believe not. When applied to trustworthiness, it may seem plausible. But we should reject Gauthier's view. It could be in our interests to have some disposition, and rational to cause ourselves to have it, but be irrational to act upon it.

2

One problem for Gauthier's view is that, at different times, different dispositions can be in our interests. This makes it hard to state Gauthier's view in a way that will suit his purposes.

In his earliest statements of his view, Gauthier assumed

   (A) If we have acquired some disposition because we reasonably believed that, by doing so, we would make our lives go better, it is rational to act upon this disposition.[8]

I challenged (A) as follows.[9] Just as it could be in our interests to be trustworthy, it could be in our interests to be disposed to fulfil our threats, and to ignore threats made by others. As before, it would be best to appear to have these dispositions, while remaining really prudent. But, to test Gauthier's view, we should accept his claim that we are too translucent to be able to deceive others. It might then be better for us if we really had these dispositions. But that would not show that it must be rational to act upon them.[10]

I gave the following example, which I shall here call *Your Fatal Threat*. Suppose that you and I are on a desert island, and we are both transparent. You become a *threat-fulfiller*. By regularly threatening to explode some bomb, you aim to make me your slave. My only way to preserve my freedom is to become a *threat-ignorer*. Since I know that you know that I am translucent, I can reasonably expect that having this disposition would be best for me. I manage to acquire this disposition. But I have bad luck. In a momentary lapse, you threaten that, unless I give you a coconut, you will blow us both to pieces. According to (A), it would be rational for me to ignore your threat. This would be rational even though I know that, if I do, you will kill us both.

Gauthier once accepted this conclusion.[11] But he later revised his view, moving from (A) to

(B) If we have reason to believe that, in acquiring some disposition, we made our lives go better, it is rational to act upon this disposition.

According to (B), for it to be rational to act upon some disposition, it is not enough that we *did* have reason to believe that, by acquiring this disposition, we would make our lives go better. We must *still* have reason to believe that this past belief was true. We need not 'adhere to a disposition in [the] face of its known failure to make one's life go better'.[12]

Gauthier intended (B) to handle my example. When you make your fatal threat, I lose my reason to believe that, in becoming a threat-ignorer, I made my life go better. On Gauthier's revised view, I need not 'adhere' to my disposition.

We can revise the example. Suppose I know that, if I had not become a threat-ignorer, I would have died some time ago.[13] Gauthier's view again implies that I should ignore your threat. Since my disposition once saved my life, my acquiring of this disposition made my life go better. True, it will now kill me. But that is not what counts. According to (B), I should deny you the coconut, and be blown to pieces.[14]

As this example shows, even if some disposition has become disastrous, (B) can still imply that it is rational to act upon it. This would be rational if this disposition brought past benefits that were greater than its future costs. Gauthier claims that we should 'adhere' to such dispositions. We should be true to our 'commitment'.

When applied to promises, such a view has some appeal. If we have gained from trustworthiness, we may think it rational to act upon this disposition, even if it becomes a burden. Talk of *commitment* here makes sense. But, in the case of threat-behaviour, it makes little sense. Why should I remain a threat-ignorer, at the cost of death, merely because this disposition once saved my life?[15]

If my alternative was to be your slave, death would hardly be a cost. But we can add a further detail to the case. Suppose that a rescue party has just landed on the beach. I know that, if I give you the coconut, I shall soon be freed.

To handle this version of the case, Gauthier must again change his view. It may have been rational for me to become a threat-ignorer. But, as Gauthier must agree, it would now be rational for me to try to lose this disposition.[16] If I could lose this disposition, it would be irrational to keep it. Since that is so, Gauthier cannot claim that it must still be rational to act upon it. Now that I could soon be free, it would be irrational for me knowingly to bring about my death.[17]

How should Gauthier revise his view? (B) could be restated so that it covered temporary dispositions. But there is a simpler formulation. Gauthier could turn to

(C) If we have reason to believe that, in having some disposition, we
      are making our lives go better, it is rational for us to act upon this
      disposition.

If he appealed to (C), Gauthier would cease to be embarrassed by my example. When I see that my disposition has become disastrous, (C) does not imply that it must still be rational for me to act upon it.[18]

I gave another example, which we can here call *Schelling's Case*. A robber threatens that, unless I unlock my safe, he will start to kill my children. It would be irrational for me to ignore this robber's threat. But, even if I gave in to his threat, there is a risk that he will kill us all, to reduce his chance of being caught. I claimed that, in this case, it would be rational for me to take a drug that would make me very irrational. The robber would then see that it was pointless to threaten me; and, since he could not commit his crime, and I would not be capable of calling the police, he would also be less likely to kill either me or my children.

When Gauthier considered this example, he seemed to accept (C). He agreed that it would be rational for me to make myself, for a brief period, insane; and he claimed that it would be rational for me to act upon this disposition.[19]

If he turned to (C), however, Gauthier would pay a price. In his defence of contractual morality, Gauthier compared only permanent dispositions. He thought it enough to show that, if we are trustworthy, this will on the whole make our lives go better.[20] But, if he appealed to (C), he would need to show more than this. According to (C), for it to be rational to act upon a disposition, it is not enough that it was in our interests to acquire it. We must have reason to believe that, *at the time of acting*, it is in our interests to have it. Gauthier must therefore show that, if we are trustworthy, this disposition is in our interests when we are *keeping* our agreements.

He does not, I believe, show this. What he shows is, at most, that trustworthiness is in our interests when we are negotiating our agreements. In some cases, when the time comes to keep one agreement, we are negotiating some new agreement. Gauthier's argument may then apply. But in other cases there is no such overlap. There are some promises that we could secretly and swiftly break, to our own advantage. When this is possible, it would be worse for us if we were trustworthy. It would be better for us if we lost that disposition, and became self-interested, even if only for just long enough to break our promise.[21]

To defend his view that it is always rational to act morally, Gauthier must claim that it would be rational to keep such promises. If he appealed to (C), however, he would lose his argument for that claim. (C) implies that it would be rational to break such promises, since we would then be acting on the disposition that we could reasonably believe to be, at the time, best for us.

Gauthier might try a different reply. He might claim that, if we are trustworthy, we would be unable to lose, or to overcome, this disposition. In the sense that is relevant here, this claim may not be true.[22] But suppose that it were true. Suppose that, because I am trustworthy, I would find it impossible to break some promise. Gauthier might appeal to the claim that 'ought' implies 'can'. He might say that, since I cannot break my promise, it cannot be true that it would be rational for me to do so. And he might say that, given the strength of my disposition, it would be rational for me to act upon it.[23]

Is this an adequate reply? Return to the case in which I am disposed to ignore your fatal threat. If I overcome my disposition, and thereby manage to remain alive until I can be rescued, Gauthier must agree that my act is rational. But suppose that my disposition proves too strong. I find that I cannot bring myself to give you the coconut. Could Gauthier claim that, since I cannot overcome my disposition, it cannot be true that it would be rational for me to do so? Could he claim that, since it is causally impossible for me to act differently, it is rational for me to bring about my death?

I believe not. As Gauthier elsewhere claims, what it is rational for us to do does not depend, in this way, on what is causally possible. We could have acted otherwise, in the relevant sense, if nothing stopped us from doing so except our desires or dispositions. If it would have been rational for me to have acted differently, it is irrelevant that, given my desires and dispositions, acting differently would have been causally impossible. Nor could I defend my act by appealing to the strength of my disposition. That may exempt *me* from certain kinds of criticism. But it cannot show that my *act* is rational.[24]

Gauthier admits as much in retreating from claim (A). Suppose that, though it was rational for me to acquire some disposition, I have learnt that doing so was a terrible mistake. Gauthier no longer claims that it must still be rational to act upon such dispositions. He agrees that, from the fact that I rationally acquired some disposition, and that I cannot overcome it, we cannot infer that it is rational to act upon it.

3

I have described one problem for Gauthier's view. Since it can be in our interests to have temporary dispositions, it is hard to state his view in a way that suits his purposes. Let us now ignore this problem, and turn to the central question. Should we accept Gauthier's view? Should we believe that, if it is in our interests to have some disposition, or rational to cause ourselves to have it, it is rational to act upon it?

In the cases with which we are concerned, though it is in our interests to have some disposition, it is against our interests to act upon it. Only here does Gauthier's view make a difference.

Reconsider Schelling's Case. Because I am temporarily insane, the robber knows that, even if he starts to kill my children, he will not induce me to unlock my safe. He will therefore soon make his getaway. This is greatly to my advantage.[25] But, while I am in my drug-induced state, and before the robber leaves, I act in damaging and self-defeating ways. I beat my children because I love them. I burn my manuscripts because I want to preserve them.

Gauthier objects that my crazy acts are, in fact, better for me. They are what persuades this man that I am immune to his threats. Since these acts are better for me, they are, on any view, rational. So this is not, as I claimed, a case of rational irrationality.[26]

To answer this objection, we can add one feature to the case. We can suppose that, to convince this man that I am crazy, I don't need to act in crazy ways. He sees me take this drug, and he knows that it produces temporary madness. Since the robber already knows that I am in this state, my destructive acts have no good effects.

Though my acts have only bad effects, they result from an advantageous disposition. That is enough, on Gauthier's view, to make these acts rational.[27]

We should note the extremity of this view. Hume at least required that, for our acts to be rational, we must be trying to achieve our aims. On Gauthier's view, we could be trying to frustrate our aims. When I burn my manuscript, or beat my children, I might be doing what I believe to be irrational, and *because* I believe it to be irrational. My acts could be as crazy as we can imagine. They could still, on Gauthier's view, be rational.[28] That is hard to believe.

4

Of Gauthier's arguments for his view, one appeals to the claim that, if we accept his view, this will be better for us. We can first ask whether that is true.

Gauthier assumes that, to be rational, we should maximize our own expected utility. He compares two versions of this view. According to the standard version of the Self-interest Theory, which I called S, we should maximize at the level of our acts. An act is rational if it maximizes the expected benefit to us. According to Gauthier's view, we should maximize only at the level of our dispositions. An act is rational if it results from a maximizing disposition. This view we can now call G.[29]

In the cases with which we are concerned, we cannot always maximize at both levels. If we try to maximize with all our acts, we cannot have maximizing dispositions. Thus, if we break our promises whenever we can expect this to be better for us, we cannot be trustworthy, which will be bad for us.[30]

When we cannot maximize at both levels, it will be better for us if we have maximizing dispositions. The good effects of these dispositions will outweigh the bad effects of our acts.[31]

Gauthier claims that, given this fact, it will be better for us if we accept not S but G.[32] In making this claim, Gauthier assumes that, if we accept S, we would maximize with our acts *rather than* our dispositions.

This assumption may be incorrect. Since it would be better for us if we had maximizing dispositions, S would tell us, if we could, to acquire them. S agrees with G that we should try to *have* these dispositions.[33] What S denies is only that it must be rational to act upon them.

Gauthier may think that, if we accept S, we would always do what S claims to be rational.[34] Or he may think that, in judging any theory about rationality, we should ask what would happen if we always successfully followed it. This may be why he assumes that we would always maximize with our acts. But, if we can change our dispositions, we cannot always do what S claims to be rational. Acquiring these dispositions would itself be a maximizing act. If we maximize with all our other acts, we shall have acted irrationally in failing to acquire these dispositions. If instead we acquire these dispositions, we cannot always maximize with our other acts.[35]

Since we cannot always do what S claims to be rational, we must do the best we can. And S implies that, rather than maximizing with our other acts, we should acquire maximizing dispositions. This is the way of acting that we can expect to be best for us. The disagreement between S and G is not over the question of whether we should *acquire* maximizing dispositions. S claims this as much as G. The disagreement is only about whether, when we act on such dispositions, what we are doing is rational.[36]

Gauthier might now say that, if we accept S, we would be *unable* to acquire these dispositions. We would believe that, in some cases, acting on these dispositions would be irrational. And we might be unable to make ourselves disposed to do what we believe to be irrational. Perhaps, to acquire these dispositions, we must accept Gauthier's view, and believe that it is rational to act upon them.

When he discusses nuclear deterrence, Gauthier does make such a claim.[37] He supposes that it would be in our interests to form an intention to retaliate, if we are attacked. Forming this intention might be what protects us from attack. Gauthier then claims that, if we believed that such retaliation would be irrational, we would be unable to form this intention.[38]

It would be implausible to claim that we could *never* acquire some disposition if we believed that acting upon it would be irrational. Schelling's Case is one exception, and there are many others. But Gauthier would not need so strong a claim. He might say that it would often be impossible to acquire such dispositions. Or he might say that, if we believe that it would be irrational to act in some way, it would be more difficult for us to become disposed to act in this way. We might have to use some indirect method, such as taking drugs, or hypnosis, both of which have disadvantages. Things might be easier if we believed that it would be rational to act in this way. We might then be able simply to decide to do so.[39]

This may only shift the problem. How could we acquire this belief? Suppose that, as Gauthier claims, we could not intend to retaliate unless we believed that retaliation would be rational. If retaliation would be both pointless and suicidal, as Gauthier concedes, how could we persuade ourselves that, as Gauthier also claims, such retaliation would be rational? How could we make ourselves believe Gauthier's view? It is not easy to acquire some belief if our only ground for doing so is that this belief would be in our interests. Here too, we might need some costly indirect method. Let us, however, ignore this problem. It might be impossible for us to acquire some useful disposition unless we can somehow manage to believe that it would be rational to act upon it. It might then be in our interests to acquire this belief.[40]

Suppose that, for these or other reasons, it would be worse for us if we accepted the standard version of the Self-interest Theory. It would be better for us if we accepted Gauthier's view. That would not yet show that Gauthier's view is true, or is the best view. To reach that conclusion, Gauthier needs another premise.

In the original version of his argument, Gauthier's other premise was – surprisingly – the standard version of the Self-interest Theory. He assumed that we should start by accepting S. We should believe that an act is rational if it will be expectably-best for us. He then claimed that it would be better for us if we changed our own conception of rationality, by moving from S to

G. Since it would be better for us if we made this change, S implies that it would be rational to do so. S tells us to believe that the true theory is not S but G. Gauthier concluded that the true theory *is* G.[41]

Shelly Kagan suggested the following objection.[42] If S is true, G must be false, since G is incompatible with S. If S is false, G might be true, but G would not be supported by the fact that S tells us to believe G. It is irrelevant what a false theory tells us to believe. Either way, Gauthier's argument cannot support his conclusion.

Gauthier later revised his argument. He no longer claimed that we should first accept S, and then move to his view. He argued directly that we should accept his view.[43]

In this version of his argument, Gauthier's main claim still seems to be that, if we accept his view, this will be better for us. What should his other premise be?

Though he no longer appeals to S, Gauthier might still say that, if it is in our interests to accept some belief, it is rational to do so. He could then keep his claim that it is rational for us to accept G.

As before, such a claim does not imply that G is true. It could be rational to accept a false theory. But Gauthier might think it enough to show that it would be rational to accept his view. He might say that, even in the sciences, we cannot prove our theories to be true. We can at most show that it is rational to believe them.

Such an argument, however, would conflate two kinds of rationality. When we claim that it would be rational to have some belief, we usually mean that this belief would be *theoretically* or *epistemically* rational, since we have epistemic reasons to have it. Such reasons *support* this belief, since they are provided by facts which either entail this belief, or make it likely that this belief is true. But Gauthier's argument does not appeal to epistemic reasons. His claim would be that, since it is in our interests to believe his view, this belief would be *practically* rational. When we have practical reasons to cause ourselves to have some belief, these reasons do not support this belief, since they are not related, in relevant ways, to this belief's truth.

The point could be put like this. Gauthier claims that it is in our interests to believe that certain acts are rational. He concludes that such acts *are* rational. This argument assumes

(D) If it is in our interests to believe that certain acts are rational, this belief is true.

Gauthier, however, rightly rejects (D). He imagines a demon who rewards various beliefs about rationality. He then claims that, if there were such a demon, it would be 'rational to hold false beliefs about rationality'.[44] Gauthier here concedes that, though it would be in our interests to hold these beliefs, they would still be false. The fact that they would be in our interests could not make them true.

Could Gauthier withdraw this claim, and appeal to (D)?[45] It seems clear that he could not. Suppose that Gauthier's demon rewarded the belief that, for our acts to be rational, we must be called Bertie, and be wearing a pink bow tie. Gauthier could not claim that, if there were such a demon, this belief would be true. Nor do we need fantastic cases to refute (D). It might be in the interests of some people to have one belief about rationality, and in the interests of others to have some contradictory belief. Gauthier could not claim that these beliefs would both be true.

Since we should reject (D), we should reject this argument for Gauthier's view. Even if it were in our interests to believe his view, or rational to cause ourselves to believe it, this would not show that Gauthier's view was true.

The argument might show something. Gauthier might still claim that it would be practically rational to believe his view. But, unless he claimed that his view was true, Gauthier would have to abandon his main aim. He could not argue that it *is* rational to act morally. He could only argue that this belief is a useful illusion.[46]

5

In his discussion of nuclear deterrence, Gauthier gave a second argument for his view. Gauthier assumed that it could be rational to form the intention to retaliate, if one is attacked. He then claimed that, since it would be rational to form this intention, it would be rational, if deterrence failed, to act upon it.

David Lewis rejected this inference. While agreeing that it could be rational to intend to retaliate, Lewis denied that retaliation would itself be rational.[47]

In his reply, Gauthier denied 'that actions necessary to a rational policy may themselves be irrational'. If we accept deterrent policies, he wrote, we 'cannot consistently reject the actions they require'. Since we 'cannot claim that such actions should not be performed', we cannot call them irrational. 'To assess an action as irrational is . . . to claim that it should not be . . . performed'.[48]

These retaliatory acts cannot be *necessary* to deterrent policies since, if these policies succeed, these acts won't even be performed. But this is a special feature of deterrence, which we can set aside. In most of the cases with which we are concerned, the relevant acts will be performed. Thus, if I become trustworthy, because this disposition will be in my interests, I must expect that I shall keep my promises. Similarly, in Schelling's Case, I must expect my drug-induced state to affect my acts. In both cases, if I adopt the policy that will be good for me, I must expect to act in ways that will be bad for me.

Note next that, even in these cases, my acts aren't *required* by my policy. They aren't necessary to my policy's success. If they were, and my policy was good for me, my acts could not be bad for me. What is necessary to my policy is not my acts, but only my intention, or my disposition. My acts are merely the unwelcome side-effects.

This distinction, I believe, undermines Gauthier's reply to Lewis. If some policy is justified despite having bad effects, we may agree that, in one sense, these effects 'should occur'. But this only means, 'Things should be such that they occur'. And, in accepting that claim, we need not endorse, or welcome, these effects. The same applies to the acts that result from an advantageous disposition. We can agree that, in one sense, these acts should be performed. Things should be such that these acts will be performed. But we can still, consistently, believe these acts to be irrational.

6

Gauthier suggests another argument in favour of his view. This view avoids, he claims, 'some of the unwelcome consequences' of the Self-interest Theory. The chief such consequence is that, on that theory, it could be a curse to be rational.[49]

This argument does not, I believe, support Gauthier's view. One way to show that is this. Gauthier says that, even on his view, it might be a curse to be *cognitively* rational. This would be so if cognitive irrationality were directly rewarded. But this unwelcome consequence could not, he claims, be avoided by any theory.[50]

That is not so. Gauthier might extend his view. He might claim that our reasoning is cognitively rational if and only if it is in our interests. On this version of Gauthier's view, cognitive rationality could never be a curse. This revision would not, however, improve Gauthier's view. When crazy reasoning would be in our interests, that does not make it rational.

Cognitive irrationality could be in our interests, as any good theory should agree. So could practical irrationality. Both kinds of irrationality could be rewarded. It is no objection to the Self-interest Theory that it assumes or accepts these facts.

Gauthier makes one other claim in support of his view. He admits that, when his view is applied to Schelling's Case, it may seem counterintuitive. We may hesitate to claim that my crazy acts are rational. But Gauthier suggests that this is no objection, since 'whatever we might intuitively be inclined to say . . . "rationality" is a technical term in both Parfit's enquiry and my critique'.[51]

That is not so. I was asking what, in the ordinary sense, it is rational to want and do. And Gauthier claims that Schelling's Case 'shows that our ordinary ideas about rationality . . . are sometimes mistaken'. Since Gauthier wishes to reject our ordinary ideas, he cannot defend his use of 'rational' by making it a mere stipulation. And that, in any case, would make his view trivial.

On Gauthier's view, acts are rational if they result from an advantageous disposition. Such acts are rational even if they are merely the regretted side-effects of this disposition, and are as crazy as we can imagine. That is very hard to believe. I have discussed what seem to me all of Gauthier's arguments for this view. None, I suggest, succeed. I conclude that we should reject this view. It could be in our interests to have some disposition, and be rational to cause ourselves to have it, but be irrational to act upon it.

If Gauthier drops these claims about rationality, he would need, I believe, to revise some other parts of his moral theory. But given the range and subtlety of Gauthier's theory, I cannot try to defend that claim here.

Notes

1. 'Reason and Maximization' , *Canadian Journal of Philosophy*, 4:411–33, 1975. This argument's fullest statement is in Gauthier's *Morals by Agreement* (Oxford University Press, 1986), henceforth *MA*.
2. In an unpublished paper 'Rational Irrationality', and later in Sections 7–8 of my book *Reasons and Persons* (Oxford University Press, 1984).
3. This paper was completed in 1994, in response to Gauthier's contribution to *Reading Parfit*, edited by Jonathan Dancy (London: Routledge, 1997). I regret that, having since become obsessed with Kant's ethics, I have not tried to take into account Gauthier's most recent work.
4. Since Gauthier means by our *utility* the fulfilment of our *present* considered preferences, what he appeals to is, strictly, the *Deliberative Theory*. But, as Gauthier remarks (*MA*, p. 6), most of his claims apply equally to the Self-interest Theory. And Gauthier often uses words, like 'benefit' and 'advantage', that refer more naturally to our interests rather than our present preferences. So we can here ignore the differences – though they are often great – between the Deliberative and Self-interest Theories. We can suppose that, in all of the cases we discuss, our present considered preferences would coincide with what would be in our own interests.
5. What is expectably-best may not be the same as what we can expect to be best. Some acts are expectably-best for us though we can know, for certain, that they will not actually be best for us. Trying to do what is actually best may be, given the risks, irrational.
6. *Reasons and Persons*, Sections 7–8.
7. Gauthier gave this reply in *MA* (especially pp. 173–4). In his contribution to *Reading Parfit*, Gauthier later gave up the claim that we could not deceive others. He suggested that, if we remained self-interested, and merely appeared to be trustworthy, that would be worse for us. Thus he writes: 'the overall benefits of being able to promise sincerely . . . may reasonably be expected to outweigh the

overall costs of keeping promises when one could have gotten away with insincerity' (p. 26). But, if we could get away with insincerity, what are the benefits from being able to promise sincerely? Gauthier might appeal, like Hume, to the benefits of peace of mind, and a good conscience. But that seems insufficient for his purposes. Gauthier also claims that, even if we were generally trustworthy, we would be able to make some insincere promises. But this merely limits the costs of sincerity. It does not suggest that there is any gain. For Gauthier's distinctive argument to get off the ground, he needs, I believe, his earlier assumption that we could not rationally hope to deceive others.

8. See, for example, *MA*, Chapter VI.
9. In *Reasons and Persons*, Sections 7–8.
10. I also supposed that it might be rational to change our beliefs about rationality. This, too, was intended to help Gauthier's argument. If we did not change our beliefs, we would be doing what we believe to be irrational, and that might seem enough to make our acts irrational. But this element need not concern us here.
11. As he wrote (like Queen Victoria), 'We are unmoved' (*MA*, p. 185).
12. Gauthier asserted (B) – which he calls his 'second level of commitment' – in *Reading Parfit*, p. 40. I discussed a similar claim, which I called '(G1)', in *Reasons and Persons* (p. 13). On Gauthier's second level of commitment, it is rational to act on a disposition 'so long as one reasonably expects past and prospective adherence to the disposition to be maximally beneficial'. This claim may seem to mean 'if one both reasonably believes that adherence to this disposition in the past has been beneficial, and reasonably expects that adherence to it in the future will be beneficial'. But this cannot be what Gauthier intends, since it would remove the difference between his second level of commitment and his first level (discussed below). Gauthier must mean: 'if one can reasonably believe that acquiring it was beneficial in one's life as a whole, taking the past and future together'.

    Gauthier's move from (A) to (B), or from his third to his second level of commitment, hardly damages his defence of rational morality. On the view defended in *MA*, for morality's constraints to have rational force for us, accepting these constraints must have been expectably-best for us. On Gauthier's revised view, for these constraints to have rational force, they must also be known not to have been on the whole bad for us. Most of contractual morality's constraints would meet this second requirement.
13. Perhaps I would have obeyed some order that would have proved fatal.
14. It may be objected that I acquired too crude a disposition. Perhaps I should have become disposed to ignore threats, except in cases in which I believed that acting in this way would be disastrous. But, as Gauthier says, 'I may reasonably have believed that any qualification [to my disposition] would reduce its *ex ante* value, so that unqualified threat-ignoring offered me the best life prospects' (*Reading Parfit*, p. 39). We can add the assumption that only the unqualified disposition would in fact have been as good for me. (There is another reason not to allow this disposition to take this qualified form. If we did, we must allow similar qualifications to the disposition of trustworthiness. As we shall see, that would undermine Gauthier's argument.)
15. Gauthier endorses the action of a would-be deterrer who, when deterrence fails, disastrously carries out her threat. He writes 'Her reason for sticking to her guns . . . is simply that the expected utility . . . of her failed policy *depended* on her willingness to stick to her guns' ('Deterrence, Maximization, and Rationality',

Ethics, 94:489, 1984). So what? Her expectation may have depended on that willingness. But why should she remain faithful now?

16. Note that, in claiming this, I need not appeal to the Self-interest Theory, S. I need not assume that this attempt would be rational because it would be likely to be good for me. Since Gauthier rejects S, that would beg the question. But even on Gauthier's theory, it would be rational for me to try to lose this disposition. Suppose that I lose my dispositions whenever they become disastrous. It would be in my interests to have this meta-disposition. So, on Gauthier's theory, it would now be rational for me to act upon it.

17. Suppose first that, if I tried, I could cease to be a threat-ignorer. As I have just argued, it would then be irrational for me to keep my disposition. If Gauthier accepts this conclusion, could he still assert (B)? Could he claim that, even though it would now be irrational to *keep* my disposition, it must still be rational to act upon it?

   There may be certain cases in which, though it would be irrational to keep some disposition, it would still be rational to act upon it. Suppose, for example, that it would be irrational for me to remain prudent. If I did, irrationally, keep this disposition, it might still be rational to act upon it, doing whatever would be best for me. (B), however, is a much stronger claim. According to (B), even if it would now be irrational to keep some disposition, it *must* still be rational to act upon it, simply because it *once* brought benefits that were greater than its present costs. This claim, I believe, cannot be true. If it is irrational to keep this disposition, why must it be rational, if I do keep it, to act upon it?

   If I have irrationally remained prudent, there is a different explanation of why it can be rational to act upon this disposition. Doing so will be better for me. The rationality of this act need not be defended by an appeal to the rationality of the disposition, or of my having kept the disposition, upon which I act. Things are quite different with ignoring your threat, in a way that I know will be disastrous for me. If this act is to be claimed to be rational, that can only be by an appeal to the rationality of the disposition on which I am acting. And if it is now irrational for me to keep this disposition, there seems no reason to conclude that, if I keep it, it must be rational for me to act upon it.

   Suppose, next, that I could *not* lose my disposition, even if I tried. Gauthier might say that, if that is true, it is not irrational for me to keep this disposition. This is not something that I *do*. But it *would* be irrational for me to keep it, if I *could* lose it. This seems enough to undermine the claim that it must still be rational to act upon it.

18. (C) is one interpretation of what Gauthier calls the 'weakest' version of his view, or what he calls his first level of commitment. On this view, he writes, one should act upon some disposition, even though one's actions are 'costly . . . only so long as one reasonably expects adherence to the disposition to be prospectively maximally beneficial' (*Reading Parfit*, p. 39).

   When Gauthier talks of 'adherence' to this disposition being beneficial, he must mean continuing to *have* this disposition. *Acting* on this disposition may be, as he agrees, costly. I shall also take 'adherence' to mean 'present adherence'. Though Gauthier might mean 'adherence now *and in the future*', that would make his claim less plausible. It would not cover cases where it would be advantageous first to acquire and then to lose some disposition. (Suppose that, while it was indeed better to acquire some permanent disposition than not to acquire it at all, it would have been expectably-best to acquire it simply for a time. Acquiring this permanent disposition was not then, as Gauthier requires, 'maximally beneficial'.)

19. My drug-induced insanity, Gauthier claims, is 'the rational disposition in such situations, and the actions to which it gives rise are rational actions' (*Reading Parfit*, p. 38). Gauthier means only that it is in my interests to have this disposition *now*. He is not here concerned with a choice between two permanent dispositions. If I had to choose my disposition, not just until the police arrive, but for the rest of my life, it would be better to remain sane and give the man my gold.

20. *MA* (*passim*).

21. Gauthier might extend his claim about translucency. He might say that we could not have reason to believe that, if we broke our promises, we could keep this fact secret. But this reply would jettison what is novel in Gauthier's view, since it would revert to the ancient claim that honesty is always the best policy.

22. There is one reading on which this claim must be true. It may be said that, if we are able to suspend our disposition, we were not *truly* trustworthy. But this reading is irrelevant since, for Gauthier's purposes, all that matters is whether we *appeared* trustworthy. It would be quite implausible to claim that, if we break some agreement, we cannot have earlier appeared to be trustworthy, even if, at the time, we sincerely intended to keep this agreement.

If this claim is to help Gauthier's case, he must make other revisions in his view. He writes: 'a disposition is rational if, among those humanly possible, having it will lead to one's life going as well as having any other' (*Reading Parfit*, p. 31). This appeal to *human* possibility seems at odds with other parts of Gauthier's view. He claims elsewhere that we should not ask which dispositions are in general rational, since the answer may depend on a particular person's circumstances. Thus he writes, 'there need be no one disposition that, independently of an agent's circumstances, is sufficient to ensure that his life will go as well as possible, and thus I do not need to suppose that there need be a single supremely rational disposition' (*Reading Parfit*, pp. 31–2). A person's circumstances can surely include what is possible for this person.

This appeal to human possibility also raises a problem for Gauthier's argument. Trustworthiness is *not* the disposition that, among those *humanly* possible, is most advantageous. It would be more advantageous to appear to be trustworthy but to be really prudent; and that is surely possible for some human beings. If Gauthier appeals to what is humanly possible, he would have to judge trustworthiness to be an irrational disposition, even when it is had by people for whom, since they could not deceive others, it is the most advantageous possible disposition.

23. At one point, Gauthier may make this move. While honesty is the best policy, Hume writes, there may be some exceptions. According to Hume's 'sensible knave', he is wisest 'who observes the general rule, and takes advantage of all the exceptions'. Gauthier replies that, to be rational, we must be disposed to keep our promises, since this disposition will be best for us. He then writes, 'such a person is not able, given her disposition, to take advantage of the "exceptions"; she rightly judges such conduct irrational' (*MA*, p. 182).

24. In the doctrine that 'ought' implies 'can', the sense of 'can' is compatible with determinism. If that were denied, and we assumed determinism, we would have to claim that *every* act is rational.

25. It would of course be better if I merely appeared to be insane. But we can suppose that this is not possible, since if I had not taken the drug, the robber would know

this. (Perhaps one of the drug's effects is a characteristic look in the eyes; or perhaps I can convince the robber only if he sees me drink this drug.) Being actually in this state is then the disposition that is best for me.

26. *Reading Parfit* (p. 37).

27. Provided, of course, that these bad effects do not outweigh the good effects of my disposition. Gauthier need not claim that, if I killed myself or my children, that would be rational.

28. It may be said that, in one respect, Gauthier's view is less extreme than Hume's. Even if my act has bad effects, these must be outweighed by the good effects of having my disposition. But we can remember here that, on Gauthier's main view, I maximize my utility if I fulfil my present considered preferences, and these need not coincide with my interests. As on Hume's view, these preferences could be as crazy as we can imagine. The difference between these views is that, on Hume's view, for my act to be rational, I must at least be trying to fulfil my aims, while on Gauthier's view, my acts need only be the side-effects of a state the having of which will achieve these aims.

29. 'Our argument identifies practical rationality with utility-maximization at the level of dispositions to choose, and carries through the implications of that identification in assessing the rationality of particular choices' (*MA*, p. 187).

30. It may seem that, if that is true, breaking our promises cannot be better for us. But this may not be so. The bad effects come, not from our breaking of these promises, but from the fact that we are both translucent and disposed to break our promises whenever this will be better for us.

31. It is worth explaining why. In our assessment of the good or bad effects of our dispositions, we include the acts to which these dispositions would or might lead. If it is best for us to have some disposition, even though this will lead to acts which are bad for us, those effects must be outweighed. Since the assessment of our dispositions includes the assessment of our acts, but goes beyond it, this is the assessment that tells us what on balance will be best for us.

32. *MA* (p. 170).

33. It may be questioned whether G tells us, if we can, to acquire these dispositions. That does not follow from the fact that, if we do, that will be better for us. If G does not tell us to act in this way, that would be an objection to G, and would again undermine Gauthier's argument. But Gauthier might claim that, in trying to acquire these dispositions, we would be acting on an advantageous, or maximizing, meta-disposition.

34. He would admit that, in practice, few of us are always rational. But he might claim that, in assessing the plausibility of these theories, we should consider what would happen if we always did what they told us to do. He might then claim that, if we fully followed S, we would always maximize at the level of our acts.

35. It may be objected that, if we cannot always do what S claims to be rational, S cannot claim that we ought to do so. 'Ought' implies 'can'. But this confuses two questions. When I say that we cannot always do what S claims to be rational, I mean that this is not causally possible. This is the kind of possibility that is relevant when we are comparing the effects of our having different dispositions. The sense of 'can' that is implied by 'ought' does not, as Gauthier agrees, require such causal possibility, since this other sense of 'can' is compatible with determinism.

36. It may seem that, if we cannot always do what S tells us to do, there is no way of predicting when we shall follow S. That is not so. Suppose that we are now

always disposed to do what we believe to be rational. If we know that we can acquire maximizing dispositions, we shall then do so, even though we know that this will cause us later to act irrationally. Acquiring these dispositions is, according to S, the rational thing to do. It is only *after* acquiring these dispositions that we shall start acting in ways that S claims to be irrational.

37. In 'Deterrence, Maximization, and Rationality', and in *The Security Gamble*, ed. Douglas MacLean (Totowa, NJ: Rowman & Allanheld, 1984).
38. 'Afterthoughts', in *The Security Gamble* (pp. 159–61).
39. Cf. Edward McClennen, 'Constrained Maximization and Resolute Choice', *Social Philosophy and Public Policy*, 5:95–118, 1988.
40. Such a claim is fairly plausible in the case of trustworthiness, the disposition that is Gauthier's chief concern. If we could not conceal our intentions, as he assumes, it might be better for us if we intended to keep our promises, even when this way of acting would be worse for us. Unless we have this intention, others might exclude us from advantageous agreements. And, for us to be able to form this intention, we might have to believe that it is rational to keep such promises.
41. 'Constrained Maximization'.
42. In a letter to me.
43. See *MA* (p. 182) and *Reading Parfit* (p. 31). (But see also *MA*, pp. 170 and 158.)
44. *Reading Parfit* (p. 36).
45. At one point, Gauthier comes close to accepting (D). He cites my book's version of (D) – there called '(G2)' – and writes, 'to this extent I accept . . . (G2)' (*Reading Parfit*, p. 40).
46. It may seem that, in making these remarks, I have presupposed a naively realistic view. Gauthier might say that a normative theory could not be *true*. But this would not rescue Gauthier's argument. Even on a noncognitivist view, we must give some content to the notion of a normative belief. We must be able to claim that an act *is* rational, and be able to assert or deny different theories. My remarks could be restated in these terms.
47. In *The Security Gamble*.
48. 'Afterthoughts', in *The Security Gamble*, pp. 159–61.
49. *Reading Parfit*, p. 30.
50. *Reading Parfit*, p. 36.
51. *Reading Parfit*, p. 38.

Are Intentions Reasons? And How Should We Cope with Incommensurable Values?

JOHN BROOME

1. Introduction

If you intend to do something, does your intention constitute a reason for you to do that thing? To put the question briefly: Are intentions reasons? Many philosophers have argued they are, but in this essay I shall argue they are not.

First thoughts are on my side. The view that intentions are reasons is implausible. If you have no reason to do something, it is implausible that you can give yourself a reason just by forming the intention of doing it. How could you create a reason for yourself out of nothing? Suppose, say, that you have no reason either for or against doing some act, and you happen to decide to do it. Now you intend to do it. So now, if intentions are reasons, you have a reason to do it. Since you have no contrary reason not to do it, the balance of reasons is in favour of your doing it. You now actually ought to do it, therefore. But this is implausible. It is implausible that just deciding to do something can make it the case that you ought to do it, when previously that was not the case.

I shall call this 'the bootstrapping objection', in honour of Michael Bratman, who raises it in his *Intention, Plans, and Practical Reason.*[1] The objection is that you cannot bootstrap a reason into existence from nowhere, just by a forming an intention.

Take an example. Suppose you are wondering whether or not to visit Paris, but have not yet made up your mind. There are reasons in favour and reasons against. Whether or not you ought to go depends on the balance of reasons. Now suppose you make up your mind to go, so now you intend to go to Paris. Ought you to go or not, now? What does that now depend on?

Before answering this question, I need to exclude some complicating

This essay has benefited from vigorous discussions at meetings in Copenhagen and Amsterdam and on the island of Raasay; I am very grateful to all those who were there. I particularly want to mention excellent written comments I received from David Donaldson, Joe Mintoff, and Howard Sobel. Most of the essay was written while I was a Visiting Fellow at the Swedish Collegium for Advanced Study in the Social Sciences. I thank the Collegium for its very generous hospitality.

factors. Your decision can create reasons in various indirect ways. Once it leads you to make some investment in going to Paris, reasons in favour of going there will begin to accumulate. If you have bought a non-refundable ticket, that adds to your reasons. Even if you have gone only as far as calling the travel agent, that effort is still a small investment and may add to your reasons in favour of going. Some people value their resoluteness, and lose some of their self-esteem if they change their minds. For these people, every decision is automatically a sort of investment, and gives them a reason to carry it out.[2] Reasons like this are the complicating factors that I need to exclude. They are consequences of your intention, but we are interested in whether the intention itself is a reason. To exclude these factors, let us suppose you have made no investment of any sort. You have simply decided to go to Paris, and so far done nothing about it. Also, you attach no particular value to resoluteness. Ought you to go or not?

The answer is intuitively clear. If the balance of antecedent reasons was in favour of your going to Paris, you ought to go there. You have made the right decision, and you ought to carry it out. If the balance of antecedent reasons was against your going to Paris, you ought not to go there. You have made the wrong decision and you ought not to carry it out. Even if the balance was only very weakly against going to Paris, still you should not go there, so long as you have not yet invested anything in getting there. Your intention itself does not count one whit in favour of going to Paris. It makes no difference to what you should do. What you should do depends only on the antecedent reasons.

Suppose there is a slight balance of antecedent reasons against going, but you made a mistake in your calculations and wrongly decided to go. A short time later, having invested nothing in the decision, you discover your mistake. Should you change your mind? If intentions were reasons, there would automatically be a reason not to, and if the balance of antecedent reasons was slight enough, you should stick to your decision. But actually you should surely change your mind. Since you have invested nothing in your wrong decision, you should change it.

Intuitively, then, your intention of going to Paris is not itself a reason to go there. The slightest balance of genuine reasons against your intention means you should not carry it out.

This is an application of the bootstrapping objection. The example shows we can add a second objection as a corollary to the bootstrapping one: There is nothing in itself wrong with changing your mind. If you have an intention, there is nothing in itself wrong with giving it up. Certainly, there would be something wrong with it in some circumstances. For one thing, there may be a good antecedent reason why you should do the thing you intend to do. If so, it is likely also to be a reason for you to stick to your intention. For another thing, having formed the intention, you may have invested in it, and your investment may constitute a reason for sticking to it. But apart from antecedent reasons and investments, there is no reason for you not to change your mind. I call this the 'objection from changing your mind'. It is a second objection to the view that intentions are reasons.

The bootstrapping objection and its corollary constitute a good *prima facie* case against this view. Many authors have offered contrary arguments, and one purpose of this essay is to answer those arguments. In view of the *prima facie* objections, I hope that will be enough to make the case that intentions are not reasons.

The essay has another purpose too. Intending to do something is not a reason to do it, but nevertheless a sort of normative relation does exist between intending and acting. I shall try to express accurately what this relation is. I hope that offering a better account of it will further reduce the attraction of the view that intentions are reasons.

Finally, I shall display this normative relation at work in a particular application. Some values are incommensurable with others. This incommensurability raises a problem for practical reason: How does a rational person act in the face of incommensurable values? I shall offer an answer, founded on my account of the normative relation between intending and acting.

2. The Pragmatic Argument

One argument for the claim that intentions are reasons is pragmatic.[3] It has two steps. The first is to demonstrate that, if indeed intentions are reasons, our lives will go better than they would if intentions were not reasons. The second is to argue from there to the conclusion that intentions are reasons.

I do not need to refute the pragmatic argument, since that has already been convincingly done by other authors. I have no quarrel with the first step; it is supported by many well-known examples. But David Velleman, for one, has convincingly refuted the second step in his 'Deciding How to Decide'. All I shall do here is add one more example in support of the first step. This example also demonstrates how implausible the second step is, so it ultimately works against the pragmatic argument.

One clarifying remark. The examples that support the first step of the argument work only if the reason created by an intention is a strong one – strong enough to defeat a significant contrary reason. A weak reason would not be enough; my example will show why not. So I slightly overstated the conclusion of the first step. The conclusion is that our lives will go better if intentions are strong reasons. Therefore, if the pragmatic argument succeeded in showing anything, it would show that intentions are strong reasons.

My example is a variation on – Gauthier might say a perversion of – one of David Gauthier's. Here it is.

You are leading your flock of sheep down from the mountain. In the last narrow defile before reaching the safety of the plain, you meet a wolf. If the wolf lunges into the flock, trying to grab a sheep, it will probably end up catching only a scrawny one. However, half the flock will die of fright or be lost over a cliff. Both you and the wolf know this, and you both know there is another course of action that would suit both of you better. It would be better for both if you handed over the juiciest of this year's lambs to the wolf, and in return the wolf allowed the rest of the flock to pass unmolested. Is there some way this desirable outcome could be achieved?

For the sake of argument, assume no contract can be made between you and the wolf, and no genuine promise issued, because no institutions of law or morality exist between the two of you. Assume the wolf is a migrant, and you will never meet it again. Assume both you and the wolf are rational, and this is known to both of you. Assume you are transparent to the extent that the wolf can accurately detect your intentions.

Now, suppose that intending something gives you a strong reason to do it (the degree of strength will appear in a moment). Then the desirable outcome could be achieved as follows. You could form the intention of presenting the best lamb to the wolf, if and when the rest of the flock has passed safely through the defile. We are supposing this intention gives you a reason to carry it out. Furthermore, the reason is strong – let us assume strong enough to outweigh the loss to you of the best lamb. Then, if the wolf allows the flock through the defile unmolested, the balance of your reasons will be in favour of your handing over the best lamb to the wolf. Since you are rational, you will do so. Moreover, the wolf will know all this. So it will know it can obtain the best lamb by letting the flock pass, whereas it will probably get only a scrawny sheep if it attacks. It will therefore not attack. Your flock will pass through, and you will hand over the lamb. The desirable outcome will be achieved.

On the other hand, if intending something is not a strong reason to do it, none of this will happen. Even if you manage to form the intention of handing over the best lamb to the wolf, the balance of reasons will be against your carrying out this intention, once the wolf has allowed the flock to pass. Being rational, you will not do so. The wolf will know this, so it will know it can gain nothing by letting the flock through. It will do best for itself by attacking and grabbing whatever sheep it can. You will lose half your flock.

In this example, therefore, both you and the wolf will do better if intentions are strong reasons. The same is true in many other examples. It seems reasonable to conclude in general that our lives would go better if intentions were strong reasons. Let us grant that. Should we then grant the second part of the pragmatic argument? Can we derive the conclusion that intending something actually is a strong reason to do it?

The example is very much against it. Suppose you successfully form the intention of handing over the best lamb to the wolf, and everything goes smoothly. The flock is safely through, and the time comes to sacrifice the lamb. Should you do so? Intuitively, it seems not. Nothing would be gained by your doing so. Your flock is safe; why should you give up a lamb? By doing so, you gain nothing and lose the lamb. You owe the wolf nothing, of course.

Gauthier evidently has the opposite intuition, but I suspect that is because he thinks of examples that are biased in the opposite direction. In his examples, carrying out your intention is generally a nice thing to do, independently of the intention. In my example, I deliberately made it a nasty thing to do. If it is not nasty enough to convince you, I can make it nastier. Let your flock be children, and the wolf a paedophile killer.

Still, this is only intuition, and the second step of the pragmatic argument needs a proper refutation. As I said, a convincing one is already available from Velleman, so I shall move on to other arguments.

3. The Argument from Instrumental Reasoning

Many authors have quite different grounds for thinking that intentions are reasons. They think that, if intentions were not reasons, they could not play the central role they do play in the management of our lives. Michael Bratman's *Intention, Plans, and Practical Reason* is an excellent exploration of this role. I shall pick out some features of it.

First, if you intend to do something, your intention normally brings it about that you do it. This is the most fundamental way in which intentions help us manage our lives. By forming intentions, we gain some control over our future actions. Without this control, we could not carry out any concerted course of action that lasts some time. We would not have coherent lives.

When I say your intention 'brings it about' that you perform an action, I mean the intention causes the action. But the process is not *merely* causal. It is also a rational process; it involves reason. This is a second essential feature of the role that intentions play in our lives. They do not cause us to act mechanically, but through our reason.

To say the process involves reason is vague. There are, more precisely, at least two ways in which it does so. Each provides a distinct argument for the view that intentions are reasons. This section explains one way, and the next section the other.

The first way is that carrying out an intention often involves reasoning.

Specifically, it involves instrumental reasoning. If you intend to achieve some end, then, commonly, by reasoning you will work out a suitable means of achieving this end, and form the intention of going about it by that means. By reasoning, we constantly derive intentions to take means from intentions to achieve ends.

It follows that our intentions must be able to figure as premises in our instrumental reasoning. It is sometimes argued that intentions could not perform this role unless they constituted reasons. This provides one argument for the view that intentions are reasons. I shall call it 'the argument from instrumental reasoning'.

It appears in Christine Korsgaard's paper 'The Normativity of Instrumental Reason'. Korsgaard asks how the pursuit of an end requires you, rationally, to take a means to this end. How can you reason from intending an end to intending a means? Her answer is that the end must be invested with normativity. She thinks you cannot otherwise be rationally required to take the means. 'Unless there are normative principles directing us to the adoption of certain ends, there can be no requirement to take the means to our ends'.[4] Instrumental reasoning can transmit normativity from the end to the means, but it cannot itself give the means normativity.

However, Korsgaard is also opposed to the realist view that some ends have normativity in the nature of things – that it is in the nature of these ends that they should be pursued. So she thinks the normativity of an end must arise from the intention to achieve it. Just because you intend an end, that makes the end normative for you: You have a reason to achieve it. Intending (willing) an end constitutes a reason to achieve it. Korsgaard says:

For the instrumental principle ['that practical reason requires us to take the means to our ends'[5]] to provide you with a reason [to take the means to an end], you must think that the fact that you will an end *is a reason* for the end. It's not exactly that there has to be a *further* reason; it's just that you must take the act of your own will to be normative for you. And of course this cannot mean merely that you are *going* to pursue the end. It means that your willing the end gives it a normative status for you, that your willing the end in a sense makes it good. The instrumental principle can only be normative if we take ourselves to be capable of giving laws to ourselves – or, in Kant's own phrase, if we take our own wills to be *legislative*.[6]

4. The Argument from Rationality

The argument from instrumental reasoning derives from one of the ways in which reason is involved in the process that leads from intending to acting: Instrumental reasoning often mediates the process. However, that does not always happen. Sometimes an intention causes an act more directly, without the intervention of instrumental reasoning. For instance, you may form the intention of patting your friend on the back, and do so, without reasoning about how to do so.

Nevertheless, even when the process that leads from intending to acting does not call on instrumental reasoning, it is still a rational process. It is part of our rationality that we usually carry out our intentions. (I say 'usually' because it is often rational to change one's mind, and not carry out an intention, as I said in Section 1. I shall make the 'usually' more precise in Section 7.) If we did not, usually, we would not be entirely rational. The process that leads from intending to acting is guided or controlled by reason, then. To put it another way, it is normatively sanctioned. This is a second way in which reason is involved in the process.

Some causal processes are rational processes. Reasoning is an example. In various ways, your existing intentions and beliefs cause you to acquire new intentions and beliefs. Some of these causal processes are normatively sanctioned as rational. Those ones constitute practical or theoretical reasoning. For instance, if one of your existing beliefs causes you (in the normal way, and not by some deviant mechanism) to believe one of its logical consequences, that process is normatively sanctioned. It is a process of theoretical reasoning.

Not all normatively sanctioned processes are necessarily processes of reasoning. If you believe you ought to do something, this belief will often cause you to do that thing. Moreover, the process whereby your belief causes you to act is normatively sanctioned, provided it occurs in a normal way. It ought to occur. If you do not do what you believe you ought to do, you are not fully as you ought to be. So this is a rational process. But we might not consider it a process of reasoning. Reasoning might bring you to believe you ought to do something, but we might not think it is reasoning that actually brings you to do it.

Similarly, the causal process that runs from intending something to doing it is a rational process, provided it occurs in the normal way. It may not be a process of reasoning, but that does not stop it from being a rational process.

Its rationality provides another argument for the view that intentions are reasons. The process that leads from intending something to doing it is a rational process. It is normatively sanctioned. But if this is so, it surely means that the intention gives you a reason to do the action. How else could it be a rational process? I shall call this 'the argument from rationality'.

In his 'Deciding How to Decide', David Velleman first dismisses the pragmatic argument for the claim that intentions are reasons. I said that in Section 2. He then goes on to offer a different argument of his own for the same conclusion. I think his argument is in effect the one I have just given.

True, he puts it differently. He stresses the autonomy of the process that runs from intending to acting, rather than its rationality. But in effect he identifies autonomous processes with rational ones.[7] Undoubtedly, the process that runs from intending to acting is autonomous as well as rational. For one thing, you can turn it off: You can change your mind and decide not to act after all. But for my purpose, it does not matter how the autonomy of the process is connected with its rationality. The argument that intentions are reasons must be founded on the process's rationality rather than its autonomy. Its premise must be that the process that runs from intending to acting is a rational one. Only from that premise does it apparently follow that intentions must be reasons. From the premise that the process is autonomous, that conclusion would follow only indirectly, at best.

5. Normative Requirements

In order to answer the two arguments I presented in Sections 3 and 4, I need first to examine rational processes in general. I shall use as an example the process of theoretical reasoning, because this one should be comparatively uncontroversial.

Suppose you believe some proposition p from which q can be inferred by an immediate valid inference. Then a rational process of theoretical reasoning will lead you from believing p to believing q. But does it follow that believing p is a reason to believe q? I shall argue that it does not.

From one point of view, this seems obvious. You might have no reason to believe p in the first place. Indeed, it might even be the case that you ought not to believe p. Then obviously you may have no reason to believe q.

Moreover, this conclusion can be supported by a simple argument. The proposition p itself follows from p by an immediate valid inference. But your believing p plainly cannot be a reason to believe p. Beliefs do not justify themselves; that would be an impossible sort of bootstrapping. So it cannot be a general principle that believing p is a reason to believe p's immediate consequences.

Still, however obvious this may seem, there is a plausible contrary thought. If you believe p, then surely in some sense or other that is a reason to believe its consequence q, when q is different from p itself. No doubt, we would not say that believing p is a reason to believe p itself, because you do not need a reason for that; you already believe it. But if you are going to believe a consequence of p that is distinct from p, you do need a reason for that, and surely believing p is one, in some sense or other.

So two plausible views seem to conflict. But fortunately they can easily be reconciled. We may say that if you believe p, *in some sense or other* this is a reason to believe the consequence q, if q is different from p itself. Expressed more precisely, the position is that a particular relation holds between your believing p and your believing q: The first *normatively requires* the second, as I shall put it.

I have examined the notion of normative requirement more thoroughly in my paper 'Normative Requirements'. Here I shall mention only its essential features. To say that believing p normatively requires you to believe q implies

$$O(Bp \rightarrow Bq), \qquad (1)$$

where 'O' stands for 'you ought to see to it that', 'B' stands for 'you believe that', and '$\rightarrow$' is the material conditional. (1) says you ought to see to it that if you believe p you believe q. But to say that believing p normatively requires you to believe q does not imply that if you believe p you have a reason to believe q:

$$Bp \rightarrow RBq, \qquad (2)$$

where 'R' stands for 'you have a reason to'.

In (1), normativity is attached to the relation between believing p and believing q, not to believing q itself. On the other hand, (2) attaches normativity to the consequent rather than the relation. This means the consequent in (2) can be detached by *modus ponens*: From Bp and (2) we can infer RBq. If you believe p, then (2) says you have a reason to believe q. A normative requirement does not allow detachment of that sort. We might say that, *in a sense*, believing p is a reason to believe q, but this sense is misleading because, even if you believe p, you do not actually have a reason to believe q. From now on, I shall not use this misleading sense. The relation between believing p and believing q is not strictly that believing p is a reason to believe q. It is that believing p normatively requires you to believe q.

It is easy to confuse a reason and a normative requirement, because they both involve a weakening of ought. A reason is a weakening of ought; it is an ought made *pro tanto* – an ought so far as it goes. If you have a reason to do something, and no reason not to do it, then you ought to do it. A normative requirement is also a weakening of ought; it is weakened by being made relative. It is easy to muddle the two types of weakening.

The difference between them can be described like this: A normative requirement is strict but relative; a reason is slack but absolute. A normative requirement is relative because it is a relation between two propositions. It is the truth of the first (such as your believing p) that requires you to see to the truth of the second (such as your believing q), and the requirement cannot be detached from its antecedent. But a normative requirement is strict because it is strictly a requirement: If you do not satisfy it, you have failed in something that is required of you. (1) expresses this strictness. It says you ought to see to it that if you believe p you believe q. So if you believe p but not q, you are definitely failing to see to something you ought to see to. On the other hand, a reason is not relative, but it is slack in that it is only *pro tanto*. If you do not do what you have a reason to do, you may not have failed in any way; you may have performed exactly as you should have. You may have had a better reason not to do this thing, and correctly followed the better reason.

The difference provides a useful test for distinguishing between a normative requirement and a reason. I call it 'the strictness test'. The relation between believing p and believing q, when q follows from p, is plainly strict. That is to say, if you believe p and you do not believe q, you are definitely failing to see to something you ought to see to. If the relation was simply that believing p was a reason to believe q, it would be slack; you might believe p and not believe q, yet still be failing in no respect. This could happen if, say, you had a better reason not to believe q. But actually this is not possible. To be sure, you might have a good reason not to believe q, and an appropriate response might be to stop believing p. That way, you can escape from the requirement that is imposed on you by your belief in p. But if you do not take this way out, and you believe p without believing q, you are not entirely as you ought to be. So the relation is strict, and it therefore cannot be that believing p is a reason for believing q. It must be the relation of normative requirement.

This explains an important feature of theoretical reasoning. Suppose one of your beliefs is one you have no reason to have; indeed, suppose you ought not to have it. Still, you can take it as a premise in your reasoning, and your reasoning will proceed exactly as it would in the more favourable circumstance where you ought to believe the premise. The nature of the reasoning is not affected by the merits of your belief in the premise. The reasoning that takes you from believing p to believing q is an example.

If reasoning had to give you a reason to believe the conclusion, this would not be possible. If you ought not to believe the premise, you may have no reason to believe the conclusion. But reasoning does not have to give you a reason to believe the conclusion. Instead, it reveals a normative requirement to believe the conclusion. Your belief in the premise may normatively require you to believe the conclusion, even if you ought not to believe this premise. For example, your belief in p normatively requires you to believe q, even if you ought not to believe p.

6. Instrumental Reasoning

With the idea of a normative requirement in hand, I can return to the argument from instrumental reasoning. The argument is that we often reason on the basis of an intention to achieve some end, to arrive at an intention to take a means to that end. Evidently, therefore, this reasoning gives us a reason to

take the means, and that would not be possible if we had no reason to achieve
the end in the first place. So an intention to achieve the end must be a reason
to do so.

Put briefly, the mistake in this argument is that instrumental reasoning does
not give us a reason to take the means. Instead, intending an end normatively
requires us to intend the means. Instrumental reasoning brings us to conform
with this normative requirement: It brings us to intend the means to an end
we intend. This is possible even if we have no reason either to achieve the
end or to intend it.

To fill out this response to the argument, I need to examine the process of
instrumental reasoning in more detail. My account is developed thoroughly
in my 'Practical Reasoning'. Here I shall be brief.

Here is an example of practical, instrumental reasoning:

	I am going to open the wine	(3a)
and	In order to open the wine, I must fetch the corkscrew.	(3b)
so	I shall fetch the corkscrew.	(3c)

I mean (3a) to express an intention of yours, rather than a belief. I mean (3b)
to express a belief. I mean the conclusion (3c) also to express an intention.

You might actually go through this process of reasoning. Suppose you
intend to open the wine, and then someone tells you the corkscrew is in the
kitchen. This information imparts to you the belief that in order to open the
wine, you must fetch the corkscrew. By reasoning, you form the intention of
fetching the corkscrew.

Like all reasoning, this process takes you from existing states of mind to a
new state of mind. It takes you from an intention and a belief to a new
intention. To describe the process in more detail, I shall assume that your
intentions and beliefs are propositional attitudes. That is to say, they are states
of mind that have contents, and the contents are propositions. I shall assume
your name is 'Pat', and I shall assume the proposition that Pat will open the
wine is the same as the proposition that you, Pat, would express by saying 'I
am going to open the wine'. So the content of your intention expressed in
(3a) is the proposition that Pat will open the wine. Expressing propositions in
the third person, we can describe your reasoning process explicitly as follows:

	I(Pat will open the wine)	(4a)
and	B(In order for Pat to open the wine, Pat must fetch the corkscrew)	(4b)
leads to	I(Pat will fetch the corkscrew).	(4c)

'B' stands for 'you believe that', and 'I' for 'you intend that'. (4) describes
your reasoning. It is a description, not a derivation. If you intend to open the

wine, and if you believe that in order to do so you must fetch the corkscrew, it does not follow that you intend to fetch the corkscrew. You might not have this intention if you are irrational, for instance.

On the other hand, (3) sets out the content of your reasoning. It has the form of a genuine derivation. Intuitively, it is valid reasoning; you are right to derive the intention of fetching the corkscrew from your existing intention and belief. Furthermore, it is indeed valid reasoning, as the following argument shows.

Start by comparing the practical reasoning described in (4) with this process of theoretical reasoning:

	B(Pat will open the wine)	(5a)
and	B(In order for Pat to open the wine, Pat must fetch the corkscrew)	(5b)
leads to	B(Pat will fetch the corkscrew).	(5c)

(To make it clear that this is theoretical reasoning concerned with beliefs, rather than practical reasoning concerned with intentions, imagine you are predicting your movements tomorrow, when you expect to be in a stupor.) Again, (5) is a description of reasoning rather than a derivation. Its content is:

	Pat will open the wine	(6a)
and	In order for Pat to open the wine, Pat must fetch the corkscrew,	(6b)
so	Pat will fetch the corkscrew.	(6c)

If you were running through this piece of reasoning, you would doubtless express it to yourself in the first person:

	I shall open the wine.
and	In order for me to open the wine, I must fetch the corkscrew.
so	I shall fetch the corkscrew.

Expressed in either the first or the third person, this content constitutes a valid inference. If its premises are true, the conclusion is true too. For this reason, the theoretical reasoning described in (5) is valid reasoning. It is valid because its content constitutes a valid derivation.

The content of the practical reasoning (4) is the same syllogism (6) as the content of theoretical reasoning (5). The difference between (4) and (5) is not in the propositions that constitute their content, but in the attitude you take towards these propositions. In the theoretical reasoning (5), your attitude is to take both premises as true. Because the conclusion is true if the premises are true, you cannot rationally take the premises as true without taking the conclusion as true. So your attitude towards the premises normatively requires you to take the conclusion as true. It requires you to believe it, that is. In the practical reasoning (4), your attitude towards the first premise is to set yourself to make it true. Your attitude towards the second premise is to take it as true. Because the conclusion is true if the premises are true, you cannot rationally set yourself to make the first premise true, and take the second as true, without setting yourself to make the conclusion true. Your attitude towards the premises normatively requires you to set yourself to make the conclusion true. It requires you to intend it, that is.[8]

Both (4) and (5) correctly track truth through the valid derivation (6). (5) tracks it in a truth-taking way, (4) in a truth-making way. Both therefore constitute valid reasoning. (5) is valid theoretical reasoning; (4) is valid practical reasoning.

I shall use the term 'conclusion-state' for the mental state that results from a piece of reasoning, and the term 'premise-state' for a mental state from which reasoning sets out. If a piece of reasoning is valid, its conclusion-state is normatively required by its premise-states. So, in my example of practical reasoning:

	I(I am going to open the wine)
and	B(In order to open the wine, I must fetch the corkscrew)
normatively requires	I(I shall fetch the corkscrew).

The relation between the premise-states and the conclusion-state is not that the premise-states constitute a reason for the conclusion-state. You might be tempted to think that, in some sense or other, you have a reason to intend to fetch the corkscrew, if you intend to open the wine and believe that to do so you must fetch the corkscrew. But to see this is wrong, we can apply the strictness test that I mentioned in Section 5. If you intend to open the wine, and believe that to do so you must fetch the corkscrew, you are definitely not entirely as you ought to be unless you intend to fetch the corkscrew. So the normative relation between premise-states and conclusion-state is strict, and therefore not the relation of being a reason for.

It is the relation of normative requirement. It does not allow a normative conclusion to be detached. Even if you intend to open the wine, and believe that to do so you must fetch the corkscrew, it does not follow that you have a reason to intend to fetch the corkscrew. Suppose, say, that you ought not to intend opening the wine in the first place, even though you do intend opening it. Then it may not be the case that you have a reason to fetch the corkscrew.

In general, intending an end normatively requires you to intend what you believe to be a necessary means to the end. It does not give you a reason to intend what you believe to be a necessary means.

This explains an important feature of instrumental reasoning. You can perfectly well reason from beliefs or intentions that you have no reason to have, and even that you ought not to have. Your reasoning proceeds in exactly the same manner whether or not this is so. If the result of the reasoning had to be that you have a reason for the conclusion-state, this would be inexplicable. Reasoning from beliefs and intentions you ought not to have could not give you a reason for the conclusion. But that is not how reasoning works. It works because the premise-states normatively require the conclusion-state.

This is the answer to the argument from instrumental reasoning. If you intend an end, you can take that intention as a premise in your instrumental reasoning, even if you have no reason to have this end. Intending the end need not give you a reason to pursue it; yet instrumental reasoning will still be possible.

7. Unrepudiated Intentions Are Normative Requirements

The idea of a normative requirement also provides the answer to the argument from rationality. The process that runs from intending an act to doing it is a rational process. The argument from rationality is that this could not be so unless the intention constituted a reason for the act. The answer is that a process does not have to provide a reason in order to be rational. Instead, it may reveal a normative requirement. But I need to identify exactly what is normatively required by what.

Could it be that intending to do something normatively requires you to do it? To do the job it needs to do, this normative requirement would have to cross time. It would have to be that an intention you have at one time normatively requires you to act on it at a later time. A trans-temporal requirement is needed, because the central role of intentions is to control our future actions, as I said in Section 3. The rational process that runs from intending an act to doing it is trans-temporal.

However, it is actually not the case that an intention you have at one time normatively requires you to act on it at a later time. That connection between intending and acting would be too strong. It would imply you ought to see to it that, if you intend to do something, you do it. So if you intend to do something at one time, but later change your mind and do not do it, you would not be entirely as you ought to be. That would mean you should not change your mind, once you had formed an intention. But I insisted in Section 1 that there may be nothing wrong with changing your mind. So, whatever is the trans-temporal normative relation between intending and action, it must be weaker than this.

We can start to work out what it is by comparing another normative requirement, which is not trans-temporal. If you intend an end, that intention normatively requires you to intend what you believe to be a necessary means to the end. This requirement holds only between intentions that you have at one time, though I have not said so explicitly till now.

I described this requirement in Section 6, and I said it does not imply that if you intend the end, you have a reason to intend the means. Still less does it imply that you ought to intend the means. But if you do intend the end, and your intention normatively requires you to intend the means, how can it fail to imply that you ought to intend the means? Because it requires you to maintain consistency among your intentions, rather than to have a particular intention. There are two ways of maintaining this consistency: Intend the means or, alternatively, do not intend the end. If you decide not to take the means, that is fine: You only have to stop intending the end. Consequently, this normative requirement puts no obstruction in the way of your changing your mind.

But if an intention normatively required you to act on it in the trans-temporal way I described, there would be no second way of meeting the requirement, once the time of the original intention was past. At a later time, you cannot make it the case that you did not have the intention at an earlier time, so you can meet the requirement only by acting on it. That is why it goes too far to claim that an intention normatively requires you to act on it.

We can arrive at an appropriately weaker claim by introducing the idea of *repudiating* an intention. You cannot change a past intention, but you can repudiate it. I suggest it is permissible to change your mind, and not carry out one of your past intentions, but only provided you repudiate it.

I suggest that if you intend to do something, and you do not repudiate this intention, your intention normatively requires you to do what you intend. In brief: Unrepudiated intentions normatively require to be acted on. I think this correctly states the normative connection between intention and action. Re-pudiation supplies a second way out of the normative requirement, and so permits you to change your mind.

How do you repudiate an intention? Not simply by stopping having it, because that would reduce the requirement to no requirement at all. On the other hand, you do not necessarily need a reason to repudiate an intention. You may have acquired the intention for no reason, and consequently need no reason to give it up. I suggest repudiating an intention must at least be done deliberately; you must at least think about it for a moment. I suggest it also requires you to distance yourself from the intention – set yourself apart from it in some way.

One implication of my view is that if you simply forget one of your intentions, and fail to carry it out for that reason, that is a normative failure on your part. Over a short span of time, this is surely correct. If you intend to bring a loaf of bread home with you, but forget, then you have not performed entirely as you ought. But it has been suggested to me that there may be no normative failure if the forgetting takes a long time. Suppose that, as a child, you intend to visit Antarctica sometime in your life. But in due course you forget this intention, and you never visit Antarctica. Perhaps this constitutes no normative failing. If not, I shall need to qualify my claim that unrepudiated intentions require to be carried out. But in this essay I shall not try to work out precisely what the qualification needs to be. I shall deal only with fairly short time spans, and ignore it.

I think mine is just the right account of the control that intentions give us over our lives. It accurately describes the degree of stability we gain from intentions, as rational people. As a causal matter, we usually carry out our intentions; once you have an intention, you usually retain it until you carry it out. Without this tendency, you would never be able to complete any course of action that takes time. Furthermore, the causal process that usually brings us to carry out our intentions is a rational one. It is normatively sanctioned. I can now say more precisely what this sanction amounts to: An intention normatively requires to be carried out, provided it is not repudiated. On the other hand, there may be nothing wrong with changing your mind and dropping one of your intentions. You have only to repudiate it.

How does this account compare with the rival view that intentions are reasons? The rival view can be similarly weakened to say that *unrepudiated* intentions are reasons: that if you have an intention and do not repudiate it, it constitutes a reason to carry it out. This is certainly more plausible than the original unweakened view. It is no longer subject to the objection from changing your mind. It makes it permissible to change your mind, and drop an intention, provided you repudiate it. So the view that intentions are normative requirements has no advantage in this respect.

However, the bootstrapping objection still stands. The weakened version of the view that intentions are reasons says that if you intend to do something, and do not repudiate your intention, it constitutes a reason to do it. This remains implausible. For instance, suppose you originally had no reason either for or against doing some act. For no reason, you formed the intention of doing it, and you have not subsequently repudiated your intention. Then this view says you now have a reason to do it. Since you have no contrary reason not to, you ought to do it. By merely intending to do it, you have made it the case that you ought to. This is implausible. Since we now have available the alternative view that intentions are normative requirements, we have no need to accept this implausible consequence.

To the bootstrapping argument, I can now add the strictness test. Is the relation between having an unrepudiated intention and acting on that intention strict or slack? Suppose you intend to do something, and you do not repudiate your intention, but you do not do what you intend. Have you definitely failed to act entirely as you should? Yes. To be sure, you might find you have a good reason not to do what you intend, so you ought not to do it. But in that case you should also repudiate your intention. Since your intention was to do something you ought not to do, you should repudiate it. If you do not, that is a normative failure on your part. This means the relation is strict. So by the strictness test, an unrepudiated intention constitutes a normative requirement rather than a reason.

8. The Practical Problem of Incommensurable Values

The rest of this essay illustrates this claim further, through an example. I shall show how it successfully handles an important practical problem.

The problem is caused by incommensurable values. Sometimes we are faced with a choice where the alternatives will realize such different values that it is impossible to weigh them against each other precisely. I shall call values like this 'incommensurable'. When values are incommensurable, it may not be determinate which of the two alternatives is better. It may be that neither is better than the other, yet they are also not equally good. When this happens, I shall say the alternatives are 'incommensurate'. I shall simply assume without argument that incommensurable values exist, and that we do sometimes encounter incommensurate alternatives.

Incommensurability can lead to a particular sort of practical difficulty. It appears most sharply if we assume teleology, and for the sake of argument I shall make this assumption. Teleology is the view that, when you have a choice among alternative acts, which you ought to choose is determined only by the goodness of the alternatives. Nothing counts apart from goodness. There are no deontic constraints, for instance.

I shall take my example from Kierkegaard's *Fear and Trembling*. I do not mean to make any comment on Kierkegaard. I simply like the example.

God tells Abraham to take his son Isaac to the mountain, and there sacrifice him. Abraham has to decide whether or not to obey. Let us assume this is one of those choices where the alternatives are incommensurate. The option of obeying will show submission to God, but the option of disobeying will save Isaac's life. Submitting to God and saving the life of one's son are such different values that they cannot be weighed determinately against each other; that is the assumption. Neither option is better than the other, yet we also cannot say they are equally good.

Abraham has to decide. How should he do so? It is hard to know. Granted teleology, nothing apart from the goodness of the alternatives can contribute to determining what he should choose. But because the alternatives are incommensurate, their goodness does not determine that he ought to choose either one. It is not the case that he ought to obey God, and not the case that he ought not to. In circumstances like these, it is hard to know how a rational person should decide. This is one problem that incommensurability of value raises. But in this essay I shall not spend time on *this* problem, because it is not unique to incommensurability.

It also arises when a person has to choose between options that are equally good. In this case, too, it is not the case that she ought to choose one, nor that she ought to choose the other. How does a rational person choose in these circumstances? Buridan's ass, standing between two equally good bales of hay, demonstrated how difficult this question is. It was a highly rational creature, and so would choose only what it ought to choose. But neither bale was one it ought to choose, so it would not choose either. It died a martyr to its rationality. It would have been even more rational had it somehow managed to choose, even though neither bale was one it ought to choose. In cases of equal goodness and cases of incommensurateness, rationality certainly demands that one make a choice. But how should one make it rationally? This difficult question is raised equally by cases of equal goodness and cases of incommensurateness. It is not a question for this essay. I shall simply assume the choice gets made somehow.

Somehow, Abraham makes his choice. Let us assume he decides to obey God, and sets out with Isaac for the mountain. However, as he travels, he can always change his mind. At any time, he can turn for home. For instance, he can turn back at the foot of the mountain. Having reached that point, he has the choice of turning back or carrying on to make the sacrifice. This is a choice he has to make.

If he turns back, Isaac will be safe, but the outcome will be decidedly worse than if he had never set out in the first place. By the time the two reach the mountain, Isaac is anxious about what is happening. He has seen his father bring the sacrificing knife, but no lamb for sacrifice. Trust between father and son is badly damaged. So turning back at the foot of the mountain is definitely worse than never setting out at all.

Let us assume, nevertheless, that turning back is incommensurate with carrying on to make the sacrifice. This is possible. There can be three options A, B, and C such that A is definitely better than B, but both A and B are incommensurate with C. This possibility is characteristic of incommensurateness, and distinguishes it from equality of goodness: If A is better than B, A and B cannot both be equally as good as a third option C. I do not need to dwell on this feature of incommensurateness in this essay, because it has been thoroughly analyzed elsewhere.[9]

Let us assume Abraham's choices are an example. Staying at home (A) is incommensurate with sacrificing Isaac (C). Turning back at the foot of the mountain (B) is also incommensurate with sacrificing Isaac, but turning back at the foot of the mountain is definitely worse than staying at home.

So, at the foot of the mountain, Abraham is faced with an incommensurate choice once again. Again it is difficult to know how he should make it. Let us imagine that at this point, somehow, Abraham decides to turn for home.

Abraham has now made two decisions. Both were between incommensurate alternatives. In neither case, therefore, was it determinate which option he should choose. So neither of his choices was wrong – contrary to what he should have chosen. He seems to have done nothing irrational, therefore. Yet he has ended up taking a course of action that is decidedly worse than one he could have taken. He could have stayed at home. This would have been disobedient to God, but at least it would have kept intact his relationship with his son. As it is, Abraham has disobeyed God and also lost Isaac's trust.

Imagine Abraham had magically been presented, all at once, with an irrevocable choice among the three alternatives: stay at home (A), set out to sacrifice Isaac but turn back at the foot of the mountain (B), and set out and complete the sacrifice (C). Then he definitely ought not to have chosen B, which is what he finally did choose. That would plainly have been irrational. Since the better alternative A would have been available, he ought not to have chosen the worse one B.

Actually, Abraham's choices were not simultaneous, but separated by time. Yet still we might have hoped that rationality would have saved him from the bad result he fell into. Intuitively, his two decisions were in some way inconsistent with each other, and we might have hoped rationality would have saved him from that sort of inconsistency. Yet neither of his decisions was wrong. The reasons that were available to determine what he ought to choose – all stemming from the goodness of the options – left him free to settle both choices either way. They therefore did not constrain him tightly enough to save him from inconsistency. So it seems he did nothing irrational. His choices were apparently rational, even though they were intuitively inconsistent, and they led to a bad result.

This sets a puzzle. Were these choices really entirely rational? I think this is the distinctive problem that incommensurability raises, from a practical point of view. When values are incommensurable, it is apparently rational to make choices that are intuitively inconsistent with each other. Is it really rational?[10]

9. One Solution

One way of solving the puzzle is to say that our decisions make our values. When Abraham faced up to his first choice, neither option was better than the other, because the relevant values were incommensurable. But when he made his decision to sacrifice Isaac, he made it the case that *for him* this was the better thing to do. He made it the case that, for Abraham, sacrificing Isaac was better than disobeying God. The values as he first considered them –

obeying God and saving his son – left the alternatives incommensurate, but his choice made them commensurate for him. We might say that objectively they were incommensurate, but subjectively, for Abraham once he had made his decision, the sacrifice was better.

On this view, making the sacrifice was better than staying at home, for Abraham. Therefore, it was certainly better than turning back at the foot of the mountain. So when Abraham faced his choice at the foot of the mountain, he ought to have stuck to his original decision. As it is, he chose the alternative that was worse, for him. This was irrational. Rationality would indeed have saved him from the bad outcome, as we hoped it would. In this way, the puzzle would be resolved.

The idea that our decisions make our values is existentialist, but the rest of this story is not. Existentialists think our decisions make our values, but we must constantly remake them. The values we make for ourselves at one time do not determine what we should do at another time.[11]

This resolution of the puzzle is not existentialist, then, but it *is* an application of the view that intentions are reasons. Abraham's decision to sacrifice Isaac makes it the case that, for him, sacrificing Isaac is the best thing to do. His decision therefore gives him a reason to carry it out. Consequently, it gives him a reason not to turn back at the foot of the mountain. That is how the puzzle is resolved.

So the view that intentions are reasons, if it were correct, would provide a possible resolution of the problem of incommensurable values. But the bootstrapping objection remains. It is just not plausible that Abraham's decision can make it the case that he ought to sacrifice Isaac, when previously it was not the case. It is no more plausible under incommensurability than in any other circumstances. A decision simply does not add to pre-existing reasons. We need a better resolution than this.

10. A Better Solution

When Abraham made his first decision, he formed the intention of sacrificing Isaac. I argued in Section 7 that, so long as he does not repudiate this intention, it normatively requires him to carry it out. In the meantime, Abraham can use it as a premise in his practical reasoning. For example, at the foot of the mountain he can reason:

I am going to sacrifice Isaac.
and In order to sacrifice Isaac, I must climb the mountain.
so I shall climb the mountain.

This is instrumental reasoning in the pattern of Section 6

It is a solution to the puzzle I posed in Section 8. There is, indeed, something in rationality that could have protected Abraham from the bad result of turning back at the foot of the mountain. The intention formed in his first decision normatively required him not to turn back. Neither of Abraham's choices was contrary to what he ought to have done, but the second choice was contrary to a normative requirement imposed on him by the first choice. So he did indeed act irrationally.

I said his choices were intuitively inconsistent in some way. Simply avoiding acting wrongly – contrary to what he ought to do – was not enough to make them intuitively consistent, because what he ought to do was too indeterminate. But if he followed the normative requirement he was under, he would have made intuitively consistent choices. The inconsistency that we identified intuitively now turns out to be a failure to satisfy a normative requirement.

However, all of this depends on Abraham's not repudiating the intention he formed in his first decision. He has no reason not to repudiate it, because he had no reason to form this particular intention in the first place. And by repudiating it he can release himself from the requirement it imposes on him. Provided he repudiates this intention, there is indeed nothing irrational about his turning back.

So the solution I have offered to the puzzle of incommensurability is extremely fragile. Rationality can save Abraham from the bad outcome, but only by the slenderest of threads. He only has to repudiate his intention, and the bad outcome can result without any irrationality on his part.

I think this fragile solution of the puzzle is the right one. It is the best that can be had. I do not think rationality could, in any more robust fashion, have saved Abraham from the unfortunate outcome of turning back at the foot of the mountain. Even if Abraham was entirely rational, he could have ended up with that result.

True, if he had been presented with all three alternatives at once, rationality would definitely have saved him from this bad outcome, as I explained in Section 8. Even then, he would not necessarily have ended up with a better outcome. He might have sacrificed Isaac, and our assumption is that that is not better than turning back at the foot of the mountain; these two alternatives are incommensurate. In any case, the fact that the decision-making was actually spread over time makes a genuine difference to the situation, so we must expect that the outcome might rationally be different.

Abraham was actually not presented with all three alternatives at once. He had an opportunity to think again about his first decision, as he rode towards the mountain. He might not have taken this opportunity. In that case, if he was rational, he would have carried on to make the sacrifice. His original decision would have remained unrepudiated, and the final result would not have been the bad one of turning back. In this case, rationality in the form of a normative requirement would have maintained consistency between Abraham's decisions.

But if Abraham did think again, there was nothing irrational in his doing so. His original decision was not made for reasons, so he was entitled to rethink it. Indeed, since he was riding to sacrifice his son, it would perhaps have been pigheaded of him not to. Moreover, if Abraham thought again, and the result of his rethinking was that he repudiated his original intention, there was nothing irrational in that either. It need not be irrational to be irresolute.

If he repudiated his decision, it was a change of heart and mind. It is an unfortunate fact about changing your mind that you often have to make the best of a bad job. You have to bear the cost of the decision you have now turned away from. Having repudiated the decision to sacrifice Isaac, Abraham should then have been pleased he had the chance to pull back. The final result was not ideal, but it was the best of a bad job.

In sum, to be rational, Abraham must not turn back without rethinking his decision. But if he does rethink it, and deliberately repudiates it, he may rationally turn back.

Notes

1. Bratman, pp. 24–7.
2. I owe this point to Howard Sobel.
3. Two proponents of the pragmatic argument are David Gauthier, in *Morals by Agreement* and 'Assure and Threaten', and Edward McClennen, in *Rationality and Dynamic Choice*.
4. Korsgaard, 'The Normativity of Instrumental Reason', p. 220.
5. This definition of the instrumental principle is implicit on p. 215.
6. Korsgaard, pp. 245–6.
7. Velleman, p. 45.
8. I am oversimplifying when I identify intending with the attitude of being set to make true. Not all cases of being set to make true are cases of intending. So here I am skating over some complications. Details are in my 'Practical Reasoning'.
9. For example, in Joseph Raz's 'Value Incommensurability'. In my 'Incommensurable Values', I argue that this is actually the defining feature of incommensurateness, which distinguishes it from equality. Raz describes this same characteristic feature of incommensurateness, but denies it is the defining feature.
10. My 'Incommensurable Values' sets out the puzzle in more detail. Ruth Chang raises the same puzzle in her introduction to *Incommensurability, Incomparability and Practical Reason*, p. 11.
11. Thanks to Philippe Mongin for this point.

References

Bratman, Michael E., *Intention, Plans, and Practical Reason* (Cambridge, MA: Harvard University Press, 1987).
Broome, John, 'Incommensurable Values', in *Well-Being and Morality: Essays in Honour of James Griffin*, ed. Roger Crisp and Brad Hooker (Oxford University Press, 1999).

'Normative Requirements'. *Ratio* 12:398–419, 1999.

'Practical reasoning', in *Reason in Nature: New Essays in the Theory of Rationality*, ed. José Bermúdez and Alan Millar (forthcoming).

Chang, Ruth, 'Introduction', in *Incommensurability, Incomparability and Practical Reason*, ed. by Ruth Chang (Cambridge, MA: Harvard University Press, 1998), pp. 1–34.

Gauthier, David, 'Assure and Threaten'. *Ethics* 104:690–721, 1994.

Morals by Agreement (Oxford University Press, 1986).

Korsgaard, Christine, 'The Normativity of Instrumental Reason', in *Ethics and Practical Reason*, ed. by Garrett Cullity and Berys Gaut (Oxford University Press, 1997), pp. 215–54.

McClennen, Edward F., *Rationality and Dynamic Choice* (Cambridge University Press, 1990).

Raz, Joseph, 'Value Incommensurability: Some Preliminaries'. *Proceedings of the Aristotelian Society* 86:111–34, 1985–6.

Velleman, David, 'Deciding how to Decide', in *Ethics and Practical Reason*, ed. Garrett Cullity and Berys Gaut (Oxford University Press, 1997), pp. 29–52.

Two Forms of Practical Generality

MICHAEL THOMPSON

This essay is an inquiry into the workings of two concepts, *practical disposition* and *social practice*, as they enter, or might enter, into moral philosophy. Or rather, it is a fragment of such an inquiry. Its point of departure is a pair of familiar tendencies in moral philosophy, the tendencies we meet with in what might be called *dispositional accounts of the rationality of morality* and *practice versions of utilitarianism*. Of course, the concepts of a practice and a disposition enter into other types of moral theory, some of them perhaps intuitively more attractive than either of these. But the deployment of our concepts in these two lines of thought is, I think, uniquely clear and intelligible. A study of their workings here can therefore be expected to supply a general elucidation of the two concepts as they are properly understood in practical philosophy and thus potentially in quite different types of normative theory.

The concepts *practice* and *disposition* appear at first sight to be quite diverse: One looks to be a concept proper to social theory, the other perhaps to psychology. A comparative treatment will, I hope, tend to burn off this dross of associated ideas and reveal an underlying kinship at least in their specifically practical-philosophical use. But further, recognition of this kinship will in turn put us into contact with a more extensive class of practical concepts and with it a larger logical, metaphysical, and normative topic, namely, *the role of a certain kind of generality in practice and practical thought*. This same field of inquiry, the problem of generality, is crossed wherever a philosopher speaks of *virtue* or *character*, of moral or other practical *principles*, of *maxims*, of *forms of practical reasoning* or of such *reasons* as bear an intrinsically general content, or, finally, of practical *conceptions*, whether they be conceptions of justice, rationality, or happiness, or of one's "self" or one's practical "identity." A certain conceptual darkness and obscurity overtake any text that deploys one or another of these phrases, an obscurity we do not find where it speaks, for example, of *action, intention,* or *desire*. The obscurity arises, I believe, from a common source in all of these cases, the peculiar "generality," as I am provisionally calling it, of the things meant. This is a feature we already find in the items captured in the concepts *disposition* and *practice* as they figure in the comparatively clear light of our two tendencies. A more remote aim of this study, not at all realized here, is thus to make sense of this larger logical and metaphysical problematic.

As a central representative of the tendency toward dispositional accounts of the rationality of morality, I will consider a number of David Gauthier's works, but especially *Morals by Agreement*.[1] I will also refer to Philippa Foot's "Moral Beliefs," which exhibits, though in a less developed way, the structural feature of Gauthier's account I want to discuss.[2] In connection with difficulties about practices and utilitarianism, the text I will mostly consider is John Rawls's essay "Two Concepts of Rules." This work is at first sight merely a defense of the utilitarian idea against certain familiar objections, by means of some consideration about practices and "rules." But Rawls's real aim was of course to redeploy these latter considerations in a more complex, and decidedly non-utilitarian, theoretical environment. (We will in fact find that this aim is not quite realized.) His attitude toward the theory under construction in "Two Concepts" is thus a model of the attitude I am taking toward both types of theory.[3]

Following the example of Gauthier and Rawls alike, the substantive focus of this essay will be on a particular moral phenomenon, namely, promising and the obligation of promises. But its more special focus is on what I will call the *act of fidelity* and its normative standing. An agent X's doing A for another agent Y is an act of fidelity where we can affirm, in a certain familiar sense, that *X did A for Y because she promised Y she would* – that is, "precisely because" or "just because" she promised this. We distinguish such acts of promise-keeping from those in which, as we say, an "ulterior motive" is at work. The Prichardian conception of a promise as potentially exhausting the agent's ground in the keeping of it is an intuitive conception, one fitted to the everyday enterprise of action explanation. It need not, I think, be supposed to impede the more articulate and philosophical analysis of the act of fidelity that our authors are attempting to supply.

This essay is a preliminary part of a longer work in which some of the logical and metaphysical aspects of the topic will be developed further and brought into connection with certain Aristotelian and, I suppose, Hegelian themes. The order of discussion here runs as follows. After an initial characterization of the two tendencies (Section 1), I attempt a preliminary articulation of the genus to which their respective "mediating elements," practice and disposition, belong. They are, I suggest, at the same time "general" and "actual" in senses I attempt to specify (Section 2). The two tendencies are then placed in the wider space of "two-level" normative theories, and some of their peculiarities are addressed. The fundamental difficulty for either tendency is to find a justification of its central claim – a "transfer" or "transparency" principle as I call it – that is consistent with the special status that the principle must be assigned within the theory. The aim of finding a suitable justification of this claim places further constraints on the apt interpretation of the concepts *practice* and *disposition* that are implicit in our theories (Section 3). I suggest that it is because neither Rawls nor Gauthier articulates a suitably narrow and properly practical-philosophical interpretation of his central concept that neither manages a proper defense of his central principle (Sections 4 and 5). I conclude with a provisional attempt to impart a "narrow" interpretation of the concept of a practice – one that might realize Rawls's ambitions – and suggest a possible parallel treatment of the object of Gauthier's intention (Section 6).

1. The Problem and the Proposed Solution

Particular doctrines manifesting either of our tendencies might cover the whole of morality, but since we are restricting our attention to the part of justice that pertains to the keeping of promises, we may say that Rawls is interested in the *moral goodness*, as he puts it, of acts of fidelity, whereas Gauthier and Foot are interested in their *individual rationality*.[4] How might these doctrines be compared?

First, they may be seen as framed in response to structurally similar problems, certain perceived *tight corners*, as we might call them, that promising tends to generate. For Rawls, presupposing a background allegiance to utilitarianism, the difficulty is the familiar Humean one that by breaking a promise we are sometimes able to do people more good than we would by keeping it; the question thus arises how it can be any good, morally speaking, to act on the strength of a promise in such circumstances. For Gauthier and for Foot, the problem is the more ancient one that, like any requirement of justice, promise-keeping will sometimes cross our *interests*, even if we take into account the irritating noise of complaint, the threat of "never being trusted again," and the like. The question is how there can be any sense in fidelity in those circumstances, or how such a thing can be rational.

It is natural to see the difficulty as arising in either case from the uncritical acceptance of a "teleological," "consequentialist," or "maximizing" understanding of morality or rationality. It is true that such ideas are in the background in these works; this is part of what makes them so clear and thus such useful theoretical models, as Rawls saw. But in truth neither conception of a tight corner depends on any very determinate "teleological" idea. The essential thing is simply this, that the goods and evils to be pursued and avoided in the tight-corner context are such as would make the faithful person's conduct either morally blameworthy or imprudent if it were performed by a similarly situated person who had not made a promise. The promise, the "dead hand of the past," is supposed to overturn that calculation and to do this without introducing any new prospect of good. How are we to make this fit with *any* form of the idea that sound deliberation is a matter of having one's sights on some kind of good?[5]

As the problems faced by the two tendencies exhibit something of a common shape, so also do their respective responses to it. On neither account is the individual act of fidelity held to acquire the relevant normative characteristic, "moral goodness" or "rationality," from the agent's setting his sights on some benefit or excellence or merit that might reside in the *individual* action itself or in the series of *individual* events it is likely to entrain. Gauthier's and Foot's suggestion is not, for example, that the faithful agent has cottoned on to some subtle, easily missed, and peculiarly moral delight to be found in individual acts of promise-keeping nor any slice of "the noble" that might tip the scales in favor of fidelity. And Rawls does not recommend, say, a "goal rights" consequentialism, nor more generally does he attempt to assign a special intrinsic value, whether "agent-neutral" or "agent relative," to the mere fact of a properly discharged promise – a "value" the faithful agent might then be understood as apprehending and seeking to realize. On neither account does the faithful agent anticipate the appearance of anything in the order of individual events that might outweigh the more readily recognizable benefits of tight-corner infidelity.

Rather, on Foot's account, the difficulty philosophers have felt about the rationality of fidelity and justice in general arises from the fact that "they consider in isolation particular just acts."[6] Their attention ought to pass from the typical individual act of fidelity to something that runs through them all, something that each of them *manifests* or *instances* or *expresses*, namely, a certain putative *virtue*. This, in our present case, is fidelity itself: a particular practical disposition, a *hexis* or *habitus*, a familiar practical "trait." Blindness to this category of practical reality is the source of the apparent difficulty about the tight corner, for the friend of fidelity can adduce nothing in its favor from the materials present in these situations considered severally or individually. But if we are granted this category, and compare the various forms of faithless vice with fidelity – each as a disposition that operates within and without the tight corner – then, Foot argues, a link to the agent's *interest* or *profit* might perhaps be found. Indeed, she argues that if no such link can be found, then fidelity, and justice in general, must lose its claim to the title of a genuine virtue.[7]

On Gauthier's account, the philosophers' difficulty about the tight corner arises from a wrong conception of the relation between individual action and the maximization of good that the rational agent allegedly pursues. A passage in "The Unity of Reason" links his thought especially clearly to our concerns. The illusion arises, he there suggests, from a temptation to pass from the correct characterization of the rational agent as one who "chooses in such a way as to maximize" to the seemingly equivalent, but wrong, characterization of her as one who "chooses [simply] to maximize."[8]

If these descriptions are heard as applying to an *individual choice*, and thus to an individual action, they are indeed equivalent: If I maximized in the particular choice I made at *t*, then I chose, at *t*, in such a way as to maximize. Gauthier's thought is that if his first characterization is to capture the idea of rational agency, it must be heard in another logical register, as expressing a formally different type of judgment. In that case, it *will* be possible to distinguish it from the second characterization similarly heard. In this other, de-individualized register, our two characterizations might be put into the past tense with the words "one who *used to choose* in such way as to maximize" and "one who *used to choose* to maximize." In the opposed "individualized" register, by contrast, they could be put into the past tense only with the words "one who *chose* (or *has chosen*) in such a way as to maximize" and "one who *chose* (or *has chosen*) to maximize."[9]

In the language of *Morals by Agreement*, an agent who falls under the second characterization, properly heard, is said to exhibit a certain practical *disposition*, namely the disposition to "straightforward maximization," an item potentially exhibited or instanced or exemplified in many individual actions. In other works, Gauthier speaks not of the agent's "disposition" but rather of her "conception of rationality" or of the "deliberative procedure" she "employs." But nothing should be made to hang on Gauthier's choice of words in any of these texts any more than on nice features of his grammar. It is necessary rather to lay hold of the function of these phrases and grammatical forms in Gauthier's argument, which is in each case fundamentally the same.[10]

Gauthier's chief effort is of course to show that only agents who have rejected the straightforward maximizer's disposition in favor of another, which he calls "constrained maximization," can satisfy his first characterization, "one who chooses in such a way as to maximize." Constrained maximization is the practical disposition that *itself* maximizes, as we see by reflecting on its effect on the choices of certain other agents. Only its bearers, then, are ideally rational. The superior disposition is supposed to be exhibited in what I am calling acts of fidelity or else in a slightly restricted class of them.

In sum, then, the philosopher's suspicion of irrationality in one who has kept her promise in a tight corner derives, on Gauthier's analysis, from an incapacity to switch conceptual registers and see past the *individual choice* to the rational *disposition* that is displayed in it – a disposition that might also be displayed in any number of other individual acts of fidelity.

For Rawls, on the other hand, the appearance that has to be overcome is that certain ends appropriate to morality itself are crossed in some acts of fidelity. And once again the trouble is said to arise from the fixation of the philosopher's attention on the individual action and the particular situation on which it bears. But in this instance the trouble arises more precisely from a failure to recognize the *practice* the individual action is said to instance or embody, and the associated failure to distinguish between "the justification of a practice" and "the justification of an action falling under it." This so-called practice is again something instanced in many individual actions, in this case in many actions of many people. In describing a practice that prevails among some class of agents, we say "what they do," in some sense, and not what any or many or most or all of them "are doing," "have done," or "will do." The thing characterized thus falls outside the order of individual events into which individual actions are fitted.

The item thus multiply realized, in our case *the practice of making and keeping promises*, is again arguably itself suited to realize certain larger ends (ends that Rawls takes over, for the duration of the paper, from utilitarianism). If, for example, we compare the practice as we have it with a variant that would permit default in tight corners, the latter will appear less beneficial, indeed destructive of the point of "giving one's word." Like the individual promises that precede them, individual acts of fidelity as they happen among us get their nature from this practice, Rawls argues, and so it is only through this practice, as it seems, that these actions can be brought into connection with any supposed ends of morality. Thus, Rawls supposes, acts of fidelity do not cross these ends even in what I have called the tight corner.

2. Two Characteristic Marks of Practices and Dispositions

The two tendencies are united at least in this, that each attributes the difficulty that arises about its particular form of "tight corner" to a blinkered focus on the individual act of fidelity together with its outcome or consequences. The further element that justifies or rationalizes even tight-corner acts of fidelity, and is so easily missed, simply does not belong to that order. Thus the peculiar appeal that our two tendencies make to the concepts of a disposition and a practice cannot come down to this, that individual acts of infidelity might lead to the *loss* of a profitable disposition or the *weakening* of a beneficial practice, while acts of fidelity help preserve these principles. The suggestion might be rejected out of hand as hopelessly uncharitable to our theories: It seems quite implausible that faithful agents must reckon on such facts. But it is in any case clear that this reading would evince exactly the point of view under attack. According to it, the concepts *practice* and *disposition* are employed in an especially sophisticated analysis of the series of events into which the individual act of fidelity is fitted – a type of analysis that must, each theory claims, sometimes favor infidelity.[11]

If this interpretation of our two types of theory is uncharitable and unsound, then how *are* we to interpret the role of practices and dispositions in them? And what exactly are these items supposed to be? These questions cannot, I think, be handled separately. The words "practice" and "disposition" are legitimately employed in any number of connections within and without philosophy, and it is clear that they often bear senses that are completely alien to practical philosophy. Consider, for example, the use of the word "disposition" in the philosophy of science. The hypothesis I have adopted is that some truth can be developed from each of our tendencies by a sort of immanent criticism: The aim of attaining this truth might thus act as our guide in seeking a suitable specifically practical-philosophical interpretation of their central concepts. It will emerge, I think, that in their practical-philosophical employments the terms must be taken to bear a much narrower sense than is customarily attached to them. But I think that no questions will be begged if we insist on two very weak marks at the outset. On any legitimate interpretation of the terms "practice" and "disposition," the occupants of the intended categories must at the same time be, as I will put it, *general* and *actual*. I will explain these two features separately.

The first mark, generality, has already implicitly been introduced. It may be elucidated by contrasting (1) the relation that an individual action might bear to anything legitimately called "the disposition it manifests" or "the practice under which it falls" with (2) the quite different relation that an individual action might bear to a *further intention* with which it is performed, or a *more inclusive action* into which it is inserted, or a *plan* or *course of action* it helps to realize.[12] A single further intention might govern a succession of individual actions, showing itself in each one of them, as a particular plan might also do. A "more inclusive action" would itself *be* such a succession of individual actions, as a so-called course of action would also be. Thus, for example, I might successively *dig a foundation, pour some concrete,* and *lay a few bricks* as so many parts or phases of a larger and more inclusive action of building a house. Similarly, I might *get out my rifle, walk across the street, take aim,* and *fire* all with the further intention of ridding the state of a tyrant. The further intention with which I act is a sort of red thread that runs throughout this manifold of individual deeds, just as the extended action of house-building maintains itself through its various phases. It is obvious that a plan or course of action might have a similar position. An item of any of these four types might "unite" the actions of several agents quite as well as the actions of any one.

But the inner tendency of an occupant of any of these four categories is precisely to wind down under its own steam, to pass away with its execution or completion. The succession of individual actions governed by any such thing will thus constitute a limited whole. The succession is related to its members or parts (the subordinate actions) as an individual animal is related to its members or parts – and not as a species of animal is related to *its* "members." By contrast, it is plainly a central characteristic of each of our two tendencies that the further element, the one supposed to favor promise-keeping even in the tight corner, is essentially one and the same, unchanged, unexhausted, and not merely similar, through a potentially unlimited series of individual acts of fidelity. A practical disposition must be something that might be exhibited in a potentially infinite series of acts of a *single agent*, all of them sharing a common description. A social practice must be something that will characteristically be exhibited in indefinitely many acts of indefinitely many agents. Thus, whatever else may be true of them and whatever exactly they are, practices and dispositions do not come to a limit in any action or event or in any totality of actions and events that could thereby be said to *satisfy, execute,* or *complete* them; they can only be said to be *manifested, instanced,* or *exhibited* in any such thing. This is the peculiar "generality" that is our quarry.[13]

But if the element that sides with fidelity in the tight corner, a so-called practice or disposition, is supposed merely to be "general" in this sort of way, how does it differ from, say, an appropriate *general concept*? Consider the general concept *act of fidelity* and the narrower concept *one of X's acts of fidelity*: Any of X's individual acts of fidelity will "instance" or "fall under" either of these concepts together with indefinitely many other individual actions. Of course, no one will suggest that we can *understand* how X's acts of fidelity (considered as such) might be rational or morally good just by pointing out that X's acts of fidelity fall under one or the other of these concepts. But more interesting ideas are available. If our two tendencies propose to accredit individual acts of fidelity by bringing them into relation to something "general," how do they differ from a so-called deontology like that of Ross, or a realism in Christine Korsgaard's sense, whether about rationality or moral goodness?[14] On a realist or a deontological conception, the element that swings things to the side of fidelity in a tight corner might be a certain general "relation of fitness," for example, or a norm inscribed in the nature of things, or the truth of a substantive general "principle" of morality or rationality that forbids infidelity. That the outward act accords with such a thing will make it "right for the agent to do" or "what she has most reason to do"; that the agent somehow adverts to it in acting will make her act genuinely "morally good" or "rational." A potentially infinite succession of actions might bear these relations to the same general norm, principle, or "relation of fitness."

Our second weak mark is meant to capture the intuitive difference between any such conception and our two tendencies. In the two tendencies, the element that sides with fidelity, the practice or disposition, bears some kind of actuality in, or among, the agents whose individual actions it is supposed to accredit. For example, a practice, however we are to understand such a thing, evidently does not exist except through people's acting and being disposed to act in accordance with it. And on any account a disposition must have some sort of explanatory standing in respect of what happens when it is manifested in an individual action. By contrast, the character of realist relations of fitness or deontological "principles" can be summed up in Hegel's ironic formula: They are "something far too excellent to have actuality, or something too impotent to procure it for themselves."[15] Such things could, for example, "act" only through an agent's granting them significance – that is, in a way in which even non-existent relations of fitness and false principles could.

On each account under discussion, then, the real presence of something somehow "general" is among the conditions of the possibility of the individual act of fidelity, i.e., of the truth of it that *X did A because she promised Y she'd do A* – just as something like an intention or wanting or other will to do B is presupposed in the truth of it that *X did A because it was a means to doing B*. The nexus of action and "consideration" that is characteristic of the act of fidelity can exist only as the phenomenon of something that might equally be exhibited in indefinitely many other instances of the same nexus. But what sort of thing can this be?

3. Two Types of Two-Level Theory

Though it is not usual in practical philosophy to speak of a "two-level," "two-tier," or "indirect" theory of *rationality*, it is clear that all of the doctrines under discussion may reasonably be brought under that familiar moralist's heading. It is to Professor Gauthier especially that we owe the idea of a two-level theory of rationality, though he does not speak in these terms. But our theories are two-level theories of a specific type. This fact will place some further constraints on the apt interpretation of their central categories, practice and disposition.

Any two-level theory is marked by two central propositions, a *transfer or transparency principle* and a *standard of appraisal*, as I will call them. Thus the transfer principles contained in our two tendencies, roughly expressed, are respectively these: that *a good practice makes the actions falling under it good*, and that *a rational disposition makes the actions manifesting it rational*. The light that falls on either sort of thing is supposed to pass through it to the individual action that comes under it. The associated *standards of appraisal* are supplied, roughly speaking, by the principle of utility and the idea of the agent's own good or interest or profit: These respectively govern the attribution of the relevant type of goodness to a practice or disposition.

But where *our* doctrines appeal, in their transfer principles, to the concepts of a *practice* and a *disposition*, another account might speak rather of a *rule*, a *principle*, a *set of principles for the general regulation of behavior*, a *practical identity*, an *intention*, a *plan*, a *plan of life*, a *course of action*, a *motive*, a *maxim*, or the like. We may speak of these as so many categories of mediating element. Thus, for example, Rawls makes the rationality of individual action (and much else) depend on the rationality of a larger *plan of life*; Christine Korsgaard might perhaps be seen as making the rationality of at least some individual actions turn on the merits of a superordinate *"practical identity."*[16] The transfer principle characteristic of a given theory will also refer to some *relation of expression* that individual actions may bear to occupants of the mediating category (*executing, falling under, manifesting, realizing, acting on, according with, being part of*, etc.). It will also, of course, refer to the particular normative quality that the doctrine represents as "transferred" from occupants of the mediating category to the individual actions that "express" them – the particular sort of light that is supposed to be refracted by the mediating element. This might be *rationality, moral goodness, moral rightness, fairness, reasonableness*, or any number of other things. In a more complex case, we might need to refer to a suitably related pair of such properties.[17] The proposition that expresses this transparency should also involve a certain explanatory direction, so that it tells us something like this: If an occupant of a mediating category has the appropriate normative property, then an individual action that bears the expression relation to it *thereby* also acquires that normative property (or another suitably associated property). Various qualifications might be admitted into such a thought without affecting its standing as a transfer principle.

Though the separation is sometimes artificial, the question what *standard of appraisal* to apply to occupants of the mediating category can, I think, always be distinguished from the question of a transfer principle, or of the "transparency" of the mediating element. How does a practice come by the excellence it is supposed to pass along to the several individual actions that instance it? In "Justice as Fairness," Rawls replaced the utilitarian standard of appraisal contemplated in "Two Concepts" with a subtle contractualist standard, all along deploying, or intending to deploy, the same underlying practice-to-action transfer principle.[18] Which standard is right? Similarly, we might consider a variant of Foot's or Gauthier's doctrine in which the disposition-to-action transfer principle mentioned earlier is retained, but the agent's profit or interest is dropped as the standard of appraisal for the dispositions in question. It might be replaced by some standard of conformity with the agent's "nature," say, or with his deepest practical self-conception, or with the principle of universalizability or anything else. I mention these possibilities to set them aside: In the rest of this essay, the emphasis will be on the question of the transparency of the mediating elements, or on the interpretation and validation of our transfer principles. I will assume that our authors are right in supposing that the practice of making and keeping promises and the disposition to fidelity meet the correct standards of appraisal, whatever they are.

These distinctions having been made, we can isolate four features that, in spite of the obvious differences, put our two tendencies in the same neighborhood within the larger space of two-level theories. We have already remarked on the "generality" and the "actuality" of the mediating elements and on the teleological, consequentialist, or "maximizing" character of the standard of appraisal – a matter we are proposing henceforth to ignore. Instead, I will emphasize a fourth feature, or rather an ensemble of related features, all pertaining to the status implicitly attached to the transfer principles themselves. First, the transfer principles characteristic of our two tendencies are intended to possess a merely *formal* or *non-substantive*, perhaps even analytic, character. Further, they are meant to express neither possible *principles of action* nor anything internally related to "principles" in that sense. Finally, their justification (in the sense of a defense of their truth) is meant to be independent of the justification of any particular standard of appraisal. That the underlying transfer principles are to have the position implied by these features places further constraints on the apt interpretation of our tendencies' central categories, practice and disposition. To make the intended status clear, I will briefly describe a few two-level theories in which the transfer principles have a quite different place.

Gauthier's "Assure and Threaten"

Of course, not all transfer principles are of the "general-to-particular" type characteristic of our two tendencies. It will help to bring out the importance of principles that *are* of our general-to-particular sort if we take as our first illustration the chief thesis of Professor Gauthier's essay "Assure and Threaten." Gauthier argues there that the rationality of an *intention for the future* tends, with certain qualifications, to be communicated to the individual action that finally executes it – even where, apart from the antecedent formation of that intention, the action would have to be judged irrational. Such an intention, he thinks, is contained in the sincere "assurance" one agent might give another; the principle will thus underwrite the rationality of some acts of fidelity or something like some of them.

The intention-execution principle is clearly a transfer principle, and the essay as a whole may be said to propound a two-level theory of rationality: Gauthier's *standard of appraisal* for intentions looks to the contribution the intention itself might make to the agent's life going as well as possible. But of course this pair of propositions does not, by itself, manifest the Gauthier-Foot tendency under investigation. The mediating element at issue, an intention for the future, is not intrinsically general or unlimited in our sense, though it is certainly "actual" in our sense. An intention for the future, like the later progress of the action it is an intention to perform – reaping someone else's corn, as it might be – is potentially *completed, carried out*, or *executed*, whereupon it passes out of existence, winding down under its own steam.

Now, as Gauthier is thinking of the matter, his rational assurance-keeper acts *on ground of* the fact that he has previously formed a suitable intention. The new "particular-to-particular" transfer principle provides one way of making articulate the connection the assurance-keeper himself sees between the past formation of an intention and the individual action he later performs. It either is, or is internally related to, a proposition with which the agent implicitly operates, and one he might reasonably be called on to defend. Gauthier is proposing to supply the necessary defense. Indeed, "Assure and Threaten" might at first sight be read as an attempt to bypass the difficulty of defending a disposition-to-action transfer principle and the associated demand for an elucidation of the obscure concept of a disposition. The concept of intention has the advantage of being perfectly clear, and Gauthier may actually prove his intention-to-execution principle.

But a closer study of Gauthier's argument will show that he makes his defense of this "particular-to-particular" transfer principle turn on a deeper principle that *is* of our "general-to-particular" type. Here is the principle: If a *deliberative procedure* is rational – if, that is, a given agent's "employment" of it makes her life go as well as possible (to apply Gauthier's standard of appraisal *for deliberative procedures*) – then any individual action the agent arrives at by use of that procedure is thereby also made to be rational. The substantive "deliberative procedure" Gauthier mostly contemplates is of course precisely that of sticking to one's prior rational intentions, subject to certain qualifications. But if Gauthier's defense of assurance-keeping is to work, the reference to the "employment" of a deliberative procedure to which this principle refers must be heard, as usual, in the right register. On his own account, after all, the whole interest of the subject resides in the fact that *individual* "employments" of the deliberative procedure he praises will often make the agent's life go *worse*. It is evidently the "employment" of a deliberative procedure *taken generally* – or taken "habitually" or "dispositionally" – that is supposed to make the agent's life go as well as possible. And so, on Gauthier's account, it is the rationality of *the disposition to employ this particular deliberative procedure* – or, equivalently, the disposition to reason practically in a certain way or the disposition to act on a certain sort of reason – that makes its indefinitely many *individual* employments also to be rational.[19]

Thus the familiar general-to-particular transfer principle of *Morals by Agreement* and Foot's "Moral Beliefs" underwrites the special particular-to-particular transfer principle of "Assure and Threaten." That no attempt is made to justify the underlying deliberative-procedure-to-action transfer principle is a sign of the purely formal character Gauthier seems to assign to that claim and, I think, must assign to it. Once it is joined to a suitable standard of appraisal, what it yields is precisely the general principle of a "pragmatic" or "Gauthierian" defense of substantive "principles of rationality." It is a fixed point around which all such arguments turn: Its own defense, if it needs one, must thus be of another kind. This defense presumably will be independent of the defense of any particular standard of appraisal for deliberative procedures (e.g., one in terms of what will make one's life go as well as possible).[20] By contrast, Gauthier's justification of the intention-to-action transfer principle of "Assure and Threaten" goes hand in hand with a defense of the associated standard of appraisal for intentions (which is also, of course, a matter of what makes for the best life possible for the agent); they are defended as a package.[21]

Rule Utilitarianism

Consider now this familiar proposition, the formula of "rule utilitarianism": If a rule of action maximizes utility and is thus (by the proposed utilitarian standard of appraisal) morally good or right, then any individual action that accords with it is also morally right. The word "rule" can be interpreted in a number of ways, but on any view rules will be *general* in some sense. On standard interpretations, though, the rules intended are merely hypothetical, and our *actuality* criterion is not met. (We will see that Rawls mentions a non-standard interpretation.) Now, on the textbook understanding of its justification, the rule utilitarian combination of a rule-act transfer principle and a utilitarian standard of excellence for rules is advanced as a doctrine of morally right action that squares best with our tutored or untutored moral judgments. This package squares with our supposed utilitarian intuitions, we say, while avoiding the counter-intuitive consequences of its act utilitarian expression. This form of argument could not be further from the one we found in "Assure and Threaten." But the result is much the same. First, there is a fusion, in point of justification, of the transfer principle and the standard of appraisal for the mediating element. There is no question of an independent justification of the transfer principle, a justification divorced from substantive moral considerations. Further, once a good rule utilitarian has been furnished with an ensemble of meritorious "rules," she will tailor her actions to fall into line with their formulae, at least on the most straightforward interpretation of the theory. Though she will act *by reference* to the rules, the *principle of her action* will be the rule utilitarian transfer principle or something internally related to that thought.

The Principle of Fairness

The situation is much the same with the practice-to-action transfer principle envisaged in Rawls's *A Theory of Justice*, namely, H. L. A. Hart's so-called Principle of Fairness.[22] This claim is, I think, very different from any envisaged in "Two Concepts." A like principle is advanced in T. M. Scanlon's *What We Owe to Each Other* under the title of the Principle of Established Practices.[23] According to either teaching, a suitable form of moral soundness in a *practice* will make the individual actions that accord with it also to be morally sound. It will also, of course, make the actions that run counter to the practice morally wrong. But what is the status of the principle itself in either case? How is it defended? And what are we to do with it? In *A Theory of Justice*, the Principle of Fairness is imagined as put directly to the parties in the original position. In this respect its status is no different from that of the Principle of Mutual Aid or the famous Two Principles – which latter supply the *standard of appraisal* for the practices at issue.[24] Similarly, Scanlon's Principle of Established Practices is defended in just the way that all substantive moral claims in the book are defended, including even a sort of Principle of Fidelity: No one could reasonably reject it, given certain aims, though someone or anyone could reasonably reject any opposed principle. Scanlon's *standard of appraisal* for particular practices is again a matter of surviving a test of reasonable rejection. There is thus no question of detaching these transfer principles from the substantive point of view articulated in either book. We might speak of a pre-established harmony of good practice and good action, rather than of a genuine transparency of practices in respect of moral goodness. Further, on each of these accounts, the ideally respectable agent is plainly to be depicted as responding to the practice and its merits as an external element of the situation in which she is operating. In this respect, she is related to the practices under which she lives as a faithful agent is related, on any view, to the past promises she has made. She acts by reference to the practice she faces, in consideration of its merits, but the practice in no sense governs her operation: Her action is rather governed by the Principle of Fairness or the Principle of Established Practices, taken now as a "principle of action" that she has internalized.

By contrast, it is plain that our transfer or transparency principles do not themselves correspond to "principles" or *archai* that might be imputed to the agent in the explanation or understanding of her action. That position is occupied rather by the practices and dispositions to which this transparency is attributed. On such an account, a practice or disposition is *itself* a "principle," if you like: We are contemplating the merits of action falling under such general *archai* in the individual case. If an agent were somehow to "act on" one of our transfer principles – and thus *in view of* the merits of one of the practices or dispositions she bears considered as a mere circumstance of her action – then her action would surely merely simulate action instancing *that* practice or disposition. If anything, it would manifest a very peculiar "transfer" disposition and perhaps an even more peculiar "transfer" practice. The proof that such an action is good, as moral or rational, would require a second (and proper) appeal to the appropriate transfer principle and would turn on the doubtful merits of that strange disposition or practice. It is clear that no such thought is contained in our two tendencies.

4. The Transparency of Practices

An argument for a non-substantive and non-action-guiding practice-to-action transfer principle is plainly among the desiderata of Rawls's "Two Concepts of Rules." He briefly considers the possibility of a non-standard, practice-related rule utilitarianism:

One might be tempted to close the discussion at this point by saying that utilitarian considerations should be understood as applying to practices in the first instance and not to particular actions falling under them except insofar as the practices admit of it. One might say that in this modified form it is a better account of our considered moral opinions and let it go at that.[25]

But this path is rejected. Rawls's preferred "logical" account is intended precisely to divorce the idea from any substantive normative theory, rendering it an independent element that can be redeployed, without further discussion, in the presence of a non-utilitarian standard of excellence for practices – as happens straightaway in "Justice as Fairness."[26]

Let us return to the individual act of fidelity: Our faithful agent X has done A for Y "precisely because" she had promised Y that she would. We do not spoil the character of an action as an act of fidelity if we enrich this common-sense description a bit, saying that the deed arose from the agent's implicit acceptance of a certain "rule" – that is, from her practical judgment that promises are to be kept, that *pacta sunt servanda*. It is not clear what is gained by adding such a thing either, of course, or how exactly we are to interpret it; but it is plain that we could not thus enrich our description of an act of promise-keeping that was founded on an ulterior motive. Rawls's approach to the question of the moral goodness of an individual act of fidelity proceeds indirectly, by way of a search for the correct interpretation of this additional element, a sort of "rule" or general practical judgment.

On what Rawls calls the "summary" interpretation, which is closely bound up with the utilitarian background of the paper, a thought like *pacta sunt servanda* is understood simply to register the fact that a type of action has often been found good or right *independently* in individual cases (as productive of utility) and to recommend it on that ground. It would clearly be absurd to carry such a thought or "principle" into a tight corner, recognized as such. Anything on the order of a transfer principle would plainly be out of the question.

Searching for an alternative interpretation of the thought upon which the act of fidelity (for example) may be said to be founded, Rawls argues that certain types of action can only take place given the "background" of what he calls a practice:

> Striking out, stealing a base, balking, etc., are all actions which can only happen in a game. No matter what a person did, what he did would not be described as stealing a base or striking out or drawing a walk unless he could also be described as playing baseball, and for him to be doing this presupposes the rule-like practice which constitutes the game. The practice is logically prior to particular cases: unless there is the practice the terms referring to actions specified by it lack a sense.[27]

A number of familiar features of Rawls's conception of a practice are joined in this passage. The claim that "the practice is logically prior to particular cases" means that some of the types of action some tokens of which instance a given Rawlsian practice can be "tokened" at all only in actions that instance this or some other similar practice. The action-types *X promises Y she'll do A* and *X is doing A because she promised Y she'd do A* would be examples. Another feature of Rawls's conception is implicit in the idea that certain "terms" "lack a sense" – and not just an application – apart from their association with a suitable practice. This means (1) that a Rawlsian practice is "instanced" not only in *actions* but also, in another way, in certain *exercises of concepts*, and (2) that certain such concepts can exist to begin with only where they have an appropriate practice-instancing exercise.[28] Examples of such *concepts* are *X promises Y she'll do A* and *X is doing A because she promised Y she would*. Note that each of these concepts is implicitly deployed by any agent X who falls under it.[29] Finally, in speaking of a "rule-like practice," Rawls means that the aforementioned practice-instancing exercises of concepts must include a certain type of general "deontic" judgment. The faithful agent's judgment that *pacta sunt servanda* would be an example. Take these judgments away and the practice falls to the ground, taking everything else with it – acts of promising, promise-keeping, and promise-breaking, for example, as well as exercises of the concepts of these things. Thus the choice the faithful agent faces, whether to keep or break her promise, may be said to presuppose the presence of a "rule" that favors keeping it, as her promise already did. It is clear that where deontic judgments have this standing, they cannot be interpreted on the summary model. The general reception of the rule enters into the constitution of the phenomena to which it pertains; it cannot be founded on a long run of experience dealing with them.

Rawls's conception of a practice is evidently much narrower than any that might arise within, say, sociological theory; there is thus some hope of showing that such practices might exhibit the transparency that would give them moral significance. But let us grant that individual promises and acts of fidelity presuppose the presence of just such a thing and that the practice of making and keeping promises satisfies whatever standard of appraisal is to be accepted, utilitarian or not. Does any of this entail that individual actions "specified" by this practice are *themselves* thereby made to be "morally good"? Rawls comes closest to a defense of this claim in the following passage:

> It follows from what we have said about the practice conception of rules that if a person is engaged in a practice and if he is asked why *he* does what *he* does, or if he is asked to defend what he does, then his explanation, or defense, lies in referring the questioner to the practice. He cannot say of *his* action, if it is an action specified by a practice, that he does it rather than some other because he thinks it is best on the whole. When a man engaged in a practice is queried about his action he must assume that the questioner doesn't know that he is engaged in it ("Why are you in a hurry to pay him?" "I promised to pay him today") or doesn't know what the practice is.[30]

But what seems really to follow from Rawls's ideas is that some sense of the question "Why are you doing A?" might be answered, and some form of defense or justification supplied, by "referring the questioner to the practice" – that is, by referring the questioner to the considerations that make the action something that is to be done under the "rules" of the practice. We may grant that the existence of a practice in Rawls's sense is coupled with the legitimacy of practice-internal forms of explanation and justification of action that are distinct from the association of an action with some prospective good. It does not seem to follow, however, that no *other* forms of explanation and justification can apply to the individual act. After all, a player who has drawn a walk might continue her progress toward first base – "because she has drawn a walk" – even though she anticipates heart failure, or even as an earthquake rumbles and the stands begin to fall. This activity can evidently be queried with several types of question "Why?" It likewise raises a demand for justification of a *type* that plainly cannot be met with a reference to the rules of baseball – that is, with a voicing of the deontic judgments that, if Rawls is right, enter into the constitution of the game.[31]

Despite Rawls's intention, the "justification" of the individual act of fidelity to which he refers is nowhere itself bound up with or colored by the necessity of the underlying practice or of the good it serves. It is not moral justification.

The reason is plain: The conception of a practice with which he operates is forcibly rendered thin enough to cover the case of games and anything else to which his great "logical priority" thesis will attach. The only forms of justification of individual action at issue must also attach to this wide genus and must therefore find application in connection even with games. Though Rawls argues that the practice of making and keeping promises is a good one, he is impeded from arguing that the "reasons" that the practice underwrites are genuine moral reasons or that the agents who act on them are thereby acting well, morally speaking. Though moral considerations make contact with the practice, they do not manage to break through to the actions themselves.[32]

5. The Transparency of Dispositions

If we pass now to the exponents of our other tendency, it will immediately strike us how little attention is devoted to the question of the transparency of the mediating element, a practical disposition, in respect of rationality. Gauthier and Foot are principally interested in showing that justice as a disposition makes a better fit with the agent's good than any of the alternatives and thus meets the standard of appraisal they propound. This fixation of attention is understandable, since the result would refute many traditional forms of skepticism about justice. The question of a transfer principle, of demonstrating that *individual acts* of justice are thereby shown to be more rational than *their* alternatives, thus appears less pressing.

In Foot's essay, the matter is left completely implicit, but Gauthier addresses it in at least two places. In *Morals by Agreement*, a section is devoted to the question "whether particular choices are rational if and only if they express a rational disposition to choose," which is precisely the question of a transfer principle.[33] But what follows appears rather to be a defense of the view that dispositions *can* be called rational, and also of the conception of rational agents as "choosing" among dispositions in accordance with the maximizing conception:

For we suppose that the capacity to make such choices is itself an essential part of human rationality. . . . At the core of our rational capacity is the ability to engage in self-critical reflection. The fully rational being is able to reflect on his standard of deliberation, and to change that standard in the light of reflection.[34]

On the face of it, though, we can agree with Gauthier that it is a noble thing to have rationally appraisable dispositions or standards of deliberation and still deny that the rationality of a disposition inevitably extends to the individual actions that manifest it.

The matter arises again in "Rationality and the Rational Aim," Gauthier's response to the skeptical remarks made in Derek Parfit's *Reasons and Persons*, Chapter 1 – remarks I have just been imitating. Parfit argues there that it is no objection to a theory of rationality or morality that it is "indirectly self-defeating." Applied to theories of rationality, this amounts to a rejection of the transparency of dispositions: A theory is indirectly self-defeating when the individual action the theory favors is sometimes not the act of the favored disposition or, equivalently, when the disposition *always to perform the favored individual action* is not the disposition that the theory "tells us to have."[35] Parfit's argument is simply this, that *every* theory of rationality must make room for such disharmony; situations like this just do arise. The official illustration is provided by Thomas Schelling: With the help of a suitable drug, a prudent father frightens off a dangerous criminal by inducing a state in which he says things like "I love my children, so please kill them" and otherwise acts "irrationally." Since the criminal now has no hope of gaining access to the family's safe, he does best to cut his losses, leaving the children – the potential witnesses – unharmed.[36] Of course, the father's strategy might equally have been implemented with a fast-acting soporific, as happens in the movie *Kiss Me Deadly*. The same wild statements might then have been uttered somniloquently. It seems plain that nothing the father "does" in either case has the status of a voluntary action, and thus that none of these "acts" can be appraised as "rational" or "irrational" in the sense that interests us. The argument appears, then, to rest on an equivocation, construing "rational" first as we understand it in practical philosophy, but then psychologically, as mere *sobriety* or *sanity*.

But even if we drop the drugged state of Schelling's prudent father's brain, we will still, I think, find that the term "disposition" is completely unanalyzed and tends, in Parfit's discussion, to take over the whole extension of the word "motive" – including, for example, habitual states of passion, appetite, or affect. A taste for chocolate, or an aversion to it, would make a respectable occupant of the category Parfit has in view. It is, however, not too surprising to be told that even where circumstances make it irrational to alter such a thing, still the individual actions it prompts might yet sometimes be irrational.[37] That a narrower understanding of the concept *disposition* might be available, that Gauthier might have intended it, that it could not find instances in a taste for chocolate, much less in Schelling's father's drug-addled state, and that it might be associated with a true transfer principle – *Reasons and Persons* appears to give us no reason to doubt any of these things.

It is therefore open to Gauthier to accuse Parfit of a second and more fundamental equivocation. But this is not the path he takes in "Rationality and the Rational Aim." There Gauthier levels two charges against the doctrine of *Reasons and Persons*: "On Parfit's view not only are some persons cursed by rationality; others are condemned to irrationality."[38] What do these charges mean? Suppose we are given a Parfitian disposition that is always manifested in rational individual actions but nevertheless itself works to the disadvantage of its bearer through its other effects. There are two further possibilities: that the bearer can't change the disposition and that he can. If he can't change it, he's "cursed by rationality," Gauthier thinks. If he *can* change it, then of course he is irrational if he doesn't; but then even if he does change it, he will often act irrationally later. So he's "condemned to irrationality" – a conclusion Parfit himself draws explicitly.[39]

Gauthier's (rather un-Gauthierian!) thought is that these consequences offend intuition and that a theory that lacks them – a theory incorporating a transfer principle – will have a better claim to our allegiance.[40]

But can Gauthier's first charge be made to stick? It does not seem clear that a theory like Parfit's must apply the name "rationality" to the disposition always to *do* what's rational, if there is such a disposition. Where other dispositions are better and would be more rational, they would seem to have as much a claim to that title. The second charge will certainly stick, but we may wonder about its own merits as a charge. Gauthier is, I think, misled by Parfit's delight in what he takes to be a novel and counterintuitive result. A theory would perhaps be counterintuitive if it entailed, for example, that some particular action was at the same time inevitable and irrational. But it seems in fact to be a traditional platitude that reasoning animals developing from infancy will inevitably act irrationally *somewhere*. As St. Thomas puts it, we can all avoid *any given* "act of sin," but it would take a miraculous intervention for anyone to avoid *all* of them.[41] If there is a genuine difficulty, it must surely arise from the way this comes about in a given theory. If I understand him, though, Gauthier points to no repulsive feature of Parfit's account apart from its bare congruity with this bit of the *philosophia perennis* and (I think) common sense.

In his controversy with Parfit, Gauthier is led deep into Parfit's territory and, it seems, away from properly Gauthierian positions. Where Parfit had denied that "dispositions" are generally transparent in respect of rationality, on the irrelevant ground that habitual states of passion, appetite, and affect aren't, Gauthier is now forced to confess the transparency even of those states. He thus commits himself to an implausibly broad transfer principle on what appear to be very slender grounds. The correct path is surely to develop the insight latent in *Morals by Agreement*: to make articulate its narrower conception of a disposition and to defend a transfer principle that is framed in terms of it.

6. Concluding Remark: What Are Practices and Dispositions in the Practical Philosopher's Sense?

In the act of fidelity, the agent's word figures as a "consideration" upon which she acts – that is, it figures as a sort of "explanatory reason" – but in a specific way. The constitution of any given case of this sort of efficacy no doubt has many conditions, some somehow within the agent and others extending beyond her. Each of our tendencies fixes on one of these conditions, the presence of a disposition or a practice. The status of the action as a case of acting on sound reasons simply or as a case of acting on morally sound reasons is then supposed to turn on the merits of the associated "general" condition. The trouble, as we have seen, is to say why the intended items should be "transparent" in this sort of way; certain features of our writers' use of the concepts *practice* and *disposition* have seemed to impede our making this out.

Consider the moral philosopher's favorite piece of casuistical wisdom: A promise to meet someone to discuss trivial matters must come to nothing if a party to that promise can save his daughter's life by breaking it. In "Two Concepts of Rules" and more extensively in *A Theory of Justice*, Rawls claims that such justifications for failure to do one's word are a part of our practice, somehow written into it, and thus also a part that might be written out.[42] My suggestion will be that the aspect of his conception of a practice that finds expression in this apparently natural idea impeded his defense of transparency in "Two Concepts" and later forced him to the quite different type of transfer principle we found in *A Theory of Justice*. But it is an aspect of his conception that might be dropped. I will conclude with a brief articulation of a possible Gauthierian parallel.

Elaborating his thought, Rawls suggests that there might be a practice of promising that is unlike our own in that it rejects the familiar battery of permissions and holds us to *any* promise "come what may." It might belong to a second alien practice of promising, he says, that its bearers are held even to "promises" they have formulated in their sleep.[43] It is only if we can imagine several possible practices distinguished in such ways that we will have any use for the idea that the excusing conditions *we* recognize are a "part" of our own particular practice: Only then would mention of these "excuses" have to enter into any complete description of it. Let us then imagine three empirically given aggregates of people, three communities, each realizing one of the three sorts of practice Rawls describes (one corresponding to our own). A practice, Rawls says, "exists in a society when it is more or less regularly acted upon."[44] In the community with the peculiar principle about sleep, then, suppose that nine out of ten people, or ninety-nine out of a hundred, can be described as accepting the thought that somniloquently produced promises bind and even as acting accordingly. They have often been found keeping their own sleep-promises and criticizing others who have failed to keep theirs. In the other alien community, the legalistic one, nine out of ten accept the proposition that one must keep one's promises though the heavens will fall, and in most cases in which *we* would take ourselves off the hook these people have done what they promised to do, though from time to time the heavens have thereby fallen. Apart from this, the general facts about the making and keeping of promises, and about the criticism of breach, are the same in each alien community as they are among us.

One apparent consequence of Rawls's account in *A Theory of Justice* is that since each deviant practice violates certain principles of justice, *no* promise falling under either of the poisoned practices can bind. Since "it would be wildly irrational in the original position to agree to be bound by words uttered while asleep," the Principle of Fairness never gets a grip even on promises falling into the central range of cases in which alien opinion mirrors our own.[45] Something similar would hold for the "Two Concepts" account. This seems a fairly counterintuitive result, and I will return to it, but it is not what principally interests me.

The notion of a "practice" that is implicit in a description of the use of *language* must be quite different from the "practical" conception of a practice we are hoping to understand. But since they must fall under a broader genus, something might be learned from a brief detour, for purposes of analogy, into some old-fashioned considerations in the theory of meaning. Consider, then, a pair of alien *linguistic* communities employing expressions pronounced as our word "gold" is. In one case the word has only ever been applied to pieces of *gold*, and whenever the question "Gold or not?" has been raised about a given bit of gold, they have almost always declared "It is gold." It is presumably *their* (linguistic) practice, then, to call gold "gold"; gold is "what they call 'gold'." In the other community things are mostly the same, but some other substance, a fool's gold, is also occasionally found, and we will suppose that individuals have called *it* "gold" in nine out of ten cases in which the question has arisen. Let us suppose further that their word "gold" is unlike our "yellow" or "valuable" in that it is fitted to be given in answer to a certain sense of the question "What *is* this stuff?" – that is, it is what was called a "natural kind term." It was a favorite suspicion of a certain line of thought that it is mere prostration before the facts to insist that it belongs to the (linguistic) practice of this second community to apply the word "gold" equally to gold and to the other stuff. A more likely story is that the practice of employing the word "gold" should receive the same description in *either* community: It is just that in the second community there is widespread error about the fake gold, a frequent mistake with no bearing on the internal description of the practice itself.[46]

Let us return, then, to the three different social formations – one of them corresponding to our own – that we imagined as fitting Rawls's three different descriptions of possible "practices of promising." Putting the original practice-descriptions out of the picture, let us view the imagined communities as would a foreign traveler bent upon learning the customs of each place. What will immediately strike us, I think, is the impossibility of our making a confident attribution of the two deviant practice-descriptions.

We have, after all, no difficulty supposing that an individual member of our society might be inclined to perform its sleep-promises when informed of these. And we are actually familiar with the legalism that sometimes leads a child to stick to the formula of its promise when circumstances have made this unreasonable, and to criticize people for not keeping promises even when they can marshal every excuse. It is easy to imagine an adult who thinks and acts in one of these ways, and even brings up his children in accordance with these ideas. If we find such a person among us, the verdict will be that he does not grasp the practice, that he has a false opinion about it, that he is in error and leads his children into error. We will say all of this even if there are quite a few such people. But if we imagine, as we have, a whole community of persons thinking and acting in such a way, then we are apt to suspect a transition from quantity to quality and to cave in before the thought that, after all, this is their practice, promising is something different for them and involves different excusing conditions. But what reason can be given for dropping our resolve? What reason can be given for rejecting a parallel with the example of words for gold? If we do hold fast, then we will say that the inner constitution of the practice itself is in all cases the same. It is just that it is *associated*, in the deviant communities, with a widespread error or a superstitious religious conviction or something on the order of a fad – a disturbance, at all events, and mere dross – propagated perhaps through mutual scandal.

It might be said that we wouldn't have any use for the notion of a practice, and wouldn't understand it, if the facts about the alien communities were not adequate for the imputation of Rawls's divergent deviant practice descriptions. What else could a practice be? I want, predictably, to recommend the opposed thesis that we won't have any use for the notion of a practice if we *do* construe it this way. Consider again that if we adopt this conception of a practice and attempt an account of the tight corner along the lines of the Rawlsian tendency – claiming that it is only the excellence of the practice that can justify keeping one's word in the face of a greater possible good – then we will have to accept the unsettling consequence of Rawls's doctrine mentioned earlier. Tight-corner acts of fidelity will not be morally justified even in the central range of cases, namely, those in which the agent was awake and the sky does not threaten to fall. Contraposing, if we insist that such ordinary acts of promise-keeping *are* justified over there, then we will not be able to appeal to the goodness or justice of the practice to make sense of tight-corner fidelity: for the practice as a whole is clearly defective.

Suppose that, hoping to avoid this consequence, we reject the practice *as a whole* as bad or unjust but attempt to divide cases. *Part* of the practice of each deviant society is good and just. The respectable portion would cover ordinary tight-corner cases, but not the ultra-tight-corner emergency situations and sleep-promising cases in which, in the alien communities, "fidelity" is still expected. This would yield the right result, but it would require a more complicated transfer principle and an account not only of the notion of a practice, which remains obscure, but also of the notion of a *part* of a practice. More importantly, any development of this appeal to a felicitous sub-practice will enable us to draw a sort of objective line through the cloud of particular instances of "fidelity" and criticism of "infidelity" that have occurred in each alien community: Only *some* of these will be expressive of the respectable sub-practice and hence themselves good. It will seem to us that the particular acts of promise-keeping that fall under the benign alleged sub-practice all "belong together," in some sense, and that the deviant acts in each community are something "fundamentally different" from these. It will thus again become difficult to reject an analogy with the linguistic community in which the word "gold" appeared to name a kind of stuff covering both gold and fool's gold. Why should we not dispense with the epicycle of the sub-practice and understand this relation, the *belonging together* that joins any two instances of ordinary promise-keeping, to be the relation *falling under the same practice*? *That* is the "unity" we intend in the practical-philosophical employment of the concept of a practice. The difference between common or garden acts of fidelity and the deviant cases will consist again in this, that the latter do not express the practice exhibited in the former.

It might be objected that such a position would contradict an opinion held universally, if implicitly, in either alien community: namely, that the self-same practice is exhibited in all of these cases; or, equivalently, that a single sort of account of action by reference to the agent's past word is found in the uncontroversial and the deviant cases alike. It's all the same to *them*. But the principle of charity implicit in this objection has little force against the account I am suggesting, for widespread error will remain even on the opposed account. There will still be the universally held false opinion that "fidelity," thus construed broadly, is morally good (the corresponding opinion will come out true on my account) and the consequent false belief about each deviant act of fidelity, that *it* is morally good.

It might further be objected that the account I am imagining must be circular: We want to say that individual acts of fidelity are morally good "because the practice is," but then, apparently, let the goodness or badness of an individual action determine whether or not it falls under the practice. But we need not accept the second clause. We need only say that if the practice makes some action good, then any action the practice cannot make good does not express the practice. This is evidently consistent with the view that such acts of promise-keeping as *are* good are made to be good only by the practice.[47] The same objection would be implicit in the idea that our remarks involve a retreat from a "practice conception" of promising – the sort of account found in Hume and Rawls and the main body of analytical moral philosophy. Again, it is not true: We can accept that promising must rest on a "convention" and still insist that not just anything can be "convened upon."[48] No one will hold that just any series of individual actions performed by some number of agents can intelligibly be reckoned to display the sort of unity we intend in bringing things under the concept *practice* or *same practice*. We must also reject the somewhat weaker idea that any general schedule of action can be fitted into a possibly denoting phrase of the form "the *practice* of doing A in circumstances C, but B in C', unless . . . , etc." – and that to any subtle distinction among such schedules there must correspond a possible distinction of practices.[49]

If what is "convened upon" in our three imagined communities and exhibited in ordinary acts of fidelity is the same in each case, then there can be no reason for supposing that the "constitutive rule" of our *own* practice needs any more elaborate formulation than is contained in the proposition "promises must be kept," *pacta sunt servanda*. No closer description of the practice could be supplied by introducing qualifications, for it would mark no distinction among practices. The thought that there is something loose and inaccurate in the formula is thus an illusion, unless it is combined with the view that the practice is pointless and realizes no good or that it has something like the position of a game.

The concept of a disposition as it arises in the Gauthier-Foot tendency evidently invites a similar treatment, though I can only outline the point here. No one will hold that just any series of actions of a single agent can exhibit the sort of unity we intend in bringing things under a single practical disposition. And again there is no reason to imagine that just any *general* schedule of action might be employed to describe such a thing, or, equivalently, that to any subtle diversity of such schedules there must correspond a possible diversity of dispositions. Let the facts about a pair of agents be tailored to meet those subtly diverse disposition-descriptions: Questions of rationality may again lead us to wonder if they were correctly described after all. Suppose, for example, that I return a deposit someone has made to me, a book for example, thinking "It is his: I must give it back" – thus manifesting a fraction of justice distinct from fidelity – and that I have often done this sort of thing. Later, though, I return some autumn leaves that have blown from someone's red maple onto my lawn, again thinking "They are hers; I must give them back." Need we hold that the practical disposition manifested in my earlier acts must or could have shown up in an act of leaf-return? Need we hold that the disposition that was manifested in those sensible earlier acts is any different from that displayed in the like acts of a more reasonable person who would have let the leaves go? That returning the book and "returning" the leaves struck me as "the same," that I didn't *feel* any difference, cannot be supposed to establish the identity. The disposition that operates in my intuitively reasonable acts of return, we might think, is no different from the one that operates in *all* the acts of return of a person who lets leaves blow by; something else is at work in me where I busy myself returning them.

My effort in this section has merely been to excite the intuition that we do operate implicitly with *such* conceptions of practice and disposition. I do not mean to deny that we are also in possession of more generic conceptions that would also cover, say, a sociological regularity or a game or – in the other case – a habitual state of appetite or whatever "disposition" characterizes those who "grasp the rules" of a given game. I have approached the question of a narrower conception indirectly by considering the outward show of an item falling under either narrower type, that is, by considering the classes of actions that might "instance" or "manifest" such a thing. Much metaphysical labor would be required to make the conceptions themselves articulate and to defend them against skeptical doubts. But if there is anything in our two tendencies, then such results as these can hardly come as a surprise. If the only available notion of a practice is a purely sociological one, and if the only available notion of a disposition is purely psychological – if, that is, practical philosophy can find no interpretation of these phrases that is proper to it, if it can find no other way of thinking a "general" and "actual" connection between an agent or agents and a form of action – then it is too much to expect that either category will combine with normative concepts in a true transfer principle. Though items of either type *may* be ranged alongside possible objects of sociological or psychological knowledge in a wider class labeled "practice" or "disposition," the workings of *this* sort of member of either class will be opaque to any resolutely value-free inquirer. Where we judge that a practice or disposition lays hold of some good – or, rather, where we judge that some good apt to be realized in a practice or a disposition *is* realized in such a thing – then, it seems, we take leave of the purely sociological or psychological domain. We reckon then with a different and specifically practical form of unity of one individual action with another; we grasp, that is, a different form of "general" element in human practical reality.

Notes

1. *Morals by Agreement* (Oxford University Press, 1986). The other works mentioned are "Reason and Maximization" and "The Unity of Reason," in David Gauthier, *Moral Dealing* (Ithaca, NY: Cornell University Press, 1990), pp. 209–33 and 110–26; "Assure and Threaten," *Ethics*, 104: 690–721, 1994; and "Rationality and the Rational Aim," in *Reading Parfit*, ed. J. Dancy (London: Routledge, 1997), pp. 24–41.
2. "Moral Beliefs," in *Virtues and Vices* (Berkeley: University of California Press, 1977), pp. 110–31, especially 125–30. It tends to be forgotten that the original rationale for Professor Foot's introduction of the category of virtue, i.e., of a certain sort of "disposition," was to account for the rationality of morality. The latter topic has remained her central theoretical interest, but it must be stressed that *only the last eight paragraphs of "Moral Beliefs" will be at issue here* and that these are paragraphs Professor Foot has long since rejected, for different reasons at different times, while always retaining the critique of non-cognitivism propounded in the bulk of the essay.
3. "Two Concepts of Rules," in John Rawls, *Collected Papers* (Cambridge, MA: Harvard University Press, 1999), pp. 20–46. I will also refer occasionally to "Justice as Fairness," ibid., pp. 47–72, and to *A Theory of Justice* (Cambridge, MA: Harvard University Press, 1971).

   Rawls's early essay is much more important to his later work than is usually recognized. His later works all preserve and complicate its central doctrine about the need to distinguish *the justification of a practice* – and, more generally, the justification of a "principle" and a practical "conception," in the senses attached to these terms in his later works – from *the justification of an action falling under it*. The former sort of justification is of course subjected to a non-utilitarian standard in all of the works in which Rawls speaks entirely in his own person.
4. Note that this means that our point of entry into this material is through an idea of "subjective" goodness in one form or other, rather than through a corresponding notion of "objective" rightness. We are in the first instance asking "Did the agent act well (or rationally) in doing A, given that she did it precisely because she promised she would?", and only secondarily "Is the agent morally required to do A (or does she have most reason to do A), given that she promised she would?"
5. Of course, any theory of the obligation of promises will allow that one is often *justified* in leaving off keeping one's word, and hence not guilty of infidelity, when it develops that to do the thing would be dangerous or somehow especially counterproductive for oneself, or when the needs of persons other than the promisee are sufficiently alarming. Neither type of circumstance would fall under my description "tight-corner situation" – neither the type that interests Gauthier and Foot nor the type that interests Rawls. But it is clear that any reasonable account of the obligation of promises must allow for genuine tight corners as well: It must allow that even where the obligation stands, the faithful person is sometimes left doing what would simply be stupid or wrong for a similarly situated person who had not given her word.
6. "Moral Beliefs" (p. 129).
7. A high-minded moralism was and is ready to oppose this constraint, together with the apparently empirical claim that fidelity considered as a *hexis* meets it. But this moralism inevitably overlooks the *specifically moral* considerations that motivate these ideas: Foot's thought, later retracted, was clearly that the rejection of

any such link is a confession that fidelity works to the disadvantage of its bearer. It is thus also the confession that to bring someone up into such "virtue," to counsel its acts, is to injure her. How could that be any more respectable, morally speaking, than binding her feet? Gauthier's motivations are similar, as we see especially in the later chapters of *Morals by Agreement*, and he, too, has had to contend with this peculiarly amoral moralism.

8. "The Unity of Reason" (p. 122).

9. I use the past tense to express the point because it is difficult to hear the English present in this sort of case as bearing anything but "habitual" or "frequentative" meaning – the natural sort to employ in the description of a disposition. Historical uses of the present fit the bill: In place of the caption "Washington crosses the Delaware," a textbook illustration might bear the words "Washington chooses to maximize" or, equivalently, "Washington chooses in such a way as to maximize." All of these formulae might describe the same choice.

10. The expression "conception of rationality" predominates in "Reason and Maximization"; its place is taken by "disposition" in *Morals by Agreement*, and then by "deliberative procedure" in "Assure and Threaten." I have opted to employ the word "disposition" throughout my discussion. It encodes less theory, and it might be, and sometimes is, given in translation of such traditional terms as *hexis* and *habitus*. The re-emergence of this traditional philosophical category in Gauthier's works is among their most striking and interesting features.

11. The idea is explicitly rejected by Rawls in his discussion of Ross ("Two Concepts," Part II), but it is equally plain that Foot and Gauthier must reject it.

12. I discuss the second sort of relation and its role in the rational explanation of action in an essay, "Naive Action Theory," forthcoming.

13. Of course this should not be understood to mean that an agent cannot lose a disposition or that a practice cannot die out; it is just that this cannot be the work of the disposition or practice itself.

It may be objected, as a point of interpretation, that in "Assure and Threaten" and other recent works Gauthier does make the rationality of promise- or assurance-keeping turn on the existence of an antecedent *intention* – namely, the intention allegedly expressed in the (sincere) assurance itself. It is not in that respect, though, that "Assure and Threaten" exemplifies the first of our two tendencies, but rather in its appeal to the idea of an agent's *deliberative procedure*. That Gauthierian deliberative procedures exhibit the "generality" that interests us will be seen later.

It may also be objected that some intentions or plans do appear to bear the "generality" we find in dispositions and practices. But this generality can at best belong to the *content* of the intention or plan, and not to the form of the "further element" itself – and the latter is what will be at issue in the "transfer principles" discussed later in this essay. It is in fact not clear, though, that an intention or plan *never to visit New York* or *always to return blows with bullets* has a genuinely general content. The particular event that would realize or satisfy it – *going to one's grave never having visited New York*, say, or *having lived one's life always having returned blows with bullets* – is simply of a very peculiar sort.

14. The notion of a deontology, which I employ for purposes of exposition, is notoriously obscure: See Barbara Herman, "Leaving Deontology Behind," in *The Practice of Moral Judgment* (Cambridge, MA: Harvard University Press, 1995). For Korsgaard's use of the notion of practical or normative "realism" (which she opposes), see, for example, *The Sources of Normativity* (Cambridge University

Press, 1996), pp. 28–48. The idea of a "deontological" theory of rationality might seem a bit surprising, but in "The Normativity of Instrumental Reason," in *Ethics and Practical Reason*, ed. G. Cullity and B. Gaut (Oxford University Press, 1997), Korsgaard contemplates but in the end rejects the possibility of a realistic or "dogmatic rationalist" interpretation even of the principle of instrumental rationality (see especially the third part of the essay).

15. *Hegel's Logic*, trans. William Wallace (Oxford: Clarendon Press, 1975), p. 9.

16. See Rawls, *A Theory of Justice*, Chapter VII, pp. 395–452, and Korsgaard, *The Sources of Normativity*, Chapter 3.

17. To handle a still more general case, we ought to speak not only of a pair of normative qualities – one appropriate to the mediating element, another appropriate to individual action – but also of something broader than a relation of expression. Then we can handle such "transfer" claims as that *the goodness, morally speaking, of a rule makes the actions that flout it morally wrong*, and so forth.

18. See especially pages 47–8 and 50–1 of "Justice as Fairness" and the associated footnotes 1 and 4.

19. See especially "Assure and Threaten," pp. 701–2.

20. In fact, Gauthier appears not to commit himself to a standard of appraisal in terms of the agent's life going as well as possible. He takes the phrase over from Parfit, apparently conscious that a similar argument might be run with a different standard of appraisal. See "Assure and Threaten," pp. 690–1.

21. See "Assure and Threaten," again especially pages 701–2. Warren Quinn's essay "The Puzzle of the Self-Torturer," reprinted in his *Morality and Action* (Berkeley: University of California Press, 1995), pp. 198–209, has the special interest of defending a very Gauthierian intention-to-action transfer principle without appeal to the "strategic" or interpersonal illustrations characteristic of Gauthier's work. Principles of the intention-to-action type are also given searching and extensive study in Edward McClennen's *Rationality and Dynamic Choice* (Cambridge University Press, 1990).

22. The Principle of Fairness is expounded in Section 18 of *A Theory of Justice*, pp. 108–14, and defended in Section 52, pp. 342–50.

23. See *A Theory of Justice*, Section 52 (pp. 342–9), and *What We Owe to Each Other* (Cambridge, MA: Harvard University Press, 1999), pp. 338–42. Scanlon outlines the differences between the two principles on page 406, note 14.

24. The Principle of Mutual Aid is explained on page 114 and defended on pages 338–9; the Two Principles are explained at length in Chapter II and defended in Chapter III.

25. "Two Concepts" (p. 33).

26. See note 18.

27. "Two Concepts" (p. 37).

28. Of course, once these concepts do exist, an observer might legitimately be said to come to possess them without becoming a bearer of the practices he observes – and she might continue to possess them after the practices that constituted them die out. Similarly, the bearers themselves might use the concepts in non-practice-instancing judgments – for example (as we will see) in false accounts of their own practice.

29. Though Rawls does not emphasize the fact, we may note that the concept-constituting or concept-interpreting feature of Rawlsian practices makes it possible to avoid the ungroundedness that seems to attach to any attempt to explain

the concept of a promise. We count it among the essential conditions of the formation of a promise that the parties to it think of themselves at least implicitly as giving and receiving *a promise*. But how do they come by the concept they are supposed thus to deploy? It seems that any explanation will have to refer to the concept explained. The answer, crudely, is that just as the presence of a practice can turn a few seconds' worth of standing upright into a case of *drawing a walk* and a peculiarly shaped piece of wood into a *baseball bat*, so can it turn a concept into the *concept of a promise* and a thought into the *thought of a promise*. [The problem of "ungroundedness," as I am calling it, is of course Humean; an especially clear formulation can be found in Elizabeth Anscombe's essay "On Promising and Its Justice," reprinted in her *Ethics, Religion and Politics* (Minneapolis: University of Minnesota Press, 1980).]

Scanlon, in his recent attempt to explain the obligation of promises without reference to a "practice," rightly sees that he must expel any deployment of the concept *promise* from the formation of his promises. In formulating the conditions under which his principle of fidelity (F) kicks in, he avoids ungroundedness by using only concepts like *intention, expectation, knowledge, cause*, etc. In my own view, which cannot be defended here, any such theory must get the casuistry wrong: No one is ever bound in fidelity except by exercise of the concept precisely of a promise. Scanlon's theory, if I understand it, comes dangerously close to turning almost any felicitous expression of intention, even the expression of an intention formed weeks earlier, into a promise – for felicity seems to require the hearer's interest in knowing what the speaker is going to do and the speaker's intention to gratify that interest. See *What We Owe to Each Other*, Chapter 7, especially page 304.

30. "Two Concepts" (pp. 38–9).
31. It is clear that Rawls is moved by features of games that have no analogy in connection with promises. For example, it is possible to restrict the idea of *playing game G* so that no activity falls under that concept unless it accords with the rules associated with the underlying practice. "If you're not following the rules," we might say, "then you're not really making a move." Action in accordance with the rules of games could then be viewed as *instrumentally* necessary to continued play. And in that case, action in accordance with the rules (considered just as such) would be rational or morally good, so long as continuing to play were rational or morally good. Rawls's confidence in his transfer principle is funded, I think, by this sort of thought. (See, for example, his reference to executing a will, and the surrounding text; "Two Concepts," p. 38.)

We may note first that here it is not the practice that is evaluated, but associated instances of play. Furthermore, where the concept of *playing game G* has not been so restricted, the conclusion clearly fails to follow. This happens wherever *playing* is understood to be consistent with *cheating*. I take it that this is how things stand with the primitive notion of play and that the restricted concept is a rather sophisticated and optional development.

However it may be with games, *this train of ideas is completely out of place in connection with the practice of promising*, for in that practice, what corresponds to the proposition "I'm playing game G" is the proposition "I promised Jones I'd do A"; that's what makes the practice-governed necessities kick in. But the continued truth of "I promised to do A" is not affected by what I later do, as the truth of "I'm playing G" might be supposed to be. The "necessity" of the corre-

sponding action thus does not admit the evasive instrumental construction we can
imagine in connection with the play of games.

32. We can only suppose that Rawls later came to see this and that the account of the
obligation of promises in *A Theory of Justice*, Section 52 (pp. 342–9), is meant
to supply the deficiency, for there he systematically distinguishes between *two*
readings of the proposition "promises must be kept" and the necessity expressed
in it. On one reading it formulates a mere "constitutive rule" of the practice –
something in the nature of a rule of a game – and expresses the concomitant
merely internal necessity. On another reading it formulates a genuine moral
principle, the Principle of Fidelity, and the necessity expressed in it is that of
moral requirement. "Two Concepts" might be diagnosed as having fused these
readings – "the tendency to conflate [them] is particularly strong" (p. 349) –
though its considerations properly pertain only to the former. (I suspect that the
reference to conflation is autobiographical.) As we have seen, though, the later
theory surrenders the earlier hope of a purely formal, non-substantive account of
the relation between *the moral goodness (however judged) of the practice that
contains this "constitutive rule"* and *the moral goodness of the individual actions
that accord with it.* Or, equivalently, it surrenders the hope of a purely formal
account of the relation between the moral goodness of the practice the "rule"
helps to constitute and the *truth* of the Principle of Fidelity.
33. *Morals by Agreement* (p. 183).
34. *Morals by Agreement* (p. 183).
35. *Reasons and Persons* (Oxford University, Press, 1984), p. 5.
36. *Reasons and Persons* (pp. 12–13).
37. Parfit does not distinguish systematically between the claim that a disposition is
rational or profitable and the claim that it would be rational or profitable to act to
cultivate it.
38. "Rationality and the Rational Aim" (p. 32).
39. *Reasons and Persons* (pp. 13–17).
40. "Rationality and the Rational Aim" (p. 37).
41. See, e.g., *Summa theologiae*, I-II. Q. 109, art. 8.
42. *A Theory of Justice* (p. 345), "Two Concepts" (pp. 31–3).
43. *A Theory of Justice* (p. 345). Rawls reasonably rejects the suggestion that the
description of these practices as "practices of promising" is usefully ruled out as
"inconsistent with the concept (meaning) of promising."
44. *A Theory of Justice* (p. 345).
45. *A Theory of Justice* (p. 345).
46. This is a rather idiosyncratic rendering of some of the points of Hilary Putnam's
"The Meaning of 'Meaning',," reprinted in his *Mind, Language and Reality* (Cambridge University Press, 1975).
47. Similarly, it was because nothing with the status of a so-called natural kind term
could be *true of* both gold and fool's gold that we had to hold that people failed
to accord with their (linguistic) practice either whenever they called gold "gold"
or else whenever they called fool's gold "gold." It is consistent with this that the
individual predications that *are* true, are true only "because of the practice," like
any other predications of conventional linguistic expressions. Given that the
practice makes the action of predicating "gold" of *gold* true, it cannot also belong
to the practice to apply "gold" to fool's gold.
48. If the position recommended here is correct, then Stanley Cavell is wrong to think

that an objection to a practice conception like Rawls's can be expressed in the question "But what might it mean to urge a reform of the practice of promising?" *The Claim of Reason* (Oxford: Clarendon, Press, 1979), pp. 295. In any event, Cavell's doctrine of promising seems much too extreme: "The very existence of human society, and the coherence of one's own conduct depend on it. . . . [P]romising is not *an* institution, but a precondition of any institution among persons at all" (p. 298). For compelling *a posteriori* counter-evidence, see F. Korn and S. R. D. Korn, "Where People Don't Promise," *Ethics*, 93: 445–50, 1983.

49. The sensible substitutions for A and C in the formulas "Everyone always does A in C" and "The rule is: to do A in C" are vastly more wide-ranging than in "It is their practice to do A in C," where it is read as I am proposing we read it. The notion of a "rule," for example, is extremely abstract and can, as we have seen, be deployed in connection with *games*. Rules of games can exhibit almost any degree of complexity possible for Fregean universal generalizations. The distinctions among games can thus be as subtle as you like. This is why it was possible for David Lyons to produce his famous reduction of "general" and "rule" utilitarianism to "act" utilitarianism in *The Form and Limits of Utilitarianism* (Oxford University Press, 1965). This is also why the notion of a "rule" fits poorly with the idea of a practice in the sense that interests us.

Psychology for Cooperators

ADAM MORTON

1. Cooperation and Psychology

Assume that human beings must cooperate to survive, and must do so extensively to flourish. Activities that require a variety of links between our actions
are essential to the full range of human life. It follows that humans need to
be able to describe and categorize actions and to attribute to one another
motives: belief, desire, character. They need a psychology.

Cooperation without psychology is possible for other species, with hard-
wired social routines that tell them when to share, when to defer, and when
to punish. We are innately social, but we do not have a fixed repertoire of
social acts with fixed instructions about when to perform them. Instead, we
have inescapable desires for company, affection, and attention from others
and an inbuilt tendency to think out courses of action in terms of the relations
we and others have to common features of the environment. That is our
evolutionary niche: to operate in groups, but to think our way through the
problems groups face. (For psychological and evolutionary evidence for this
diagnosis, see Chapters 8 and 9 of Byrne [1995] and the first three chapters
of Baron-Cohen [1995].) Each person thinks what to do, but must do so
strategically, taking account of the decision-making of others. Strategic thinking is impossible without concepts to represent the paths of reasoning that
lead from motives to acts and outcomes. (It need not use the concepts of
"reasoning," "motive," "act," "outcome," and their friends, but it must use
concepts that represent reasoning, motive, act, and outcome.) So it needs
psychology.

People learn psychology, largely as children from older people and largely
in the form of the doctrines, habits, and cognitive tricks of their cultures. We
now have reason to believe that human beings are adapted to pick up such
folk psychologies, and it is a natural conjecture that there is some relation of
mutual support between the psychological conceptions current in a culture
and its patterns of cooperation and interaction. (Teasing out this relation is a
focus of my current research.) Actual human cultures clearly sustain an
imperfect degree of mutual cooperation among their members, and there is

most likely a very imperfect fit between their norms and their folk psychologies. The question this essay asks is, What would constitute a perfect fit? What conception of action, motive, and outcome might be used by idealized rational agents maximizing their individual good by thoughtful cooperation?

2. Conventional Psychology

Each agent possesses a folk psychology, a selection from the space of possible psychologies, which she uses to interpret, explain, and predict the actions of others and of herself. If a number of interacting people have the same folk psychology, and no one of them could do better by possessing a different one, given that the others possess the psychology in question, then the psychology is theirs by convention. I shall call this the conventional psychology of the people in question. More precisely, a conventional psychology for a set S of people consists of a scheme P for supplying explanations for actions, such that for each person p in S the two marks of a convention apply: (a) If most other people in S subscribe to P, then it is in p's interest also to subscribe to P. (b) If p subscribes to P, then the more other people in S subscribe to P, the more it is in p's interest also to subscribe.

Conditions (a) and (b) make adherence to P a kind of convention, in the spirit of Lewis [1968] and Sugden [1986]. Condition (b) is important in making the situation conventional, as it requires that it be in each subscriber's interest that others subscribe. A mere equilibrium needs only an (a)-like condition, that it be in each person's interest that she subscribe, if others do. One might choose a stronger definition, in which "most" would be replaced by "all." But while that would better fit the definition into the tradition of game theory, it does not seem realistic. One might also choose a weaker definition, without (b). Then the psychology would occupy an equilibrium position that would not be a convention. One reason for such a weaker definition could be that it might be in person p's interest that others have a different psychology, for example, one that did not give them the resources to see what person P was planning. But I shall assume that the dynamics of social life will force the psychology adopted by a coherent social group to be a convention. In effect, if there is a psychology that it is in most people's interest to have most other people subscribe to, then they will find a way of making most people subscribe to it.

The definition leaves basic things unspecified, also. It does not define adherence to P, nor specify how P produces explanations of actions, let alone what is to count as an explanation. And it does not ask what is to count as being in a person's interest. (In particular, it neither asserts nor denies that adherence to P may change what is in a person's interest.)

These unspecified factors are going to be left unspecified in this essay. However, it is essential to say more about the uses to which explanations of actions are put. The relevant uses center on the capacity of a person to think about the motivation of another. Suppose, for example, that two people find themselves in a situation described by a payoff matrix such as the following. I shall call it Domcord I, because one agent is reasoning by dominance, choosing acts that the other has reason to coordinate with.

$$B$$

		b_1	b_2
		b_1	b_2
A	a_1	2, 0	0, 1
	a_2	0, 0	2, 2

Domcord I

Here B can think through his actions entirely in terms of the possible outcomes. And in terms of them, b_2 is the obvious choice. [Throughout this essay, agent A will be female, and agent B male, and pairs of utilities will be in the order (for A, for B).] A, on the other hand, has no dominant choice. Her choice is undetermined until she takes account of B's situation. Then it will be clear to her that B will choose b_2 and that she therefore should choose a_2. The use of a psychology lies in the difference between B's situation and A's. To make her choice, A has to think in terms of the reasoning that may lie behind B's choice: She has to see B not just as choosing options but as choosing them for reasons. (Many situations – most real situations – are thoroughly strategic, in that each interacting agent has to take account of the reasoning of all other agents, and in fact very often of the reasoning by which others take account of their own and others' reasoning. And so on.) The most basic requirement on a conventional psychology is that it allow agents in situations like A's in Domcord I to go through reasoning like A's.

This means, first of all, that outcomes and actions must be identified. There are no intrinsic pausing points in the ongoing flux of events, except perhaps the death of each agent. So in thinking of choices in the terms used earlier, we are already assuming that we can impose a conceptualization on the world that marks some possible effects of our actions as salient. This is not yet psychological. Psychology enters when an agent thinks of another agent as carving the world into a specific set of outcomes and actions. Very often agents think of others as using the same conceptualization that they do. (Presumably this is the default for real humans.) Many coordination problems would be very hard to solve were this not the case. As David Gauthier has observed (see also Sugden [1995]), it is very often the case that "We must convert our representation of the situation into one with but one best equilibrium. This restriction in our conception of what we may do, far from being disadvantageous, is what makes successful coordination possible" (Gauthier [1975, p. 210]).

The situation can become very complicated when there are large numbers of acts and outcomes and each agent has to think about which outcomes are the objects of consideration by the other agent. Then, if the other is not aware of an outcome, in a coordinative situation there is no point in considering it oneself. (You and I are both approaching an intersection as the light turns yellow for me. My obvious options are to rush through the intersection or to stop. But I could also do a U-turn, or reverse back up the road, or get out and do a dance on the car's roof. If you consider all the things I might do, you'll never decide what you should do.) More subtly, even when another agent is in some sense aware that an option is open to her, it is important to know how she thinks of it. Is it thought of as one action or a set of actions? Is it thought of in terms that make it salient, or make it likely that she will think it is salient to you? On the other hand, it is worth noting that there are situations in which it is in an agent's interest not to reason in terms of the outcomes in terms of which she understands the other person's reasoning. Consider, for example, the following situation:

		B		
		b_1	b_2	b_3
	a_1	2, 2	2, 0	1, 0
A	a_2	0, 4	3, 3	1, 1
	a_3	1, 2	1, 1	1, 1

If we suppose that both agents are considering all three options, then A knows that B will choose b_1, and she will therefore herself choose a_1. But suppose instead that the option b_1 is not in B's list of things he might do, and A knows this. Then B will choose b_2. Knowing this, A will choose a_2, so that the resulting situation (a_2, b_2) will be better for both than the outcome (a_1, b_1) that would have resulted if B had known that a_1 and b_1 are options. (Sound familiar? The issues return in Sections 4 and 5.) In practical terms, this can be described by saying that it is sometimes best to pretend you don't know that an option exists. More abstractly, this suggests that one conventional psychology might sometimes be more in the interests of its adherents than another when the former fails to provide a description of some actions. A less rich conceptualization might sometimes have advantages.

A conventional psychology, then, will provide characterizations of acts and outcomes and will allow agents to relate one another to the same act and outcome types when it is in their interest to do so. This is only the very beginning of any psychology, though. Situations like Domcord I require participants also to consider the patterns of reasoning that others may be following. We – people like this book's contributors and readers – naturally think of this in terms of specific kinds of interactions between preference orderings and degrees of belief. But, of course, not all people think through their strategic situations in these terms. It is not obvious that it is sensible for all people so to think, that it forms part of a conventional psychology for them. And there is the worrying thought that there might be better ways of thinking out strategies. There might be better ways of describing them and thinking out what might pass through one's own and other people's heads that would be even less related to the folk psychology of our culture or the psychologizing tendencies of humankind than game theory is. The aim of the next section is to show that there are constraints on the kinds of conventional psychology that extremely rational agents will use. They are unlikely to be as exotic as this paragraph might suggest.

3. Game Theory Backwards

Assume that we have agents who are optimally adapted to their social and physical environment. That is, each agent has a consistent set of preferences, and in each situation there is a best, or co-equal best, preference-maximizing choice for each agent, which that agent will choose. Many of these situations are strategic, in that the best choice for an agent will be a function not just of the agent's preferences and the physical facts but also of the choices of other agents, which may themselves be functions of the choices of the first agent. Assume that agents' choices are determined by facts about situations and that agents can represent choices and outcomes and can carry out quite complex conditional thinking ("If A or B happens, then as long as C does not happen, the result will be D," etc.). Assume also that agents can think about possible situations and what it would be best to do in those situations.

But do not assume that the agents determine the best choice in terms of the preferences or reasoning of other agents. Simply assume that they possess some way of determining the optimal choice in each situation. It might consist of advice from a mystical infallible oracle, or it might consist of an ability to pick up cues from the behavior of others that contingently correlate with optimal choices in situations involving them. Or it might consist in some knowledge of the nervous system that cannot be expressed in terms of preference and decision. The aim is to show that even such oracle-guided agents will have the capacity to think in terms of the preferences and reasoning of others.

Consider an agent A confronted with a situation S in which a number of acts a_i are available to A and a number of acts b_j are available to another agent B. The agent represents one act a* as choice-worthy. A's choice may

reveal nothing about the preferences or choice of B. This will be so when a*
may be determined by considerations of dominance, that is, when for each b_j
that B may choose, a* is the best choice for A. In this case, B's preferences
are irrelevant to A. Thinking – as we may, though not as A does – in terms
of the situation as a game in normal form, we can determine a* in terms
simply of the payoffs to A of the given outcomes, without considering those
to B.

But this is not usually the case. Usually, if you know what the optimal
actions are, then basic facts about the preferences of the agents are determined. Given a strategic situation – which we can think of in terms of the
preferences of the agents, but which they represent in some other way –
agents have a way of knowing what is the best action for each participant.
Then very often agents can deduce what one another's preferences must be.

The simplest typical cases are those like Domcord I, whose matrix was
given earlier. There the optimal choice for A depends on B's choice, which
is itself determined by dominance. Thinking strategically, A must take account of the reasoning to which B's preferences will lead. Thinking in terms
of her oracle, A simply gets as a datum that her best action is a_2. But she can
reason from this datum, with a little further help from the oracle. First of all,
she can know some complex facts about her situation that we would express
by saying that her own choice is not dictated by dominance. And in fact she
can grasp facts that amount to representing some of her preferences. Let us
see why this is so.

Agent A can consider a variant on the actual situation in which b_1 is
available to B, but both of a_1 and a_2 remain available to A. (She can query
the oracle: Suppose that I was in a situation like this, except that. . . .) This
reduced situation would have the two outcomes resulting from the product of
$\{a_1, a_2\}$ and $\{b_2\}$. And the oracle would tell her that the right choice in this
sub-situation would be a_2. Similarly, it would tell her that the right choice for
her, if b_1 but not b_2 had been available to B, would be a_1. But the fact that the
right choice is different in these two sub-situations can be taken to represent
the fact that A's choice in the whole situation is not dictated by dominance.
(For us, it is that fact.) And the fact that the right choice in the first of them
is a_2 can be taken to represent the fact that (a_2,b_2) is preferred by A to (a_1,b_2),
just as the fact that the right choice in the second is a_1 can represent the fact
that (a_1,b_1) is preferred by A to (a_2,b_1). So she can learn something that is in
effect a translation into the language of optimal choice of what we would
express in terms of her preferences.

By pushing the same reasoning a bit further, A can know similar facts
about B's preferences. Since A does not have a dominant choice and yet there
is a single best action for A, this must be because one slice of possibilities is
eliminated by B's choice, and thus (this being a game of 2 agents with 2 acts

each) there must be a dominant solution for B. This is either b_1 or b_2. If it were b_1, then in order to have chosen a_2, A would have to have preferred (a_2,b_1) to (a_1,b_1), which is not the case. Therefore B's dominant solution is b_2, and (extending the reasoning) B prefers (a_1,b_2) to (a_1,b_1) and (a_2,b_2) to (a_2,b_1). Or that is how we would put it, at any rate. Agent A simply realizes these complex facts about B's actual and possible choices, which are extensionally the same as B's preferences.

Several things are worth noting about the procedure so far. First of all, there is a symmetry between ascriptions of preferences to oneself and to others: One starts with situations and the optimal actions they determine and then one figures out what constraints this puts on the states one can ascribe to all parties involved.

Second, these considerations provide a defining condition for preference: An agent prefers one outcome to another if given a choice between an act producing the one outcome but not the other, and an act producing the other but not the first, the first act is the best for her. This is a very constrained definition: It says that if some conditions are met, then an agent prefers the one act to the other. Most often the conditions are not met. The more complicated preference-eliciting procedures to be discussed later can produce more complex defining conditions.

Third, this reasoning applied to these situations results in only a partial determination of the agents' preferences. Thus, in Domcord I, all that is required of B's preferences is that he prefer (a_1,b_2) to (a_1,b_1) and (a_2,b_2) to (a_2,b_1). The orderings "in the other direction" between (a_1,b_1) and (a_2,b_1), and between (a_1,b_2) and (a_2,b_2), are irrelevant to B's choice of action. There are two distinct aspects to this underdetermination. First, some preferences, such as B's ordering of (a_1,b_1) and (a_2,b_1), are simply left unspecified. But, also, even when the ordering of outcomes is determined, there is incomplete information about their relative degrees of desirability. Thus in Domcord I and in surprisingly many other situations we can characterize agents' preferences in terms of the two-unit scale 1, 0, or "want/don't want." In terms of this, we and they can know all they need to know about their best choices. And as a result, reading back to preferences from best choices in many situations the finest grid we can impose on them is "want/don't want."

The two underdeterminations are closely linked. The greater the number of preference-comparisons that can be made between outcomes, the finer the grid that can be imposed on their relative degrees of preference. But even starting from a comparatively simple situation such as Domcord I we can deduce somewhat more about the agents' preferences if we allow ourselves more elaborate reasoning. Suppose a situation in which act b_2 (the same b_2) is available, but only if a_1 is not, and in which b_1 is available, but only if a_2 is not. [Another way of describing it: B has b_1 and b_2 available, and A has the acts (a_2 if b_2) and (a_1 if b_1) available. Or, equivalently, B has available b_3 and b_4. If B performs b_3, then b_1 becomes available to B, and a_1 to A, and if B performs b_4, then b_2 to B, and a_2 to A.] If in this situation b_2 is the best choice for B – as it is – then (a_1,b_2) is preferred by B to (a_2,b_1).

The underdeterminations are not surprising. After all, Domcord I is a very simple situation, and so it can be expected to yield only limited information about the agents' preferences, even over the actions found in it. So one might expect that by considering more complex strategic situations we should be able to impose a finer triangulation on preferences. This is indeed the case.

Consider what happens when we add another option for each of the participants, to get Domcord II:

$$
\begin{array}{c c}
 & \text{B} \\
 & \begin{array}{c c c}
b_1 & b_2 & b_3
\end{array} \\
\text{A}\ \begin{array}{c}
a_1 \\
a_2
\end{array} & \left|\begin{array}{c c c}
3, 0 & 0, 2 & 0, 1 \\
0, 0 & 2, 1 & 2, 2
\end{array}\right.
\end{array}
$$

Domcord II

This situation is to be seen through B's eyes. Thinking in terms of preferences and reasoning, B's decision is made as follows. Option b_1 is dominated by (b_2 or b_3). But the choice between b_2 and b_3 cannot be made in terms of B's preferences alone. On the other hand, A's preferences make her coordinate with B: If she expects B to choose b_1, A will choose a_1, and if she expects B to choose (b_2 or b_3), then A will choose a_2. A knows that B will not choose b_1, and thus A will choose a_2. Knowing this, B's preferences are coordinative, leading him to choose b_3.

In deciding what to do, B has to consider A's reasoning about his reasoning. Some of the effect of this reasoning about reasoning about reasoning can be recaptured by thinking backwards, from choice to preference. Suppose, again, that B has the use of an oracle, which announces that b_3 is the best choice for him. Then, knowing that b_3 is his choice, B can know that (b_2 or b_3) dominates b_1, by reasoning like that used earlier. B knows that if A's best choice were a_1, b_3 wouldn't be his best choice, and so B knows that A's best choice is a_2. B can know that this choice is not dominant for A, and so it must be motivated by coordination. So A must prefer (a_1,b_1) to (a_1,b_2) and (a_2,b_2) to (a_2,b_1).

So B can ascribe "horizontal" preferences to A, in effect preferences between the results of B's actions. Coordinative aspects of situations elicit preferences between results of the other person's actions, and dominance aspects elicit preferences between results of one's own actions. Note also that the reasoning that B applied to Domcord II reveals some of A's beliefs as well as her preferences, since A's choice of a_2 reveals her belief that B will choose b_2 or b_3, and thus that neither (a_1,b_1) nor (a_2,b_1) will occur. In fact, this can be taken as giving the practical content for B of A's belief about these outcomes.

It is not hard to construct a Domcord III in which domination is embedded within coordination within domination (just as in Domcord II coordination is embedded within domination), and in which an agent's choice of action depends on another level of embedding of motives. And in this situation even more of the structure of the agents' beliefs and preferences is revealed. And so on, with increasingly complex situations and – unfortunately – increasingly complex reasoning inverting the usual game-theoretic considerations to deduce from what acts are optimal for agents what their preferences are. The conclusion is that given a sufficiently rich variety of strategic situations in which an agent has knowledge of her best action, the preference and belief structures of that agent and others interacting with her are determined. If an ideally rational agent were equipped with an oracle that told her the optimal actions in all possible strategic situations involving herself and a given other, then she could deduce all the facts about the other's preferences that would be relevant to determining those optimal choices.

I believe this is a very significant conclusion, with consequences in the philosophy of mind. (Eliminative materialists should take note of it, for it says that if you can make good choices in strategic situations, then you can ascribe beliefs, desires, and thinking, and thus have the core of folk psychology.) One intriguing aspect of the analysis is that attributions of preferences to self and other are interdependent: You have to conceive of others as having preferences in order to attribute them to yourself. Another is that attributions of finer-grained preferences to self and other depend on considerations about embedded reasoning, about one person's thinking about another person's thinking about the first person's thinking, and so on. One might think that attributions of even very finely grained preferences would be conceptually more primitive than such involuted thinking. But the patterns of reasoning described in this section suggest the possibility that the attribution of rich preferences may depend on that of complex reasoning about reasoning.

These are suggestive possibilities in the philosophy of mind. But for the argument of this essay, the important conclusion must be that agents making optimal choices are in a position to ascribe beliefs and preferences to one another. The minimal objects of these ascribed states are acts of interacting agents and the consequences of combinations of those actions. Thus we can expect that a conventional psychology that gives its subscribers the resources to make good decisions will also allow them to ascribe beliefs, desires, and reasoning to one another.

4. Harvestless in Humeston

The aim has been to see what kind of a psychology would best aid people in negotiating the problems of strategic interaction. A standard understanding of "best" has led us by an interesting route to a fairly unsurprising bottom level of such a psychology. It will describe actions in terms that people can generally share, and it will allow people to attribute to one another beliefs about actions and preferences between actions and outcomes. That is obviously only the very bottom level; any workable set of psychological ideas will be much richer, and one would expect it to facilitate the interactions of its subscribers in more complex and subtle ways. In particular it would be natural to consider whether or not a shared psychology could bring advantages in connection with those interactions in which the pursuit of individual self-interest seems self-defeating. The obvious test cases are situations like the prisoner's dilemma, where a non-equilibrium outcome is intuitively something the agents ought to be able to aim for.

Questions about how agents can cooperate for mutual advantage are often framed in terms of rationality. Then we ask whether or not it is, for example, ever rational to cooperate in a prisoner's dilemma. I have not used the R word in this essay until this paragraph. I have spoken of what is in agents' interests, and of how they can get more of what they want. I am suspicious of theories that put too much weight on what is or is not rational. I doubt that the concept of rationality can bear the weight. My aim in the rest of this essay is to show how a conventional psychology can ease the route to cooperation. But psychology is not needed if logic will do the job. David Gauthier has famously argued that as long as agents are equipped with the psychological concepts of the preceding section, they ought to be able to see that it is rational of them to act cooperatively, under suitable circumstances. (See Gauthier [1986], especially Chapters V and VI.) I agree, but I think the claim is best understood as one about conventional psychology rather than about rationality. I must explain why this is so.

The simplest characterization of rational action is as action that will, on average, give optimal results. So if it is sometimes rational to cooperate, then it should follow that cooperators will sometimes do better than non-cooperators. There are two crucial ambiguities here. Optimal by what measure? And averaging over what range of possibilities, with what weighting? Standard choice theory answers both these questions by relying on the agent's own states: Optimality is measured in terms of satisfaction of the agent's preferences, and the averaging is over all states to which the agent assigns a degree of belief, weighted by those degrees of belief. Clearly these are not the only ways of resolving the ambiguities, and clearly they raise problems of their own. The degrees of belief are normally inaccurate; the preferences may be bizarre. (So why should we define "optimal" in terms of an averaging weighted by false probabilities? Or give points to outcomes that will make the agent miserable?) Even more threateningly, both preferences and beliefs are, for anything like a real person, defined on only a tiny subset of the range of possible future outcomes. So it is almost inevitable that the expected value of an act, in terms of the agent's own preferences and beliefs, may be utterly different from the average outcome for the agent. (And it is almost inevitable that on many occasions agents doing the "irrational" thing will fare better than agents doing what the theory calls rational.)

But these problems fade into insignificance when we move to strategic choice, for there the crucial factors affecting a choice are the choices made by others. And an agent has no degrees of belief about these. Degrees of belief about other agents' choices cannot be data for strategic choice, for two reasons. First, the agent's reasoning is centered on forming conclusions about what the other agents may do. Once you get to that point, the decision becomes a standard non-strategic one. And second, there is a symmetry between interacting agents. Each is trying to conclude what the others may choose: So if you could start with probabilities about their choices, they could start with probabilities about your choice, and knowing this you would have probabilities about your choice and could spare yourself the effort of reasoning.

So the definition of optimality for strategic choices is deeply problematic. It is hard even to understand what is meant by the choice that will, on average, give the best results. Realizing this should help to prevent us from being too deferential to game-theoretic solutions to real-life problems. But it should also prevent us from thinking that we can solve practical problems simply by deciding what we are to count as rational.

To illustrate both these points, consider an example from Gauthier [1994] and ultimately from Hume. It is not a prisoner's dilemma, but a situation that I, at any rate, find rather more disturbing and thought-provoking. Analyzing it while trying to avoid pointless disputes about what might or might not count as "rational," we find ourselves led to conclusions about what psychologies agents might profitably use to describe one another.

Dave and Tom are graduate students at Pittsburgh. Jobs in philosophy are scarce, and so they leave to become farmers in Humeston, Iowa. (It exists, not far from Princeton and Pleasantville.) They buy neighboring farms so that they can talk philosophy on winter evenings. One year Dave plants X, and Tom plants Y. X needs to be harvested a month earlier than Y, and each crop is best harvested by two people. So Tom proposes that each help bring in the other's harvest. Dave likes the idea, especially since this will be his last harvest: As a result of their winter discussion, he has published an article on dynamic choice that has attracted so much attention that he has been offered a tenured position at the University of Hawaii. Knowing that there will be no more Dave & Tom harvests leads Tom to some sober reflection. His motive for helping Dave had always been the expectation that Dave would in turn help him. But what motive will Dave have for helping him, since Tom will no longer have available the sanction of withdrawing his help? It seems that Dave has no reason to help Tom. But if that is so, Tom has no motive to help Dave. So they will each bring in their harvest alone.

Tom's conclusion is uncomfortable, not just because they seem headed for more laborious harvests. That is the practical problem, but there is also an intellectual difficulty. Dave seems to lack a motive for helping Tom next month. So he will not, and so Tom will not help him this month, and so he will be worse off than if he had had a motive to help. This does not seem right: Surely the fact that he would be better off if he had a motive gives him a motive. (This reasoning presupposes that the cost of helping is less than the benefit from being helped. For one set of utilities bearing this out, see Gauthier [1994, p. 714].) In response to this thought, Gauthier presents a very subtle analysis of the conditions under which it would be rational for someone in a situation like Tom's to commit himself to an action like that of helping Dave. Gauthier summarizes his discussion as follows:

[S]ometimes my life will go better if I am able to commit myself to an action even though, when or if I perform it, I expect that my life will not thenceforth go as well as it would were I to perform some alternative action. Nevertheless, it is rational to make such a commitment provided that in so doing I act in a way that I expect will lead to my life going better than I reasonably believe that it would have gone had I not made any commitment. As a rational agent I shall be able to offer and honor assurances when it is advantageous for me to do so. [Gauthier, 1994, p. 707]

Suppose that this is right. Suppose that it is rational for Dave to commit himself to helping Tom and then actually to help on harvest day. How much of the puzzle does this remove? Suppose that you are Tom, and it is the night before Dave should arrive to help you, in return for your help of a month earlier. Suppose that you are convinced, from your studies in Pittsburgh, that it was rational of him to promise and will be rational of him to keep his promise. Does this allow you to sleep easily, confident that he will be there in the morning? I must confess that if I were Tom, I would pass a sleepless night, worrying what my philosophical friend would decide to do. And my sleep would not be helped (much) by the conviction that it would be rational for Dave to be there. This conviction would not help me as long as I could imagine Dave calculating what course of action it would pay for him to take, and then considering taking it even if it were irrational.

Or imagine that you are Dave, wondering whether or not to turn up for Tom's harvesting. You have nothing to gain from it; nevertheless you believe that it would be rational to help, given your earlier commitment. Then a thought strikes you: Sometimes one can gain from doing an irrational action. You remember your Aunt Florence, who set fire to the office of a salesman who had sold her a defective truck. She didn't get her money back on the truck; in fact, she had to pay a substantial fine. But the fact that no one could predict her occasional uncalculating fits of self-expression meant that few people tried to cheat her. Perhaps not helping with Tom's harvest would be a profitable irrational act. If rationality were a matter of maximization, then the cases where irrationality pays should be fairly exceptional. But Pittsburgh taught you that rationality is more complex than that. So you waver; you spend the night in internal debate. It would be irrational not to help Tom, but perhaps it would be the most profitable, most sensible, or simply the best thing to do.

The general problem is that an analysis that cuts the link between what is rational and what will generally turn out best for an agent also cuts the link between thinking that something is rational and seeing a reason to do it. And as a result it cuts the link between thinking that it will be rational for someone else to do something and expecting that if he reflects enough he will be likely to do it. These are vital links. They are central to the use of the concept of rationality. In particular, they are central to its psychological use, in anticipating the reasoning and actions of others. That *psychological* aspect is vital here. Agents need to have information about one another that gives them reason to be confident in the cooperative or uncooperative aspects of their future actions.

What information could Tom and Dave have about one another that would give them the confidence they need? That must depend on what the facts are about Tom and Dave. Suppose that their minds are such that there is some act that each can perform at one time that will make it impossible for them not to perform a given action at a later time or under specified conditions. Call this "strong binding" (see Kavka [1983], Bratman [1986], and McClennen [1990]). Then their problem is just to know that strong binding has taken place. To know this, they will first of all need to have the concept of binding: They will need a conventional psychology that describes it adequately. Then they will need to have seen adequate evidence of binding. A conventional psychology will be essential here too. Strong binding could take many forms. They could be capable of getting into a state of mind in which the consequences of not doing the act would be unbearable. (Remorse.) Or they could be capable of forming a kind of intention that would have automatic priority at a later time. Or they could be capable of getting into a state in which preferences at an earlier time could be the basis for actions at a later time. (Will.) Or they could have beliefs about the rationality of acts subsequent to an act of binding, beliefs that would be so strong that no amount of perceived self-interest could overcome them. (Faith.) Creatures who would be capable of strong binding would have advantages over creatures who were not. Promises would be easier for them.

They might not be capable of strong binding. But they might still *believe* that they had the capacity. Conventional psychology would play a larger role then. (And the label "conventional" would be more appropriate.) Suppose that they have the concept of binding and believe that binding is effective, and in fact when an agent is bound there is a good chance, though not a certainty, that the action in question will be performed. Call this "weak binding." Then many forms of cooperation will be possible for them. They will trust each other's promises. Sometimes these attempted cooperations will fail, and conventional psychology will come in again, to give case-by-case reasons for the failure, which do not undermine the belief that binding works. Suppose, on the other hand, that though they have the concept of binding and believe that it is effective, it in fact quite often fails. Then some profitable cooperation will still be possible. Tom and Dave can trust each other's promises, and Dave's harvest will get gathered. Then Tom's harvest may or may not get gathered, depending on the details of the case. Often it will be, and even if it is not, Dave's harvest has at any rate been gathered.

Finally, they might not even be capable of believing in binding. Each sees himself and the other as making decisions in a moment-to-moment way influenced by the information and preferences of the moment. These beliefs may be true, but they will make it harder to achieve some mutually beneficial cooperation (see Frank [1988]). The remedies are well known, though. As each case in which assurance is vital comes along, they can try to set up a penalty for non-cooperation. (Dave can plant marijuana among Tom's crop, and they can jointly send an anonymous letter to the FBI in Washington, which, the U.S. Postal Service being what it is, will arrive in a month. Both will then be in deep trouble unless Dave has come over with his tractor to help harvest both the crop and the evidence.) Or they can join with others to set up a system of commercial law, with courts to enforce contracts, thus providing a single device for guaranteeing a wide range of mutually beneficial arrangements. All these remedies have costs, but the more intelligent Tom and Dave are, the smaller they can make the costs. Since it is in everyone's interest to have such remedies, it is in everyone's interest to make the costs minimal.

In each of these four cases there is information that Tom and Dave can have that will ease their problem. Which would they be best advised to try for? That depends on the facts about them. If they are capable of strong binding, then they should use it when appropriate. That is, instead of simply harvesting or planning to harvest they should first bind themselves: With this additional option the situation will not have the structure of the original game. But of course they may not be capable of this. Perhaps ideally rational agents would be capable of strong binding. Edward McClennen can be read as arguing for this (McClennen [1990]), and, with a little imagination, so can Gauthier. But it does not follow that humans should try for strong binding if humans will fail at it. (In this connection, see Jackson and Pargetter [1986].) Given their limitations, it is possible that humans should try something they can actually do. So in order to come to a conclusion about rationality, we need a psychological premise.

Rational agents might also find themselves in the last case. Their very rationality might show them options and show them how others might see these options, which would block both binding and belief in it. In that case they would have the corresponding remedies: setting up penalties or binding contracts. These could be quite demanding of their thinking powers, though. They would have to see non-cooperation traps coming and head them off, and they would have to devise suitable low-cost remedies for them. Rational agents of arbitrarily great intelligence would have little difficulty here. They would be caught in the occasional trap by unpredictable random events, but in most cases they would have seen a problem coming and would have devised a solution to it at minimal expense. But we humans have very limited intelligence. When we adopt this strategy we seem to oscillate between expensive substitutes for foresight and very fallible substitutes for ingenuity. We go either for overbearing institutions, which enforce cooperation in a large range of cases but at a high cost in resources and loss of liberty, or for happy-go-lucky improvisation, which can produce low-cost solutions but which allows many uncomfortable situations to come upon us unexpectedly.

5. Psychology to the Rescue?

If we had one kind of ideal rationality we would be able to bind ourselves to cooperative actions. If we had another we would be able to devise cooperation-enforcing transformations of our situations, at minimal cost. In either case we would need enough psychology to understand the solution adopted. We are not ideally rational. We waver in our resolutions, and we do not see problems until they are upon us. (So the facts described by Cherniak [1986] are very relevant to moral philosophy, and indeed to the practical design of institutions. See also Slote [1989].)

That may be the end of the story. There may be only two rational solutions to one of the fundamental problems of human life, and we may not be very well equipped for either of them. However, in this final section I shall argue for a third solution, a more intrinsically psychological one. It corresponds to the second and third cases described earlier, in which agents are not capable of strong binding but do understand what it would be like to be bound. I think that, for better or worse, this is the solution adopted by most human cultures.

It is easy to think of characteristics people could have whose presence would bind them to present or future cooperative behavior. There could be states of character, innate or acquired, that would make it impossible for their bearers to renege on a promise or act on a narrow construal of their own interest. There could be kinds of pride or self-respect that would be unbearably damaged by letting down another person. There are important differences between these and other similar characteristics, but they share the feature that if a person had such a characteristic, her cooperation could be relied on, even when on the particular occasion cooperation would not be in her interest. Of course, it does not follow that people can or do have characteristics with these features. A variant on these familiar ideas can be got from Gauthier. There could be a characteristic C such that if a person had C, and if she believed that someone else had C, then she would choose an option with a particular cooperative feature in some specific range of strategic interactions with that other person. (The wording is meant to avoid the circularity problem described by Smith [1991].) Or there could be a characteristic that would ensure that a person would follow through with certain commitments. Call the person "Jane." If John has performed an action A on the assumption that Jane will later perform an action B, and Jane expects that her life will go better if she performs B than it would have had John not performed A, then she will perform B. A culture could have a name for these two characteristics. It might even refer to one or both of them as "rationality." (The term would then be on the border between the psychological and the ideological – *rough* connections with Gauthier [1977] and Chapter X of Gauthier [1986].) Ascriptions of them could then play a large role in people's decisions whether or not to enter into various interactions.

In some circumstances, if all interacting people believe that each of them has the characteristic, then cooperation will be assured, whether or not the beliefs are true. In others, the result will be one-sided cooperation (which may or may not produce more total benefit than no cooperation at all, depending on the details). There is something worrying about this, though, even when the result is cooperation. Could rationality result, after consideration of accurate evidence, in false beliefs, however useful?

The beliefs may not be false. There are two reasons for this. The first is that it is in each person's interest that others believe that she has the characteristic. But it may be hard to fake. It may be linked to contingent features of human psychology that are very difficult to acquire except by going through a certain developmental process. That is, the easiest way to get people to think you have the characteristic may be actually to have something much like it. (The easiest way to have the result of rational dispassionate dealings with people may be actually to like them, for example. See Bertram [1995].) I said "something much like it" because the process one has to go through for the characteristic to be plausibly applied to one is unlikely all by itself to have the required effect. The effects of self-attribution are also likely to be needed. For example, if the characteristic is the simple sense of shame, then cooperation may need not only a tendency to disquiet at broken promises but also an anticipation of the shame one expects will follow treachery. That anticipation is itself unpleasant, but it results in part from the belief in the conventional psychology. And if the characteristic is the Gauthier-style commitment-fulfilling disposition described earlier, then a person will keep her commitments not just because she has acquired the frame of mind needed to convince others of her trustworthiness but also because she expects herself to keep them. Believing that she has the characteristic in question, she will not make the contingency plans necessary to follow up broken promises or failed expectations. Very occasionally she may find an opportunity for improvised unreliability that can be taken on the spot, surprising herself with what she takes to be out-of-character behavior. But much more often, in order to take advantage of another you have to plan in advance, which you will not do if you do not believe yourself capable of it.

There is another reason why the beliefs engendered by a suitable conventional psychology may not be false, for there is another, subtler way in which a conventional psychology can induce mutually beneficial choices. The psychology supplies the vocabulary used to describe actions and strategic situations. As I pointed out in Section 1, echoing Gauthier [1975], it can make a large difference to the ways agents approach a strategic situation how the acts are described. It can also matter how the situation is described. Any strategic situation, occurring at a particular moment between particular people, is an instance of infinitely many situation-types. Which types a vocabulary for predicting acts and ascribing motives will make salient to those people at that moment can influence the way they think through their possible actions. The influence can be crucial.

A situation that happens to be a prisoner's dilemma, for example, will also be many other things. It will be an instance of a non-zero-sum game, a game with one equilibrium that is not Pareto-optimal, and a situation in which each person will hope the other is not paying attention. It may also be an instance of a situation in which one person wants to get an advantage over another, or a situation in which they each desperately hope they can trust one another. The psychological vocabulary of the people involved may not have any simple concept picking out all and only prisoner's dilemmas (PDs), for if we classify social interactions in ways that would be natural for people in almost any society – as buying and selling, building, reporting, hunting, or whatever – we find that most of them involve ranges of situations, many of which have

PDs as special cases within the range. The result is that many PD-shaped situation-instances occur, but PD-shaped situation-types are rarely described.

I imagine this is a very plausible claim. But to reinforce it, consider two types of situations. The first might be called cumulative cooperation. Here there is some shared good that can be created by cooperative action. It may be produced in proportion to the number of cooperative acts performed or in some more complex way (in particular, it may be a non-linear function of input: twice as much cooperation may produce more than twice as much of the good). There is a cost to individuals for cooperative action that is compensated for if enough others cooperate. (The cost may simply be physical tiredness.) In any such action the payoff matrix in the two-person case will have the form

	C	D
C	$g(2) - c, g(2) - c$	$g(1) - c, g(1)$
D	$g(1), g(1) - c$	$g(0), g(0)$

where $g(n)$ is the amount of the good produced when n cooperative acts are performed, and c is the cost to the individual of performing a cooperative act. This will not, in general, be a PD. It will be a PD only when $g(2) - c < g(1)$, $g(1) - c < g(0)$, and $g(2) - c > g(0)$. On any particular occasion it will usually be quite hard for agents to know whether or not the situation-instance is a PD, although they are conceptualizing it as, in effect, cumulative cooperation and know the form of $g(n)$ and the size of c.

Another large class of types of situations might be called foul-dealing (taking the term from Pettit [1986], but generalizing to cover cases that Pettit did not intend to cover). Here there is an aggressive action that one person can direct at another in order to gain some benefit, or can refrain from. If two people both act aggressively toward one another, then the effect may be that both will gain the benefit, or that both will be harmed, or that both will be protected by their aggression, or something in between. The payoff matrix will be like this:

	C	D
C	$0, 0$	$0 - a, b$
D	$b, 0 - a$	$0 - sa + tb, 0 - sa + tb$

Here a is the harm done by an aggressive action, b is the benefit to be gained by aggression, s is the proportion by which harm is reduced by counter-aggression, and t is the proportion by which benefit is reduced by one's victim's counter-aggression. These situations, too, will be PDs only in special cases. Assuming that all these factors are always positive, they will be PDs when $a > sa - tb$ and $tb < sa$.

In real life there are other types of situations whose instances include simple or generalized PDs (especially when one moves beyond two agents and two options). The consequence should be obvious. Suppose that people operate with a conventional psychology that prompts them to classify situations as buying and selling, building, reporting, hunting, and so on, and then at a higher level as cumulative cooperation, foul-dealing, and so on. The concept of a PD lies in between these two levels of description. Suppose that they do not have any simple characterization of it. Then when they find themselves in a PD, they will usually think of it as, for example, a house-building situation of a cumulatively cooperative sort. And thought of that way, the cooperative option usually will be the one that each will expect the other person to choose and will choose herself. Or, to put it differently, each will know that the other is committed to a cooperative action, because each will know that the other is engaged in an activity for which cooperation is the reasonable and profitable choice.

Rational beggars can't be choosers. We do have some resources both to bind ourselves to future actions and to anticipate cooperation-traps so that we can devise low-cost transformations of them. But these resources have definite limits, and to that extent we have to find ways of solving our problems with more primitive means. The two uses of conventional psychology in this section do not make extravagant demands on our rationality. In fact, they both exploit our cognitive limitations. The first builds on the fact – if it is one – that the easiest way for a limited agent to give the appearance of a cooperative disposition is actually to have one. And the second builds on the fact – if it is one – that the classifications of situations that fit most easily into the decision-making heuristics that mere humans must use assimilate many situations in which non-cooperation would be advantageous to situations in which it would not be. As a result, a sufficiently intelligent human will always be able to find some situations in which by thinking around the concepts used by others she can take advantage of them. But there will never be too many such situations (rarely as many as hopeful intelligent humans persuade themselves they can find). One reason is that no person is that much smarter than those around her. Another is that too original a way of thinking will break a person's link with the conventional psychology she needs to anticipate the actions of others. You can't exploit people unless you know how they are thinking, and you can't do this unless you can use the same descriptive and explanatory concepts that they do.

References

Baron-Cohen, Simon (1995). *Mindblindness* (Cambridge, MA: MIT Press).

Bertram, Christopher (1995). Self-effacing Hobbesianism. *Proceedings of the Aristotelian Society* 94:19–34.

Bratman, Michael (1986). *Intention, Plans, and Practical Reason* (Cambridge, MA: Harvard University Press).

Byrne, Richard (1995). *The Thinking Ape* (Oxford University Press).

Cherniak, Christopher (1986). *Minimal Rationality* (Cambridge, MA: MIT Press).

Frank, Robert (1988). *Passions within Reason* (New York: Norton).

Gauthier, David (1975). Coordination. *Dialogue* 14:195–221.

(1977). The Social Contract as Ideology. *Philosophy and Public Affairs* 6:30–52.

(1986). *Morals by Agreement* (Oxford University Press).

(1994). Assure and Threaten. *Ethics* 104:690–721.

Jackson, Frank and Robert Pargetter (1986). Oughts, Options, and Actualism. *Philosophical Review* 95:233–55.

Kavka, Gregory (1983). The Toxin Puzzle. *Analysis* 43:33–6.

Lewis, David (1968). *Convention* (Cambridge, MA: Harvard University Press).

McClennen, Edward (1990). *Rationality and Dynamic Choice* (Cambridge University Press).

Pettit, Philip (1986). Free Riding and Foul Dealing. *Journal of Philosophy* 83:(7):361–80.

Slote, Michael (1989). *Beyond Optimizing: A Study of Rational Choice* (Cambridge, MA: Harvard University Press).

Smith, Holly (1991). Deriving Morality from Rationality, in *Contractarianism and Rational Choice*, ed. Peter Danielson (Cambridge University Press), pp. 229–53.

Sugden, Robert (1986). *The Economics of Rights, Co-operation, and Welfare* (Oxford: Blackwell).

(1995). A Theory of Focal Points. *The Economic Journal* 105:533–50.

Which Games Should Constrained Maximizers Play?

PETER DANIELSON

Much of the response to *Morals by Agreement* has focused on David Gauthier's most philosophical claims: Is constrained maximization rational? Is it moral? While these traditional questions are important, they might lead us to overlook two features of Gauthier's innovative project. First, he develops Rawls's *constructive* approach to moral theorizing, seeking to invent new devices and principles that can meet pragmatic and moral demands. In particular, Gauthier offers his constrained maximizer as a new kind of agent who benefits by her moral constraint. Significantly, *Morals by Agreement* ends with a discussion of Nietzsche's question: " 'To breed an animal *with the right to make promises* – is not this the paradoxical task that nature has set itself in the case of man?' . . . Such an animal is able to interact with its world in a new and distinctive way, which we have sought to capture in the conception of constrained maximization."[1] But mention of Nietzsche and Rawls reminds us that moral innovation is often controversial. As in the case of Rawls's difference principle, Gauthier's principle of constrained maximization has struck some critics as less demanding than morality requires. This leads to the second feature of Gauthier's approach: His appeal to rational choice suggests new ways to address such criticisms, by allowing a sophisticated pragmatic theory to select the best among various approaches (moralized and not) to problematic interaction.

My own research program presses these two features further. First, I have argued (Danielson 1988, 1992) that an even less morally constrained principle, reciprocal cooperation (RC), which cooperates only when necessary and therefore exploits unconditional cooperators (UC), is pragmatically superior to the conditional cooperation (CC) that Gauthier built into constrained maximization (CM).[2] The difference between CC and RC is exactly the sort of moral dispute within the instrumental approach that its methods should be able to resolve. The question is which of these two principles "can be

I wish to thank the Social Science and Humanities Research Council of Canada (SSHRC) for research support for my project "Evolving Artificial Moral Ecologies," of which this essay is a part, and Chris MacDonald for comments on several drafts.

generated as a rational constraint from the non-moral premises of rational choice" (Gauthier 1986, p. 4). But deciding among several moral principles is not so simple as the choice between a unique moral principle and straightforward maximization (SM) that Gauthier discussed. So I suggested that evolutionary game theory and computer simulations were needed to deal with the complex interactions of various more and less constrained agents.

However, my criticisms were not so novel as I thought. Howard (1971) had earlier argued for the RC strategy (under a different label) in a game extended like the one I introduced. More recent critics (LaCasse and Ross 1998; Binmore 1994) have pressed versions of my criticism even further, by making dispositions to cooperate into explicit moves in the game. Substantially, LaCasse and Ross argue that RC is simply rational; it calls for no moral constraint. On the methodological side, they argue that traditional game theory suffices for this result; no appeal to evolutionary methods is needed. Section 1 sketches these criticisms and elaborates the game the critics see constrained maximizers playing. Section 2 introduces a new device, equivocation, by which agents who would like further moral constraint on their interactions might achieve that. This new device complicates the situation, but preliminary evolutionary simulation suggests that the new device is stable.

1. Which Game?

Part of the dispute arising from *Morals by Agreement* concerns which game it is at which morally constrained agents are supposed to outperform rational agents. Gauthier focuses on the one-shot prisoner's dilemma, where the problem of obtaining optimal outcomes is known to be unsolvable by straightforward maximizers. Were this problem solved by constrained maximizers, their superiority would be demonstrated thereby. But Gauthier's solution depends on conditional dispositions, and several critics argue that there is no room in the one-shot game for disclosing whatever these dispositions are conditional upon. Taylor is especially clear that "asymmetry is of course essential to the resolution, for if both players use conditional strategies of the same order, then some conditional strategy combinations do not yield determinate outcomes" (1987, p. 183).[3]

1.1. The Extended Prisoner's Dilemma

To avoid the problem of symmetry, I introduced the extended prisoner's dilemma (XPD1; Figure 1).[4] This game has one player (P1) make her move publicly at T-1, and the second (P2) then make his at T-2. These two moves determine the payoffs to P1 and P2 listed at the bottom. Notice that the XPD is not an iterated game; P2's move is terminal. I went on to argue that a P2

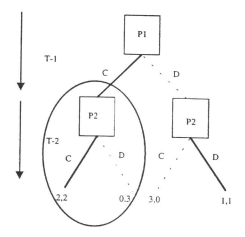

Figure 1. Extended Prisoner's Dilemma (XPD1).

who was committed to respond to C with C would induce P1 to choose C (straightforwardly, for her own benefit), thus showing the advantage of moral constraint. (These choices are shown by the solid diagonal lines; P2's non-maximizing constrained choice is in the circled left-hand node.)

The XPD thus attempts to model counter-preferential constraint. P2 would do better to choose D in any case. In addition, it separates the two ingredients of constrained maximization – constraint and its perception – localizing them in the two roles P2 and P1, respectively. Finally, it allows us to introduce the dispositions that P1 is able to perceive, and P2 to choose among. According to my critics, this is where I went wrong. If P2 can be committed to various strategies, they should appear explicitly as options in the game before analysis proceeds.

1.2. LaCasse and Ross's XPD2

Recently, Binmore (1994) and LaCasse and Ross (1998) have developed similar criticisms of Gauthier and myself, respectively. I shall focus on La-Casse and Ross because they begin with my extended game and they press their conclusion further, arguing that my RC strategy is rational but not morally constrained.[5] Figure 2 shows the XPD2, where the four strategies available to P2 are made explicit.[6] P2 can respond to P1's choice of C or D by C or D, yielding four strategies, which I shall represent by ordered pairs: ⟨CC⟩ responds to C or D with C (this is unconditional cooperation), ⟨CD⟩ responds to C with C, but to D with D (this is conditional cooperation), and so forth.

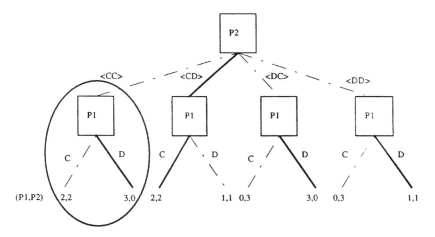

Figure 2. Extended Prisoner's Dilemma (XPD2).

Since P1 knows about these four strategies when she moves, she is modeled as moving *second*. Her strategy is a vector of four choices (e.g., ⟨CCDD⟩ for a conditional cooperator, who responds to ⟨CC⟩ and ⟨CD⟩ with C and to ⟨DC⟩ and ⟨DD⟩ with D). P2 has the first move when he chooses a disposition. The great advantage of this fully explicit extended game is that the standard game-theoretic method of backward induction suffices to select equilibrium strategies for P1 and P2.

... the first task of analysis ... is to find the subgame perfect equilibrium in the XPD2. We proceed by backwards induction. That is, we first find the strategy for P1 which maximizes her payoff at each of her information sets; then, we find P2's best reply to this strategy. ... [I]n the context of this game, each information set for P1 is identified with a disposition adopted by P2; therefore, backwards induction allows us to find the best *action* against each of P2's [four] possible dispositions. Taking the vector of these actions identifies a *strategy* or decision procedure for P1; this decision procedure maximizes her payoff against a mixed population of UCs, UDs, and CCs. [LaCasse and Ross, 1998, p. 361]

Then (a rational) P1 looks only at the first element (the P1 score) in each of the eight available outcomes and chooses the four indicated in Figure 2 by the solid lines at the bottom. This yields the choice vector ⟨DCDD⟩, meaning: Choose D when P2 chooses ⟨CC⟩, C when P2 chooses ⟨CD⟩, and so on. In turn, P1's choices induce simple outcomes for P2's four choices, {0, 2, 0, 1}, so P2 maximizes by choosing his second strategy element, ⟨CD⟩. Combining the P1 and P2 strategies, we get ⟨DCDD⟩⟨CD⟩ as the rational choice of strategies in the whole game. This is the strategy that I have defended as

RCC, in contrast to Gauthier's recommended conditional cooperation, CC, which is ⟨CCDD⟩⟨CD⟩ in this model.[7] (They differ in the circled node.)

LaCasse and Ross's analysis confirms my criticism of Gauthier: A less constrained variation of CC is what instrumental rationality requires. Following the backward induction, the rational superiority of choosing D in the first (circled) node in Figure 2 is evident. Here constraint is unmotivated, even indirectly, so RCC's unconstrained exploitation of UC is obviously an instrumental advantage over CC's more constrained strategy. On the other hand, the *moral* appeal of CC is also brought out by this analysis. Compare the circled decision nodes in Figure 1 and Figure 2. In each, the player has the opportunity to exploit the cooperative choice of the other player. *Morals by Agreement* requires that one resist this temptation in cases where the cooperative outcome is fair. So the moral reasoning that supported the ⟨CD⟩ strategy for P2 in the XPD1 similarly supports the ⟨CCDD⟩ strategy for P1 in the XPD2. Thus a gap reappears between moral constraint and maximization. My proposed strategy, RCC, fills this gap by combining (less) constraint with maximization.

1.3. Moral Constraint?

However, perhaps I should not be too quick to enlist LaCasse and Ross's analysis on my side. They go even further, claiming that the difference between CC and RC is not a matter of degrees of constraint. They put their point in terms of the superfluousness of morality in the fully extended game: "when [Danielson's] tournament . . . is properly represented as a game, RC[C] turns out to be the rational strategy according to the received definition of rationality. Thus RC[C] . . . is unconstrained according to Danielson's own concept of constraint" (p. 353).

I cannot accept LaCasse and Ross's skeptical conclusion, although I accept much of the argument leading them to it. First, their game theoretic analysis is much better than my own, making explicit the flow of information in an extended game with dispositions. Second, I agree that *in this game* (the XPD2) there is no need – indeed no room – for moral constraint. But that is because the model assumes this need away.[8] By making ⟨CC⟩ and ⟨CD⟩ available as moves, the model assumes that P2 will choose C after P1 chooses C. LaCasse and Ross write that "what is crucial is simply the *ability* of agents to commit" (p. 370). The model doesn't specify whether P2 will choose C because it is wired to do so, has a side bet making this instrumentally best, is threatened by the Sovereign to do so, or applies some moral principle. There would be a place for moral constraint only if the model were extended to include P2's move as well as P2's strategy choice. Then we would be faced with the issue of how P2's two choices are related. As is well known, there are roughly three positions on this issue, namely, that a rationally chosen strategy is rational to enact, that it is rational to choose only strategies that it is rational to enact, and that the two choices are unrelated.[9] Some of the ways of relating the two choices involve moral constraint.

However, we should not lose sight of the more general point: Which game is being played is not objectively given by the players' environment. It is a function of their cognitive abilities as well. Some environments will, for example, force agents to play single-play games, but in other environments, that *permit* more extended interaction, agents who cannot remember their encounters, or cannot identify themselves to others, will be fated to play less efficient isolated games. Thus the ability of players to constrain themselves, for example, by communicating and keeping a promise to cooperate, changes their situation; it allows them to play the XPD2 instead of the XPD1 (Danielson forthcoming).

This leaves us with a puzzle. If moralized devices (among other factors) determine the game to be played, why would morally inclined agents choose a game in which rationality makes RCC the preferred strategy? Why can't they do better, that is, make their world safe for unconditional cooperators? There is, of course, a plausible answer – indeed, the general lesson of social science. Interacting agents must settle for equilibria; they can't choose outcomes directly. But this invites the rejoinder of the social contractor: They should choose to get the best equilibrium outcome. One suspects that the resources of moral theory have not yet been adequately deployed. Are there ways to structure the XPD situation to allow a morally better game to be played? The mention of social contracting also suggests an answer to this question: Agents collectively decide to play a new game and construct institutions (norms, etc.) to support it. But to maintain our focus on Gauthier's internalist approach to morality, we shall consider only what agents can do individually, by means of changes in their motivation and perception, or, as we shall suggest in the next section, by means of the information that they are willing to reveal.

2. Communication Games

In the XPD2, RCC does better than CC. None the less, doubts remain about the XPD2, as the (wealth of) information available clearly benefits RCC. For example, in a (cognitively) simpler world, where P1 agents could find out if P2 would reciprocate only P1's choice of C, but not of D, CC agents would do better than unconstrained agents. CC would do best in this world, because RCC would not be available. But this is a weak argument for CC. As we have seen, when both strategies *are* available, RCC does better. So all the weight of the argument falls on the assumption that less information would be communicated, and this assumption has not been argued for. In this section, I shall construct a model that supports an information strategy leading to (a variant on) CC.

Another route into this issue comes from noticing that RCC is a compromise, combining an unconstrained strategy for P1 and a more constrained CC for P2. But our discussion thus far provides no argument for this constraint; players have no alternative but to treat all P1 cooperators the same. The question arises whether or not the element of constraint for P2 would remain were the additional information available to inform a more discriminating P2 choice. Again we look to LaCasse and Ross for instructive elaboration of our apparatus. They take up the task of extending the game (to the XPD3, on pp. 364–9) to allow the needed information, and they argue that a full RC will be the rational strategy in that game.

However, I suggest that we not follow them down this path, but rather back up a step. We should wonder about the extra information needed to allow full RC. This is not a criticism of LaCasse and Ross. Elsewhere (Danielson 1992) I assumed full transparency, and they are simply trying to model explicitly what I crudely sketched. Indeed, once we raise this question, it takes us back to an earlier stage: Why is the information needed for RCC, as distinct from CC, available? In effect, we are asking what disposition/perception pairs are available to provide moves in the extended game.

One might address this question empirically, to try to find out which cognitive abilities are available to agents.[10] However, we shall continue along a more *a priori* path here. In an evolutionary simulation, we can make alternative dispositions and abilities available to our modeled agents and seek to discover which sets do better in interaction.

2.1. The Strategic Aspect of Communication

Another way to support this approach is to see dispositions and the ability to perceive them more dynamically. We have supposed that agents have dispositions and that it is rational to have the ability to perceive this feature of the world. But this misses the strategic aspect of communication. Constraining dispositions are useful to the agent only if communicated; the ability to perceive is the ability to receive a useful message. So we should expect messages to be sent and received only if they are strategically in equilibrium. In other words, while attention to the strategic aspect of communication complicates the picture (we can't assume dispositions and perception as given facts), it also allows us to apply well-developed tools to establish equilibrium behavior. For the general problem of evolving communication, see Skyrms (1996, Chapter 5); we shall focus on the special case of communicating the extent of one's cooperative disposition.

Earlier (Danielson 1992) I had assumed that morally constrained agents would benefit from transparency, that is, full and open communication. But I remained focused, with Gauthier, on the need to do better than straightforward maximizers. Once RCC becomes the problematic predator, the situation changes. SM needs no communication (it has a dominant strategy), but RCC needs more information than CC and needs it for exploitative purposes. In the new situation, structured by the agent I introduced, it is no longer clear that a would-be moral agent should communicate so freely. In particular, when asked if one will reciprocate D with D, one might better reply, "I won't say; all you need to know is that I will return C for C." That is, this is all a CC agent needs to know; it suffices to provide *assurance*.[11] However, it falls short of providing the information RCC needs to distinguish its victims. Note that CC does not withhold this information to protect itself; the CC strategy is safe against exploiters under full information. Withholding information is here motivated by another reason: to maintain solidarity with RCC's intended victims: UC. Lacking the extra information, RCC can't separate CC from UC and presumably will not attempt to exploit either.

If players could refuse to give more than assurance, how might things work out with regard to CC and RCC?

2.2. A New Device: Equivocation

To give agents a new alternative, we must specify the device that structures it and then extend the game they play to reflect the new strategies. We want to change the game minimally, so we shall continue to force agents to be truthful. Therefore the new device will not introduce deception, but instead, optional partial revelation. If one's P2 strategy is $\langle CD \rangle$, one may reveal $\langle CD \rangle$ or merely $\langle C? \rangle$. In the latter case, one's revealed strategy is indistinguishable from that of a $\langle CC \rangle$ who also reveals only $\langle C? \rangle$. With this device, players can *equivocate*, that is, communicate something "unclear or misleading, sometimes as a result of a deliberate effort to avoid exposure of one's position."[12] A technological example – from which I got the idea – is the Global Positioning Satellite system. It provides the U.S. military with higher-precision location data than it provides other users, also for strategic reasons.

2.3. Extending the Game

We extend the game by allowing agents to reveal more or less of their P2 strategies, shown to the right and left, respectively, in Figure 3.[13] This yields eight initial moves: CC/reveal C part; CC/reveal all, and so forth. Note that on the left branches, P1 can no longer distinguish all of P2's moves; they are combined in two information sets, shown by the dashed boxes. Since P1

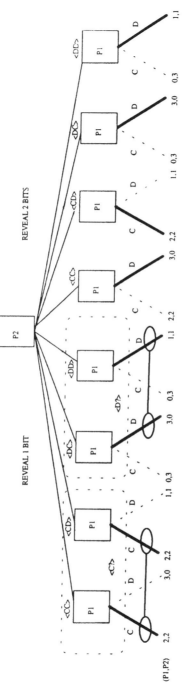

Figure 3. Variable communication (XPD2.5).

knows whether P2 is revealing all or only some, her choice can be conditioned on how candid P2 is. So P1 has to specify a response to six features (and so has 2^6 alternatives): the four original features ($\langle CC \rangle$, $\langle CD \rangle$, etc.) plus, in case only 1 bit is revealed, $\langle C? \rangle$ and $\langle D? \rangle$. (Notice how the leftmost pairs of choices are tied by connecting bars.)

The effect of restricting information is that P1 must choose between $\langle D \rangle$ and $\langle C \rangle$ in the leftmost information set $\langle C?; \rangle$ the more discriminating RCC component $\langle DC \rangle$ is no longer an option. This allows a P2 CC to throw its lot in with less discriminating UC, forcing P2 agents to cooperate or defect with both, as a class, thereby blocking RCC's cream-skimming exploitative strategy. So if C is the best choice in the first information set, CC, not RCC, will prevail.

But calculating an equilibrium strategy in this game is more complex than it was in the simpler XPD2 case. The effect of introducing partial information is to force agents to choose under uncertainty on the left hand side of the game. If P2 reveals $\langle C? \rangle$ only, and P1 chooses C, it can expect 2, but if it chooses D, it can expect $3p + (1-p)$, where p is the probability that P1 is hiding that it is an unconditional agent. Notice that uncertainty makes no difference in the second information set $\langle D? \rangle$ D dominates regardless of P2's choice. But in the first set, P1's choice depends on whether P2 has chosen $\langle CC \rangle$ or $\langle CD \rangle$, and P1 doesn't know this. This uncertainty undermines our ability to use simple backward induction to solve this game, since that procedure depends on fixing these expectations for any choice of P2. However, since unconditional cooperation (i.e., $\langle CC \rangle$) never does better than CD, and sometimes worse, we predict that there will be more $\langle CD \rangle$ than $\langle CC \rangle$. If P1 expects more $\langle CD \rangle$ than $\langle CC \rangle$, a C response is best. So we predict that the best strategy in this game for P1 will be $\langle CD \rangle \langle DCDD \rangle$, that is, CC if given less information, and RCC if given more. The best P2 strategy remains $\langle CD \rangle$, and the choice of revealing 1 or 2 bits of P2 strategy appears underdetermined, since either information strategy yields the same outcome, 2. Hence it is difficult to predict the outcome, even with the extended game before us.

2.4. Evolutionary Dynamics

We would like to consider a number of variations on CC strategies, as well as variations on RCC, that might do better. We can model our communicative agents by giving them extra bits to control the information they reveal, and then further bits to react to receiving more or less information. So a CC agent now looks like this:

(1) CD CCDD 0 CD

Move1 (partial)	Move1 (full)	Show all?	Move2
CD	CCDD	No (0)	CD
98	7654	3	21

The new bits are numbered 1–9 from the ¬ight. Bit 3 controls whether only the first (0) or both (1) of the Move2 bits are communicated.[14] If two are communicated, these select from the four bits at the front. If only one is communicated, they select from the two new bits at the very front. For example, our full-CC agent (1) sends only ⟨C?⟩ (due to bit 3) and reacts to this by cooperating (using bit 9). It also will cooperate if the other sends two bits, which include ⟨CC⟩ or ⟨CD⟩ (because of bits 7 and 6). This is not the only CC strategy. Consider these others:

    (2) CD CCDD 1 CD (CC-1)
    (3) CD CDDD 0 CD (CC-2)
    (4) CD CDDD 1 CD (CC-3)

RC also comes in different strengths.

    (5) DD CCDD 1 CD (RC-1)
    (6) DD DCDD 1 CD (full-RC)

Where (5) refuses to cooperate with 1-bit showers, and (6) is closer to RC, these two RCs refuse to cooperate with CCs that show only one bit. Conversely, this enforcer refuses to cooperate with RCC or CC that shows two bits:

    (7) CD DDDD 0 CD (enforcer)

The basic evolutionary model – the replicator dynamics – tests strategies by generating all possible strategies, testing them in interaction, building a new population by replicating strategies proportionally to their payoffs, and repeating this process. The process eliminates strategies that do poorly, and thus it also reduces the influence of strategies that do well only against strategies that do poorly. Unfortunately, given the extra bit to determine how much of Move2 to reveal and the extra 2 (for the two new information sets) to specify P1's move, there are 2^9 or 512 strategies to consider, which is too many for analysis of the replicator dynamics of the entire population. So we shall sketch the dynamics of an interesting subset of the population.

To test these strategies, we put them together in a small and balanced population of twelve agents, where ⅓ are P1 UC and ½ show one bit. The results are shown in Figure 4. The main results are encouraging. All four successful agents are broadly CC; they cooperate with any 1-bit cooperator.

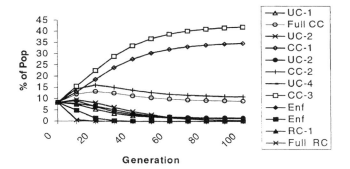

Figure 4. Dynamics of CC and RC.

Conversely, the RCs that would exploit 1-bit UCs fail. On the other hand, the most successful agents are CC-3 and CC-1, both of which tolerate 1-bit UCs but show two bits, so they do not fully support solidarity. CC-2 and full-CC, which do, come in third and fourth. And, not surprisingly, no strategy using UC in its P2 move survives.

3. Conclusions

Our conclusions from this partial analysis are encouraging. Our proposed communication strategy is not eliminated by evolution. However, solidarity does exact a cost, even in this selected population; the full-CC strategy appears to be weakly dominated. Finally, remember that this is a partial analysis, with a population that I selected. For example, it included two enforcers, which were quickly eliminated but kept the population of RC strategies down. These results need more general testing. In particular, revealing less is safer in our deception- and error-free models than in more realistic situations.[15]

Nonetheless, we can draw some further conclusions. First, our model of equivocation sheds new light on the topic of transparency. I had assumed, following Gauthier, that increased transparency would favor morality. This has proved naïve. One way to induce morally constrained behavior is to make *less* information available. This, of course, is not news to the contractarian tradition, one of whose central devices is the veil of ignorance, whereby lack of information induces rational choice of moral principles or outcomes. However, our device is not a veil of ignorance that would block information about herself from the agent doing the choosing. In contrast, our device keeps the chooser (P1) ignorant about her partner in interaction. Our device is quite rudimentary, yet in one respect it goes further than most in the contract tradition, by showing that imposing (partial) ignorance is itself motivated and effective even when merely a few agents use it. Some agents would individually choose to apply a filter to information about themselves and have all agents cooperate with others revealing less than full information.[16]

Second, we should separate the device from some complications introduced by our argument. To avoid begging the question about CC, we introduced our device in the larger context of a game that allowed both equivocal and full communication. We have argued that equivocal CC players do no worse in that game than any other strategy. But we do not wish to argue for the complex device that allows both full and equivocal communication. Given the pragmatic success of various CC strategies, including equivocators in the more complex game, we can propose that the simpler device of cooperative communication, for which simpler agents would suffice, would likely evolve and be stable. Moreover, for these simpler agents, equivocation is not an issue. Since they cannot reveal more, they do not reveal less by choice. (That choice was introduced for the sake of our argument.) They may be seen as having a simpler concept scheme that distinguishes P2 partners as cooperative or not.

Third, focusing on equivocation may mislead. We began with the moral appeal of more generous and tolerant conditional cooperation. This suggested the morally inspired strategy of solidarity – casting one's lot with the less fortunate.[17] Equivocal communication provides the means to this (intermediate) end in the setting of XPD games. But solidarity is the more general and morally more informed strategy that may, for these reasons, have application wider than the particular strategy of equivocal communication.

Finally, we return to LaCasse and Ross's moral skepticism with which we began. We have argued that the morally more attractive strategy, CC, can be made rational by introducing a partial-information strategy into the extended PD. But notice that in the XPD2.5, $\langle CD \rangle \langle DCDD \rangle * \langle CD \rangle$ is just the rational strategy, as RCC was in the XPD2. By LaCasse and Ross's analysis, one is no more moral than the other. This shows how little can be gleaned from the extended form of the game. The 9-bit game is one that allows more moral agents to be rationally selected, but in the extended game only the rational aspect of this double conclusion shows. Rationality remains crucial as the selector of players, but the task of generating the games they play falls elsewhere. We have suggested that moral theory can play a role here by suggesting morally structured dispositions and forms of communication and perception that can structure rationally stable but also morally acceptable forms of interaction.

Notes

1. Gauthier (1984, pp. 344–5), quoting Nietzsche (1967, p. 57).
2. Sobel (1996, p. 249, note 2) criticizes my basis in Gauthier's text for associating CC and CM. But as Gauthier (1988, p. 402) allows that the RC/CC distinction is useful to mark our difference, I shall persist with this simplifying move.
3. I have argued (Danielson 1988, 1992, p. 36) that there are ways around this indeterminacy, so conditional strategies can be applied to a less extended game. But this game still is not the one-shot PD, as a prior stage of mutual revelation of dispositions is needed. In this essay I shall discuss only the simpler extended game.
4. Danielson (1992, §2.1.2).
5. One can follow the argument using Gauthier and Binmore instead (Binmore 1994, §3.2.1).
6. This diagram combines notation from LaCasse and Ross (1998, p. 357, Figure 2) and Binmore (1994, p. 176, Figure 3.1) and my own notation. Since LaCasse and Ross are careful to consider several objections I might have to their representation, I should explicitly state that I accept it, and note that I am greatly simplifying their argument in this section.
7. This strategy is RCC, not RC, because it does not exploit UC when UC moves first (in role P1). The RCC name reflects the fact that it and CC have the same P2 component, namely ⟨CD⟩. CC's extra constraint is in the first bit of ⟨CCDD⟩, which selects C on the leftmost branch of the XPD2 tree.
8. Thanks to Joe Mintoff for the suggestion that LaCasse and Ross "beg the question" of morality.
9. With their emphasis on external devices (see pp. 370f.) to keep commitments, one suspects that LaCasse and Ross hold the middle position, but this is not part of the model under discussion. More could be said about this debate, but I have nothing to add to it here. See Gauthier (1984) and Lewis (1984)) and, more recently, Gauthier (1998) and Bratman (1998).
10. Perhaps this is the basis of Heath's suggestion (1996) that Gauthier must be assuming that his agents use telepathy, although he cites no evidence for such a narrow view of human abilities. More constructively, elsewhere (Danielson 1996, 1998) I show that for some ways of perceiving constraint in artificial agents, CC has an advantage, and with others, RC has.
11. On the assurance game, see Sen (1974).
12. *The American Heritage® Dictionary of the English Language*, 3rd ed., copyright © 1992 by Houghton Mifflin Company. Electronic version licensed from INSO Corporation. All rights reserved.
13. It is difficult to number this game; I call it XPD2.5 to avoid confusion with LaCasse and Ross's XPD3.
14. In addition, communicating none or only bit 1 could be added for a complete model. Thanks to Chris MacDonald for this suggestion.
15. We also need to explore the consequences of withholding information on a richer model, which includes, for example, Gauthier's bargaining procedure. We have simplified, in effect, by labeling an outcome as cooperative, but in a richer model agents would need to calculate the features of outcomes. If they need information about the non-cooperative outcomes, this may conflict with withholding information. For example, in a game without several cooperative outcomes, an agent may need to know what the other would do in the event of D to discover whether or not the particular cooperative outcome offered is fair.

16. Game models of ethics usually assume that cooperative agents favor more information. An instructive example is that of Orbell et al. (1996), who investigate the contrast between two decision procedures for the optional PD: *projecting* one's own strategy on the other player versus *predicting* the other player's strategy. When they discuss the effect of allowing deception into the model, they assume, as is common, that "dissembling is particularly useful for those intending defection" (p. 96). This is true, but given their main result, that populations of cooperative projectors may be invaded by perceptive agents, projectors have an indirect interest in blocking perceptive players' discrimination. This is similar to CC's indirect interest in blocking RCC's discrimination. Of course, CC and RCC are both perceptive in Orbell's terms, but the point remains: The additional information that RCC requires may be denied to block RCC's exploitation of others. Similarly, less cooperative projective strategies might not provide the information that perceptive strategies need to exploit more cooperative projective strategies.

17. Hegselmann (1996) models a richer conception of solidarity as cooperation in spite of differing risks for needing aid.

References

Binmore, K. (1994). *Game Theory and the Social Contract. Vol 1: Playing Fair* (Cambridge, MA: MIT Press).

Bratman, M. (1998). "Following Through with One's Plans: Reply to David Gauthier," in *Modeling Rationality, Morality, and Evolution*, ed. P. Danielson (Oxford University Press), pp. 55–66.

Danielson, P. (1988). "The Visible Hand of Morality." *Canadian Journal of Philosophy* 18: 357–84.

(1992). *Artificial Morality* (London: Routledge).

(1996). "Evolving Artificial Moralities: Genetic Strategies, Spontaneous Orders, and Moral Catastrophe," in *Chaos and Society*, ed. A. Albert (Amsterdam: IOS Press), pp. 329–44.

(1998). "Evolutionary Models of Cooperative Mechanisms: Artificial Morality and Genetic Programming," in *Modeling Rationality, Morality, and Evolution*, ed. P. Danielson (Oxford University Press), pp. 423–41.

(Forthcoming) "How to Evolve Rationality and Something Better," in *Twentieth Century Values*, ed. K. F. T. Cust (Lanham, MD: University Press of America).

Gauthier, D. (1984). "Deterrence, Maximization, and Rationality," in *The Security Gamble: Deterrence Dilemmas in the Nuclear Age*, ed. D. MacLean (Totowa, NJ: Rowman & Allanheld), pp. 101–22.

(1986). *Morals by Agreement* (Oxford University Press).

(1988). "Moral Artifice." *Canadian Journal of Philosophy* 18: 385–418.

(1998). "Intention and Deliberation," in *Modeling Rationality, Morality, and Evolution*, ed. P. Danielson (Oxford University Press), pp. 41–54.

Heath, J. (1996). "A Multi-Stage Game Model of Morals by Agreement." *Dialogue* 35:529–52.

Hegselmann, R. (1996). "Social Dilemmas in Lineland and Flatland," in *Frontiers in Social Dilemmas Research*, ed. W. Liebrand and D. Messick (Berlin: Springer), pp. 337–61.

Howard, N. (1971). *Paradoxes of Rationality* (Cambridge, MA: MIT Press).

LaCasse, C., and D. Ross (1998). "Morality's Last Chance," in *Modeling Rationality, Morality, and Evolution*, ed. P. Danielson (Oxford University Press), pp. 340–75.

Lewis, D. (1984). "Devil's Bargains and the Real World," in *The Security Gamble: Deterrence Dilemmas in the Nuclear Age*, ed. D. MacLean (Totowa, NJ: Rowman & Allanheld), pp. 141–54.

Nietzsche, F. (1967). *On the Genealogy of Morals* (New York: Random House).

Orbell, J., A. Runde, et al. (1996). "The Robustness of Cognitively Simple Judgment in Ecologies of Prisoner's Dilemma Games." *BioSystems* 37:81–97.

Sen, A. (1974). "Choice, Orderings and Morality," in *Practical Reason*, ed. S. Korner (Oxford: Blackwell), pp. 54–67.

Skyrms, B. (1996). *Evolution of the Social Contract* (Cambridge University Press).

Sobel, J. (1996). "Must Constrained Maximizers Be Uncharitable?" *Dialogue* 35:241–54.

Taylor, M. (1987). *The Possibility of Cooperation* (Cambridge University Press).

The Strategy of Cooperation

EDWARD F. McCLENNEN

1. Introduction

Starting with Adam Smith, and running like a bright thread throughout virtually all the subsequent theoretical literature on political economy, one can mark a preoccupation with the conditions under which public structures can emerge that will permit individuals to cooperatively transact with one another to their mutual advantage.[1] The good news that there are in fact conditions under which such structures do emerge has to be tempered, however, by the bad news (1) that historical processes of institutional development tend to be path-dependent in ways that work against adaptive efficiency and (2) that virtually all institutional arrangements are subject to manipulation by special interests, to the short-term advantage of some, but often to the long-term disadvantage of all.[2] Recent work in political economy has in fact identified deep pressures on human interaction that tend to prevent anything like the full realization of the mutual gains that cooperation can make possible. A truly optimal arrangement would seem, then, to be an ideal that is remote from social reality.

In one sense, there should be nothing surprising about this. After all, the historical record hardly supports any other picture. What is surprising, however, is that many of these conclusions are driven by models of *ideally* rational beings who have substantial and common knowledge of each other's rationality and preferences and the strategic structure of their interactions. On the accounts offered, Pareto-suboptimality does not flow just from assuming that some are less than fully rational, or possess limited or asymmetrical knowledge. Mutually disadvantageous free-riding and conflict over the distribution of goods are taken to be natural to the way in which even hyper-rational and fully informed individuals interact.

This raises the questions that I want to address in this essay: How does it happen that even thoroughly rational and knowledgeable agents manage to do worse rather than better? And should we not consider, then, whether a better model might not be provided for ideally rational agents?

What I shall argue here is that the standard models of rationality fail to provide a basis for something that is essential to really effective cooperative interaction between individuals. This is for such individuals to have a commitment to act in accordance with rules, to see their mutual arrangements as defining a practice that calls for principled as distinct from purely strategic choice.[3] I shall also suggest how the standard account of rationality can be modified so as to allow for such a commitment. The proposal I shall make for modifying the standard model is parallel to, and very much in the spirit of, the one proposed by Gauthier (1986). Like Gauthier, I shall argue that thoroughly rational persons are capable, under appropriate conditions, of constraining their natural disposition to maximize, and to choose instead to act in compliance with (mutually agreed upon) rules. Whereas Gauthier seeks to establish this by appeal to the principle of utility maximization adjusted to the level of choice among dispositions to choose, I want to motivate our shared conclusion in a somewhat different way, by exploring, first, how purely cooperative situations might be reconceptualized.

2. Schelling's Model of Cooperative Interaction

My ultimate objective is to offer an alternative model of rational, interactive choice that will apply to dynamic, ongoing interaction, involving a mixture of conflict and cooperation, and taking place under conditions that approximate to real-life situations. It will prove useful to begin, however, as most other theorists have, with simple one-stage cooperative games, and, in particular, with a special class of such games, namely, *pure-coordination* games. The *locus classicus* for how to think about such games is to be found in Schelling's *The Strategy of Conflict*. Here is one of his examples of such a game:

You are to meet somebody in New York City. You have not been instructed where to meet; you have no prior understanding with the person on where to meet; and you cannot communicate with each other. You are simply told that you will have to guess where to meet and that he is being told the same thing and that you will just have to try to make your guesses coincide. (1960, p. 56)

Here there are only two relevant outcomes: You and the other person meet up, or you do not meet up. Meeting up has the strong property that it is *maximally preferred* by each: There is no other outcome that *either* player prefers to this one.

It is the presence of multiple pairs of strategies, all of which will yield a maximally preferred outcome, plus the restriction on communication, that defines what Schelling and others take to be the pure-coordination-game *problem*. Given a common understanding of the structure of the game and each participant's preferences with regard to outcomes, if there is a unique set of strategy choices, one for each player, whose outcome is maximally preferred by each, then there is an obvious choice for each: Do one's part to ensure the realization of that outcome. Schelling does not explicitly make this point in the context of pure-coordination games. But he does argue it explicitly in connection with mixed games. His illustration is that of a game involving reciprocal fear of surprise attack:

	Attack	Don't attack
Attack	0, 0	.5, −.5
Don't attack	−.5, .5	1, 1

Game 1

Mutual refraining in this instance results in what is maximally preferred by each, and this, he suggests, suffices to resolve the game:

> ... part of our behavioral hypothesis is that, if the two players both perceive that a joint policy of no-attack is the best of all possible outcomes for both of them, they will recognize this "solution" and elect to abstain. . . . This seems to be a fairly modest demand on the rationality of the two players. (p. 210)

Correspondingly, the existence of multiple pairs of strategies whose outcomes are maximally preferred by each player poses no problem if they can communicate with one another, for in this case they have only to agree on which of the indifferently valued pairs to coordinate upon, and then proceed to execute that agreement.

Suppose, then, as in the example given, communication is ruled out, and there are many pairs of strategies that will yield maximally preferred outcomes. That is, any one of many meeting points will do, so long as both go there. How, then, to coordinate on one of them? Schelling's own, and much-discussed, proposal is to appeal to considerations of psychological saliency, which the players can use as a signal to effect a coordination of their strategies. That approach, however, presupposes that one can provide a precise characterization of the set of qualifying strategy pairs upon which principles of saliency will operate. It is this feature of Schelling's theory that needs to be examined with care.

Within the main text of *The Strategy of Conflict*, no such precise characterization is explicitly given. In Chapter 4, Schelling begins by modeling the way in which a player would deliberate, given a belief that there is common knowledge of the rationality, preferences, and choices of each participating agent, and perhaps also, at least in some cases, certain psychological "cues." Such a situation, he argues, calls for strategic deliberation – for recognition that the "best" choice of action for a player depends on what that player expects the other player to do, and where the choice of the other is guided by similar considerations:

. . . the pure-coordination game is a game of strategy in the strict technical sense. It is a behavior situation in which each player's *best choice of action* depends on the action he *expects* the other to take, which he knows depends, in turn, on the other's expectations of his own. This interdependence of expectations is precisely what distinguishes a game of strategy from a game of chance or a game of skill. In the pure-coordination game the interests are convergent; in the pure conflict game the interests are divergent; but in neither case can a choice of action be made *wisely* without regard to the dependence of the outcome on the mutual expectations of the players. (p. 86, emphasis added)

Successful coordination, on this account, will involve a convergence of choice and expectation: What each expects the other to choose is what the other does choose. But no specification is offered at this point as to what is to count as a "best" or "wise" strategy.[4]

3. Some Basic Properties of Pure-Coordination Games

Before turning to examine how Schelling chooses to characterize the solution to a pure-coordination game, it will prove helpful to briefly summarize the pertinent logical features of such games. To return to Schelling's basic example, any pair of strategies that results in meeting up yields an outcome that both strictly prefer to what would result from not meeting up. That is, it yields an outcome that Pareto-dominates the other outcome. But, since not meeting up is the only other relevant outcome, any such pair of strategies yields an outcome that Pareto-dominates every other possible outcome. Second, every such pair of meeting-up strategies is in equilibrium. Each strategy in such a pair maximizes the preferences of the player choosing that strategy, given that the other player chooses the counterpart strategy in the same pair. We can generalize here. For *any* pure-coordination game, we can establish all of the following:

(1) By definition, a game of pure coordination is one in which the preferences of the two players over alternative possible outcomes completely coincide. If one player weakly prefers an outcome o_i to another outcome o_j then the other player also weakly prefers o_i to o_j.

(2) There exists at least one outcome that is Pareto-optimal and Pareto-efficient relative to what each could expect to transpire, if no coordination takes place.

(3) Any pair of strategies that yields a Pareto-optimal outcome is an equilibrium pair.[5] The converse, of course, is not necessarily true: A strategy pair can be in equilibrium without its outcome being Pareto-optimal.

(4) If we identify the outcome that it is reasonable to expect that players will be able to achieve in the absence of any effective coordination of

their strategies, then any Pareto-optimal outcome is also Pareto-efficient relative to that "non-coordination" outcome. More generally, whatever is taken as the benchmark point that represents what each can achieve without coordination, every Pareto-optimal outcome is also Pareto-efficient relative to that point.[6]

(5) There may be, of course, many outcomes that are Pareto-optimal, but they are all equivalently ranked by both players. This means that there is no distributive issue that arises in the context of games of pure coordination.

As one might expect, these findings have led theorists to focus their attention on equilibrium and optimality pairs as potential components of a conception of a rational solution to a game of pure coordination. But it should also be noted that these findings do not yet tell us just how equilibrium and optimality considerations are to be dealt with vis-à-vis one another in the framing of such a solution concept. Indeed, it is not until we reach Appendix C that we learn how Schelling thinks the concept of a solution should be formally spelled out. There Schelling begins by making reference to a much wider class of games, namely non-zero-sum games, and to the Luce and Raiffa (1957) characterization of a "solution in the strict sense" for such games. Such a game is said to have a solution in the strict sense *iff* (1) there exists an equilibrium pair among the jointly admissible strategy pairs *and* (2) all jointly admissible equilibrium pairs are both interchangeable and equivalent. A strategy pair is jointly admissible if and only if there exists no alternative pair such that both players would prefer its outcome to the outcome of the pair in question. That is, joint admissibility is Pareto-optimality. What this concept of a solution invokes, then, as one might expect, are the *dual* conditions of Pareto-optimality and equilibrium.[7] If the set of equilibrium pairs is disjoint from the set of Pareto-optimal pairs, the game is not solvable in the strict sense. What if there are multiple pairs that are both in equilibrium and optimal? Solvability then hinges on whether or not the Pareto-optimal equilibrium pairs are interchangeable and equivalent.[8] Schelling suggests that the interchangeability requirement is introduced by Luce and Raiffa to rule out *confusion* in the case of non-unique jointly admissible equilibrium pairs (p. 292). Just such confusion, he goes on to argue, lies at the heart of pure-coordination games. That is, these are games that do not have a solution in the strict sense. And it is just where solvability in this sense fails to obtain that Schelling thinks the notion of saliency can be usefully invoked.

This discussion of the Luce and Raiffa concept of "strict solvability" tells us that for Schelling the solution to a pure coordination game is to be characterized as an equilibrium point that has certain other features, specifically, one that is Pareto-optimal.[9] But the only argument offered as to why being in equilibrium is a necessary condition of being a solution comes in a footnote (p. 96, fn. 12) that discusses the difference between the intellectual processes involved in games of pure conflict and games of pure coordination. There Schelling discusses a particular *mixed* game (involving both conflict and cooperation) and remarks that the game "has no equilibrium point; interests do not converge" (p. 97). But this is not followed up by any analysis of why convergence can take place only at an equilibrium point.

4. The Need for an Even More Ambitious Reorientation of Game Theory

In the pivotal chapter of *The Strategy of Conflict* (Ch. 4, "Towards a Theory of Interdependent Decision"), Schelling argues that while game theory (as conceptualized up to that point) has yielded important insights concerning games of pure conflict, it has had little to offer by way of insights into non-zero-sum games, games in which some sort of collaboration or coordination is needed, if only to ensure the avoidance of disaster. The theme note struck there is that game theory needs to be reoriented. One must recognize that there is not just one limiting case, but rather two limiting cases – the case of pure coincidence of interest as well as the case of pure conflict of interest – and that the intellectual process of choosing a strategy in a pure-coordination game is something quite distinct from that of choosing a strategy in the case of a game of pure conflict of interest:

. . . if *pursuit* epitomizes the zero-sum game, *rendez vous* may do the same thing for the coordination game. (p. 85)

This contrast is re-emphasized just a few pages later:

. . . it becomes increasingly clear that the intellectual [processes] of choosing a strategy in pure conflict and choosing a strategy of coordination are of wholly different sorts. . . . In the pure-coordination game, the player's objective is to make contact with the other player through some imaginative process of introspection, of searching for shared clues; in the minimax strategy of a zero-sum game – most strikingly so with randomized choice – one's whole objective is to avoid any meeting of minds, even an inadvertent one. (p. 96)

Correspondingly, the mixed game is to be seen as requiring for its analysis both the perspectives appropriate to games of pure conflict of interest and those of pure coordination. On Schelling's own account, what the theory of coordination games contributes is the role played by "perceptual and sugges-tive elements" (psychological saliency) *and* various strategies involving threats, enforcement, and the manipulation of communication.

Despite the extraordinarily interesting and helpful analysis of these neglected features of many games, the reorientation that is effected falls short, I think, of what is needed. The theory that emerges has not much to say about how consideration of the possibility of mutual gain, and the avoidance of mutual loss, can motivate persons. This impacts significantly on the kind of theory that emerges for the case of mixed games of conflict and cooperation. What Schelling has crafted is a theory that sets the stage for what became the paradigmatic way to think about interaction in general, namely, as a process in which "non-cooperative" dimensions play the central role.[10]

Consider once again a game of pure coordination. What shapes one's strategic problem in this kind of game? As Schelling himself argues, the organizing idea is not avoidance but rendezvous. Failure on the part of the other to correctly anticipate what one is going to do proves costly to oneself (as well as to the other player). Thus one has an interest in a meeting of minds. But one's task is not just to achieve a meeting of minds, but one that avoids a suboptimal outcome. If coordination takes place on a suboptimal outcome, then there must be some other outcome such that coordination on it would be preferred by one of the players and not dispreferred by the other. But by the assumption that it is a pure-coordination game, in which there is complete coincidence of preferences, if there is another outcome that is preferred by one of them, then it is preferred by both of them. To settle for a meeting of minds on a suboptimal outcome, then, is to settle for less than one could have, under conditions in which the other player is also settling for less than he or she could have. Both, that is, forgo an opportunity, which both players would prefer, and in the absence of a special reason why they should collectively forgo such a mutually preferred outcome, passing up such an opportunity would be irrational. Recast in positive terms, any given player is naturally motivated to seek a more, rather than less, preferred outcome. But, in a game of pure coordination an outcome's being more preferred than another by one player means that it is also more preferred by the other player. It is thus plausible to suppose that cooperation will be forthcoming from the other, if only signals permit a convergence of choice and expectation. That is, each player realizes that he or she cannot achieve a more preferred outcome unless the other does also, and unless the two players can coordinate. Thus a player is led to explore what cues each can exploit in parallel fashion to effect that coordination.

Notice also that in a pure-coordination game a given player has an interest not only in choosing an appropriate strategy but also in the other player choosing appropriately as well – for only then will the two end up meeting, end up coordinating on an outcome that will be maximally preferred by each. Suppose the first player has decided that a particular pair of strategies is salient, and thus thinks it reasonable to expect that it can be the focus of attention for both players. By definition of a pure-coordination game, the first player could not hope to do better if the second player chose any other strategy, for in that case the outcome of the salient combination of strategies would not be maximally preferred by the first player. If the first player expects to do just as well if the second player chooses some other strategy, then the first player will be indifferent as to which of the two (or more) strategies in question the second player chooses, but the first player will still be concerned that the second chooses in such a way that an outcome maximally preferred by each is achieved. But clearly the first player has this concern in any case in which it is possible that the first player will do worse if the second player chooses to play otherwise. Thus the first player not only has an interest in how he or she chooses, but also in the two of them meeting up.

I conclude, then, that the appropriate concern for a rational players in a game of pure cooperation is to coordinate strategies so that the outcome will satisfy the Pareto condition. It is true, of course, that outcomes satisfying the Pareto condition satisfy the equilibrium condition. But from the perspective of the strategic problem that players face in a game of pure coordination, this additional property is purely accidental. That is, the equilibrium concept adds nothing that illuminates the nature of the deliberation that persons face in such games. In this context, it does no work.

Not only does being concerned to achieve an equilibrium seem out of place in a theory of pure-coordination games, concerning what it means to intend to coordinate on a desired outcome, but also reliance upon the reasoning behind it appears to be out of keeping with the basic orientation that von Neumann and Morgenstern (1953) adopted for the analysis of games in general. At the very outset of their landmark work, they argue that one encounters a conceptual, as distinct from a technical, difficulty in moving from the study of the isolated individual (the proverbial Robinson Crusoe) to the study of interacting persons. Crusoe's task, given his wants and resources, amounts to a simple maximization problem, complicated at most by the need to incorporate probabilistically defined outcomes. In the case of social interaction, however,

... the result for each will depend in general not merely upon his own action but on those of the others as well. Thus each participant attempts to maximize a function ... of which he does not control all the variables. (p. 11)

This poses a problem that cannot be overcome simply by appeal to probabilities and expectations:

Every participant can determine the variables which describe his own actions but not those of the others. Nevertheless these "alien" variables cannot, from his point of view, be described by statistical assumptions. This is because the others are guided, just as himself, by rational principles – whatever that may mean – and no *modus procedendi* can be correct which does not attempt to understand those principles and the interactions of the conflicting interests of all participants. (p. 11)

Picking up on this crucial point, Karl Kaysen (1946–47), in a very early review of von Neumann and Morgenstern's work, argues that in the case of games,

> ... there is no possibility of what we have called parametrization that would enable each agent (player) to behave as if the actions of the others were given. In fact, *it is this very lack of parametrization which is the essence of a game.* (p. 2, emphasis added)

But the way in which the equilibrium requirement has been made central to a theory of games, as exemplified by the *a priori* argument to which Luce and Raiffa appeal (1957, pp. 63–4), involves solving the problem of choice in the context of a game by assuming, in effect, that under the stated conditions, contrary to von Neumann and Morgenstern's suggestion, parametrization is possible. The assumption is that if there is a well-worked-out theory of rational interdependent choice, then a rational player will be able to anticipate what the other player(s) will do, and an appropriate stance for the rational player to then take will be to maximize against that expectation of how the others will choose. But that simply begs the question in favor of a denial of the very point that von Neumann and Morgenstern insisted upon, that the essence of a game is that such parametrization is not possible.[11]

My conclusion is that Schelling's call for a reorientation of game theory is most appropriately realized by a theory that makes the set of Pareto-optimal outcomes, and not pairs of strategies in equilibrium, the focus of the attention of rational players in a pure coordination game. Stated somewhat more carefully, the following would seem to be basic to a theory of pure-coordination games:

> *The Pareto condition.* Rational agents who know each other to be such will, *ceteris paribus*, confine their choices to strategies that can, in combination with the choices of the other agent(s), generate outcomes that will be Pareto-optimal and Pareto-efficient relative to what each could expect to be the outcome were neither player to attempt to coordinate with the other.[12]

Focusing on the set of outcomes satisfying the Pareto condition leaves in place all of what Schelling has to say about the role of psychological salience. Within the framework of the pure-coordination game, where there is a barrier to communication, there is a need for some way of sorting through the alternative combinations that satisfy the Pareto conditions. This model also leaves in place their notion of a process by which expectations are drawn to a focus. Suppose that there is common knowledge of each other's rationality, as well as the strategy and payoff structure of the game, and that both players perceive their task as effectively coordinating their choices so as to achieve what is mutually perceived to be a best outcome. Suppose, in addition, that there is a strategy combination (r_i, c_j) that is salient among the multiple combinations that satisfy the Pareto conditions. To say that (r_i, c_j) is salient is to say that Row expects Column to choose c_j, and that Column expects Row to choose r_i. And given such an expectation on the part of each, and an understanding that the task is to coordinate on a combination that satisfies the Pareto conditions, Row now has a reason for choosing r_i, and Column has a reason for choosing c_j. Moreover, each can replicate the reasoning of the other. It is because (r_i, c_j) is salient that each expects the other to play for this combination. But then each also expects that the other expects that they will play for this combination, etc., etc. Finally, just as on the standard account, coordinated choice involves conditional strategies: One's best choice depends upon what one expects the other player to do. There can be no *coordination* of choices unless the each party seeks to anticipate what the other party will do. But it is not part of the logic of this alternative model that one expects that the other player will unilaterally choose to maximize utility in response to what one does, any more than that one is required to always choose so as to maximize utility in response to what one expects the other to do.

5. Extending the Argument to Mixed Games

The graph of a game of pure conflict of interest (with utility payoffs to the two players on the horizontal and vertical axes) consists in a set of points that lie on a straight line with negative slope (i.e., it has only NW–SE dimensionality). The graph of a game of pure coordination consists in a set of points that lie in a straight line with positive slope (i.e., it has only NE–SW dimensionality). Every game that lies in between these two extremes, including the prisoners' dilemma game, is a mixed-motive game, which involves, then, both a conflictual dimension and a cooperative dimension. The graph of such a game consists in a set of points that has both NE–SW and NW–SE dimensionality. The potential for cooperation is to be found in its NE–SW dimensionality, and the potential for conflict in its NW–SE dimensionality.

The potential for mutual gain or loss does not correspond, of course, to any particular player's potential for gain or loss. One may be able to gain by being able to effect a NW–SE dimensional shift in outcome (in which case, one's gain is matched by a loss on the part of the other player). Within this framework, moreover, there is no simplistic identification of cooperative, as distinct from conflictual, interaction with whether or not the gains from coordination are shared equally. The potential for mutual gain is defined by the fact that the game has NE–SW dimensionality. Coordination could result in any number of different outcomes, each of which would improve the position of each player, relative to some specified status quo situation, but each one of which would have different distributive implications.[13]

Let us, however, abstract for now from this dimension of a mixed-motive game.[14] The simplest way to do that is to confine attention to games in which, when agents cooperate, they do so on distributive terms that are not subject to negotiation, but are fixed by the structure of, or the rules defining, the interactive situation. Specifically, one can specify that the game is a simple one-off, simultaneous-choice game in which no side-payments are allowed. By way of a first, and diagnostically important, example of a mixed game to which the proposed model can be applied, consider the following matrix:

$$
\begin{array}{c|cc}
 & c_1 & c_2 \\
\hline
r_1 & 1,1 & 0,1 \\
r_2 & 1,0 & 0,0 \\
\end{array}
$$

Game 3

All pairs of choices are in equilibrium, but each such equilibrium is a weak equilibrium. From the standpoint of the standard theory, there is nothing that a player can do to improve his or her payoff: Both strategies have the same expected return, regardless of how the other player chooses. Correspondingly, the *ex ante* expected return to each is $1/2$.[15] But on the alternative model, the Pareto conditions call for coordination on (r_1, c_1), for an expected return to each of 1. Of course, (r_1, c_1) is also an equilibrium. Thus, the issue between the standard theory and the proposed alternative is not yet joined.

It is, however, joined once we turn to consider the standard prisoners' dilemma game, where once again it is specified that no side-payments are allowed, by appeal to which the two parties can negotiate how the benefits are to be distributed:

$$
\begin{array}{c|cc}
 & c_1 & c_2 \\
\hline
r_1 & 3,3 & 1,4 \\
r_2 & 4,1 & 2,2 \\
\end{array}
$$

Game 4

The claim I want to advance is that the alternative model of coordination presented earlier plausibly extends to this case as well. That is, here, no less than in the case of a pure-coordination game, ideally rational persons who have common knowledge of their rationality and the game they are playing will be disposed to cooperate to ensure a Pareto-efficient and Pareto-optimal outcome. What this means is that rational agents who know each other to be such will not confine their attention to equilibrium combinations of choices. Specifically, if parametric or equilibrium reasoning leads to a suboptimal outcome, and there is an unambiguous combination of coordinated choices that is Pareto-efficient relative to the equilibrium outcome, then they will coordinate on it. Thus, for example, the revised model holds that in Game 4 rational players will choose to cooperate with one another and coordinate on (r_1, c_1), even though this pair is not in equilibrium.[16]

There is another natural extension of the model. Suppose that there is not a unique alternative satisfying the Pareto conditions, but rather a number of alternatives between which the agents are indifferent. If communication is not possible, we may suppose, in keeping with Schelling's own analysis, that successful coordination will turn on considerations of psychological saliency. But suppose instead that the agents can communicate with one another and that they agree on a coordination scheme. The proposed model of rational coordination implies that this scheme will be regulative of the choices that each then makes, despite the fact that it does not prescribe an equilibrium set of choices for the participants.

6. Extending the Argument to Dynamic Contexts

With this last remark we are now in a position to extend the argument to extensive games, in which the choices of the players are sequentially ordered. It has always been recognized that the principle of dominance that is appropriate (on at least the standard way of thinking) to simultaneous-choice games does not necessarily apply in sequential-choice games. If one chooses first, one may be able, by selecting a dominated strategy, to induce the player who chooses second to make a choice that will yield one a greater payoff than could be secured by playing the dominating strategy. Correspondingly, the concept of a simple (Nash) equilibrium must be reformulated if it is to apply in a dynamic context.

On the alternative model proposed here, however, there is a much more radical reconceptualization of rational choice. Within the context of games in which there is an outcome that uniquely satisfies the Pareto conditions, and under conditions of common knowledge, Pareto considerations will prevail. In particular, then, under conditions of common knowledge, rational players will cooperate in one-shot *sequential* prisoner's dilemma games.[17]

Most importantly, however, the alternative model has significant implications for more realistic settings of ongoing, open-ended interaction, where the idealizing assumption of common knowledge will have to be relaxed. This sort of setting is the focus of the recent "folk theorems" concerning indefinitely repeated games. Here the question of assurance is bound to loom large, even for agents who are, as fully rational beings, otherwise predisposed to cooperate. What is characteristic of indefinitely iterated games is that multiple (sub-game-perfect) equilibria can be identified, equilibria that typically are Pareto-suboptimal, while combinations of strategies that do satisfy the Pareto conditions are not sub-game-perfect equilibria. Now, intuitively, the fact that any given player will repeatedly encounter other members of the group suggests that it should be possible for them to work out, tacitly or explicitly, coordination schemes that would ensure that they would not have to settle each time for a mutually disadvantageous equilibrium.

But the commitment that the folk theorems make to the standard theory of rationality means that in this iterated framework there can be no assurance that rational individuals will voluntarily comply with such coordination schemes. It is precisely voluntary compliance with the rules or practices that define such coordination schemes that the standard account of rationality cannot accommodate. Parametric reasoners cannot make even this very modest sort of commitment to act in accordance with a practice or rule. For such a reasoner, the only consequentially defensible policy will be a flexible policy of making exceptions to following the rules, whenever allowing for such exceptions contributes to the realization of the very ends for which that reasoner agreed to coordinate his or her actions with others. On this account, rules are to be understood as maxims – rules of thumb. The only relevant question will be whether the expected utility of acting in conformity with that plan or rule is greater than the benefits to be secured by deviating. But since each will be disposed then to free-ride on the coordination commitments of the others, they typically will have to arrange to have the coordination scheme backed up by some sort of enforcement device.[18] And since enforcement devices typically are costly, their arrangement typically will constitute only a second-best way to realize the gains that cooperation can make possible.

The work in this area is quite technical and not easy to summarize, but, very roughly speaking, a number of different types of sanction systems can be distinguished. An *informal* arrangement (expressing a norm of reciprocity) may emerge in which each participant is motivated to conform to a cooperative agreement governing pairwise interactions by an expectation that defection will be met by retaliations whenever that same partner is encountered again, retaliation whose expected costs outweigh the immediate gains to be secured by defection. These results are, however, sensitive to the probability that one will encounter the same player again, one's discount for the future, and the severity of the loss involved in having that other player refuse to cooperate on future encounters. Some of these limitations can be overcome if there is more widespread reporting and punishment of defectors, specifically if there is an *informal institutional* arrangement under which others in the community will also retaliate against anyone identified as a defector. This presupposes, in turn, some sort of communication system between the participants, so that all members of the group can identify the defectors. Since the costs of such a communication system are non-negligible, efficient community (as distinct from individual) enforcement typically will require the centralization of the reporting system (as, for example, takes place in the case of a centralized credit bureau reporting system). Finally, of course, one may sustain cooperation by employing *formal institutional* arrangements, that is, an enforcement mechanism involving third-party surveillance and apprehension, and a legal system dispensing appropriate punishments. What has become increasingly clear, however, is that whichever method of enforcement is employed, there are significant associated costs of surveillance and enforcement. A central concern, then, becomes that of comparative costs of alternative schemes.[19]

Notice also that within the iterated game context, it is almost inevitable that there will be any number of different arrangements that could be reached, differing from one another in terms of their distributive implications. The formal work in this area, however, does not address this problem at all. The thrust of the theorems is simply to establish that if there are outcomes that are Pareto-superior to what could be expected to be the outcome of purely non-cooperative interaction, there will exist ways to arrange sanctions such that any one of those Pareto-superior outcomes can be achieved as a result of a strategic plan that satisfies appropriate equilibrium conditions.

Against this background, the proposed alternative model of rational interaction carries significant conceptual implications. We are now in a position to return to a theme introduced in the opening section – that of the rationality of rule- or practice-governed choice. Within the context of ongoing interaction between individuals, we need not suppose any longer that individuals will have to use cues of psychological saliency in order to "tacitly" coordinate on mutually advantageous outcomes. With the extension of the proposed alternative model of coordination to cases in which there is ongoing interaction between individuals, we can now suppose that such individuals can explicitly agree upon various coordination schemes, and with this, sense can now be made of a quite different way to think about rule-governed choice. Within that context we can imagine persons who are capable of tacitly or explicitly identifying a coordination scheme and then choosing in a rule-governed manner, even when that choice is not supported by standard (expected) utility-maximizing considerations. For such persons, the central question is *not*, What available alternative is mandated by expected utility reasoning? Rather, it is, What course of action is called for here, given some coordination scheme on which we have explicitly agreed?

This also means that we can recover the more commonsense notion of the rationality of being trustworthy. Despite the way in which most decision theorists proceed – see, for example, Hardin (1993) – we can insist, following

Morris (1999), that trustworthiness among agents is not something that is secured by establishing conditions under which conformity to some rule is utility-maximizing for each agent, given how each other agent chooses (i.e., it is not just a matter of ensuring that the coordination scheme is in equilibrium). On the contrary, trustworthiness involves being rule-governed in one's choice behavior.

But, even more importantly, there are consequential implications. The persons described in this alternative model will be able to voluntarily guide their choices by certain (agreed upon) arrangements, and thus they can secure the gains to be associated with not having to expend scarce resources on enforcing such agreements. These are benefits that could be distributed among the participants in such a way that every participant would be a gainer. That is, for virtually any cooperative arrangement that can be achieved in the way described in the folk theorems (by organized systems of surveillance and sanction), a counterpart system of voluntary compliance can be described whose costs to the representative participating individual will be less, and hence which will be Pareto-superior to the arrangement established by the folk theorem.

This takes us part of the way toward the conclusion that a system of voluntary compliance is rational. But it remains to consider that the disposition to be rule-guided in one's choice, whose credentials as a rational disposition I have been concerned to establish here, must be understood as a *conditional* disposition. Within the context of "ideal," one-shot games, the assurance problem was resolved (if you will, quite artificially) by the framework assumption of common knowledge. The question now, however, is whether or not the case for resolute cooperation can be extended to more realistic settings, where the issue of assurance is pressing.

As it turns out, the iterated game framework provides a setting in which the epistemological problem of assurance can be resolved. If interaction is sufficiently ongoing, then for many kinds of encounters, a given individual can have the requisite assurance regarding the dispositions of other participants. The history of past encounters between participants typically will provide the needed information. It is plausible to suppose, moreover, that for many such contexts, the requisite information will be securable from anecdotal sources – that is, it will be unnecessary to resort to formal mechanisms for the compiling and transmission of this information. At the "street level," each typically will be able to consult personal experience and informally shared information with friends and family members to determine whether or not the level of voluntary cooperation in more impersonal, "public" settings has been great enough to warrant voluntary compliance on one's own part.[20]

The recent work on the folk theorems of iterated games, then, prepares the ground for a significant extension of the alternative model. It describes a whole range of much more realistic settings within which one can expect, following the standard line of reasoning, not only that various surveillance and enforcement systems will emerge but also that conditions will be right for the emergence of purely voluntary systems of cooperation.

7. Summarizing the Argument

The problem of coordination characteristically calls for one to think about how to meet up with another, and not simply maximize against one's best estimate of what the other is likely to choose. That point carries over to the problem of coordination that is posed by mixed games, as discussed in Section 5, but in that context a quite distinct consideration emerges to militate against the standard model. Agents who deliberate in the standard manner do less well than those who can interact with one another in the manner described in the alternative model. Under both the ideal conditions discussed in Sections 4 and 5 and the more dynamic and realistic settings discussed in Sections 6 and 7, the standard theory implies that compliance typically will require a comparatively costly system of surveillance and sanctions in order to ensure that participants will abide by the terms of a mutually advantageous arrangement. Those who can act voluntarily in accordance with such arrangements and rules can thus expect to realize savings with respect to enforcement and surveillance systems. This is to say that such a way of organizing their joint activities will be more efficient. This, it is important to recognize, is a *consequentialist* argument for not approaching every interdependent choice situation from the perspective of the standard theory. A rule-governed or practice-oriented approach to certain interactive situations is one that will better serve the interests of the participants than one that is not so governed or oriented. This is not simply a conceptual point. On the contrary, the argument is that those who are capable of rule-governed choice do better in terms of furthering whatever interests they have than those who are not, and this has direct bearing on the credibility of claims about what counts as a rational approach to various forms of interaction.

Notes

1. In the more formal literature, this concern culminates, in the middle of the twentieth century, in a fundamental theorem of welfare economics – see, for example, Arrow (1974) – according to which individuals will, given the special conditions of perfectly competitive market exchange, achieve an outcome that is Pareto-optimal and Pareto-efficient relative to the outcome of no transactions (that is, each does better as a result of such transactions). The theme of Pareto-efficient changes in institutional structures is also central to Coase's important work, both on the theory of the firm (1937) and on the problem of social cost

(1960), Posner's economic analysis of law (1986), the public choice tradition initiated by Buchanan and Tullock (1962), Axelrod's work on iterated prisoners' dilemma games (1984), and Ulmann-Margalit's study of the emergence of norms (1978). The Pareto conditions also figure centrally in virtually all axiomatic bargaining and social choice models. To be sure, these explorations are sometimes accompanied by the suggestion that the Pareto conditions are perhaps best secured indirectly, rather than by any deliberate attempt on the part of participating agents. This is, of course, the idea that is so strikingly captured by Adam Smith's "invisible hand" metaphor and reproduced in the formal work on the welfare theorems referred to earlier: the wealth of nations is an unintended by-product of each person pursuing his or her own personal interests. It also finds powerful reincarnation in some evolutionary accounts of the emergence of institutional structures (Alchian, 1950; Hayek, 1967; Axelrod and Dion, 1988; Sugden, 1989; Nelson, 1994). Finally, where satisfaction of the Pareto conditions is not assured, much effort is invested in the search for mechanisms that will overcome this problem. The recent "folk" theorems on indefinitely repeated games are cases in point. The objective is to show that Pareto-efficient outcomes can be secured by backing up coordination schemes with appropriate sets of surveillance and enforcement devices. For a recent survey of this work, see Fudenberg and Tirole (1992).

2. The former theme is central to the work of Arthur (1994) and also to the new institutional theory associated with North (1990). The latter theme is central to the literature on "rent-seeking" (Buchanan, Tollison, and Tullock, 1981), as well as to the work of North (1990), Olson (1982), Knight (1992), and Hardin (1995).

3. I use the term "practice" here in roughly the sense introduced by Rawls (1955).

4. Later in the same chapter (pp. 95–9) the coordination problem is recast in terms of game theory matrices, but the notion of a wise choice for each is treated simply as one in which both "win" (p. 95).

5. Given condition (1), that the preferences of the two players are completely coincident, it follows from the assumption that a given pair of strategies will yield a Pareto-optimal outcome, that the pair will be in equilibrium. Suppose that a pair of strategies is Pareto-optimal, but not in equilibrium. Then one of the players can achieve a more preferred outcome by a unilateral shift to some other strategy. But since the preferences of the two players coincide, the other player must prefer this outcome as well; but then the new outcome is preferred by both to the original one, and this contradicts the hypothesis that the original one was optimal.

6. To see this, note that the plot of all outcome points in the graphic representation of a two-person game of pure coordination, with payoffs for the two players measured along the horizontal and the vertical axes, is simply a straight line with positive slope, i.e., a line moving from mutually inferior outcomes in the southwest to more mutually superior outcomes in the northeast.

7. Oddly enough, it is not until very late in the book that the equilibrium concept is even explicitly defined (p. 226). The index lists only two prior places in the book where the concept is even mentioned, both being footnotes, one of which (p. 97) I discuss later, and the other being one in which merely passing reference is made to Luce and Raiffa's notion of a "solution in the strict sense" (p. 210).

8. What is easily overlooked is that this criterion is fully applicable to the other limiting case of games as well, that is, strictly competitive games, since for such games *all* pairs of outcomes are Pareto-optimal!

9. Moreover, given the way that saliency can operate to reduce confusion, it turns

out that optimality considerations will have to be relaxed in some cases. Here is
the type of game that explicitly motivates this move on Schelling's part:

	c_1	c_2	c_3
r_1	2	0	0
r_2	0	1	0
r_3	0	0	2

Game 2

Here the combination (r_2, c_2) yields an outcome that is suboptimal, but the pair
is in equilibrium, and it possesses a saliency that is lacking in the case of the
pairs associated with the two optimal outcomes. On Schelling's account, (r_2, c_2)
may, in virtue of its saliency, emerge as the solution to this game. All of this
serves to remind us that Pareto-optimality and saliency can conflict. Could one
still insist here that it is a type of Pareto consideration that drives the argument?
Were the "salient" combination of strategies to yield the worst outcome, or a very
inferior one, there would be little incentive to play for it. In Game 2, the "second-
best" outcome is a solution candidate in virtue of its assuring one that one can
thereby avoid an even worse outcome. As it turns out, however, in his Appendix,
Schelling rejects this line of reasoning (p. 297).

10. One need only recall here that the title of the work is *The Strategy of Conflict*,
    not "The Strategy of Cooperation"!
11. One can also mark in von Neumann and Morgenstern's *Theory of Games and
    Economic Behavior* (pp. 506ff.) a remarkable suggestion that provides a frame-
    work in terms of which the role of mutual-advantage (Pareto-type) considerations
    can be integrated into a theory of non-zero-sum games. They suggest that any
    non-zero-sum n-person game can be shown to be formally equivalent to a *zero-
    sum* $(n + 1)$-person game. This is accomplished by supposing that one can add
    to the n-person game an additional fictitious player who has no move to make
    herself, and who, then, cannot influence the outcome of the game by making any
    choice, but who is assumed to lose, in any play of the game, an amount equivalent
    to what the totality of the other, real players win, and *vice versa*. The most natural
    interpretation of this game, of course, is that the $(n + 1)$-th player is Nature and
    that if the real players can manage to act in a concerted, cooperative way, they
    can maximize the gains that they can collectively secure.
12. The proviso recognizes the force of Schelling's suggestion that in a game in
    which there is a unique "second-best" combination of choices, and many "first-
    best" combinations, one can expect players who cannot communicate with one
    another to converge on the second-best combination. For an example, see note 9.
13. Exactly similar distributive implications are to be associated with the even more
    general, dynamic case in which interaction takes place over time, with various
    types of sequences of encounters between the various participants. And that
    indeterminacy in turn extends to the case in which, in addition, the institutional
    constraints under which the participants interact are themselves subject to strate-
    gic manipulation.
14. I take up this aspect of the problem elsewhere (McClennen 1989, 1990).
15. Can one interpret the standard theory as allowing saliency considerations to select
    out (r_1, c_1) as the solution to this game? I think not! Saliency may direct the
    players to (r_1, c_1), but within a theory predicated on the idea that a rational player
    will always choose to maximize expected utility against what he or she expects

the other player to do, neither player will have sufficient motive to coordinate on that point, given that the player expects the other to coordinate on that outcome. That is, the problem of weak equilibrium points remains. See McClennen (1992) for a further discussion of this point.

16. It also means, of course, that rational players will, under these conditions, sometimes choose strategies that are strictly dominated by other strategies.

17. Thus, from the perspective of the model presented here, the standard backward-induction arguments, both for sequential games and for finitely and determinately iterated games, must be rejected.

18. To be sure, an obvious functional substitute for social sanctions or a formal enforcement system is a set of shared cultural beliefs regarding the "appropriateness" or "correctness" of acting in accordance with the rules in question. Careful accounts usually acknowledge this point. But the appeal to shared cultural values is an appeal to what is not a matter of a deliberate, and voluntary, agreement between persons. It involves an appeal to a "non-rational" or ideological factor. For a further discussion of this, see McClennen (in press).

19. For an excellent survey of some of the more recent work in this area, see Calvert (1995).

20. See Hardin (1993).

References

Alchian, A. A. 1950. Uncertainty, Evolution and Economic Theory. *Journal of Political Economy* 58:211–21.

Arrow, K. 1974. General Economic Equilibrium: Purpose, Analytic Techniques, Collective Choice. *American Economic Review* 64:253–72.

Arthur, W. B. 1994. *Increasing Returns and Path Dependence in the Economy* (Ann Arbor: University of Michigan Press).

Axelrod, R. 1984. *The Evolution of Cooperation* (New York: Basic Books).

Axelrod, R., and Dion, D. 1988. The Further Evolution of Cooperation. *Science* 242: 1385–90.

Buchanan, J. M., Tollison, R. D., and Tullock, G. 1981. *Toward a Theory of the Rent-seeking Society* (College Station: Texas A&M University Press).

Buchanan, J. M., and Tullock, G. 1962. *The Calculus of Consent* (Ann Arbor: University of Michigan Press).

Calvert, R. L. 1995. Rational Actors, Equilibrium, and Social Institutions. In *Explaining Social Institutions*, ed. J. Knight and I. Sened (Ann Arbor: University of Michigan Press), pp. 57–93.

Coase, R. H. 1937. The Nature of the Firm. *Economica* 4:386–405.

1960. The Problem of Social Cost. *Journal of Law and Economics* 3: 1–44.

Fudenberg, D., and Tirole, J. 1992. *Game Theory* (Cambridge, MA: MIT Press).

Gauthier, D. 1986. *Morals by Agreement* (Oxford University Press).

Hardin, R. 1993. The Street-Level Epistemology of Trust. *Politics and Society* 21: 505–29.

1995. *One for All: The Logic of Group Conflict* (Princeton University Press).

Hayek, F. A. 1967. Notes on the Evolution of Systems of Rules of Conduct. In *Studies in Philosophy, Politics, and Economics* (University of Chicago Press).

Kaysen, K. 1946–47. A Revolution in Economic Theory? *Review of Economic Studies* 14:1–15.

Knight, J. 1992. *Institutions and Social Conflict* (Cambridge University Press).

Lewis, D. 1969. *Convention* (Cambridge, MA: Harvard University Press).

Luce, R. D., and Raiffa, H. 1957. *Games and Decisions* (New York: Wiley).

McClennen, E. F. 1989. Justice and the Problem of Stability. *Philosophy and Public Affairs* 18:3–30.

   1990. Foundational Explorations for a Normative Theory of Political Economy. *Constitutional Political Economy* 1:67–99.

   1992. The Theory of Rationality for Ideal Games. *Philosophical Studies* 65:193–215.

   1997. Pragmatic Rationality and Rules. *Philosophy and Public Affairs* 26:210–58.

   In press. An Alternative Model of Rational Cooperation. In *Justice, Political Liberalism, and Utilitarianism: Proceedings of the Caen Conference in Honour of John Harsanyi and John Rawls*, ed. M. Salles and J. Weymark (Cambridge University Press).

Morris, C. 1999. What Is This Thing Called Reputation? *Business Ethics Quarterly* 9:87–102.

Nelson, R. R. 1994. Evolutionary Theorizing about Economic Change. In *Handbook of Economic Sociology*, ed. N. J. Smelzer and R. Swedberg (Princeton University Press), pp. 108–36.

North, D. C. 1990. *Institutions, Institutional Change and Economic Performance* (Cambridge University Press).

Olson, M. 1982. *The Rise and Decline of Nations: Economic Growth, Stagflation and Social Rigidities* (New Haven, CT: Yale University Press).

Posner, R. A. 1986. *Economic Analysis of Law* (Boston: Little, Brown).

Rawls, J. 1955. Two Concepts of Rules. *Philosophical Review* 64:3–32.

Schelling, T. C. 1960. *The Strategy of Conflict* (Cambridge, MA: Harvard University Press).

Sugden, R. 1989. Spontaneous Order. *Journal of Economic Perspectives* 3:85–97.

Ulmann-Margalit, E. 1978. *The Emergence of Norms* (Oxford University Press).

von Neumann, J., and Morgenstern, O. 1953. *Theory of Games and Economic Behavior*, 3rd ed. (Princeton University Press).

We Were Never in Paradise

CANDACE VOGLER

1. Contractarianism

Liberal contractarian political and moral theory, based in accounts of practical rationality, sets itself the task of identifying a reasonable set of conditions under which individual persons, conceived as having no necessary tie to one another, can form orderly societies for the sake of mutual benefit. Clearly, if individuals have no necessary tie with one another, there is no reason to expect that they will protect each other's interests. Nor is there any reason to suppose that one individual or group will gladly sacrifice its private good for the common weal, or for the well-being of another. And clearly, we cannot expect to have a stable, well-ordered society if each of us is prepared to do anything in her power to get what she wants, no matter what the cost to her fellows.

While it could turn out that every potential citizen in the desired commonwealth would just happen to be a lovely person who never would want a thing that would jeopardize others' interests, there is no reason to *expect* this happy turn of events, and, anyway, the aim of contractarian theory is to determine what rational social life would be like no matter how good-natured or ill-tempered the members of the society might be. The question for contractarian theory becomes, What kind of concessions should individuals make for the sake of cooperative social life? Or, When is it reasonable to forgo self-interest for the sake of the general welfare? Or, more simply, Why be moral? (understood as the question, What reason is there to constrain the pursuit of my own ends for the sake of just social life?). The work of building a contractarian theory, accordingly, is the work of arguing that it is in any man's interest to accept some specified set of constraints on his choice of ends and means as is compatible with like constraints on others' choices.

I am grateful to Jeremy Bendik-Keymer, Lauren Tillinghast, Daniel Brudney, Ian Mueller, and Michael Thompson for extremely helpful comments on the deconstructive reading of Rousseau offered toward the conclusion of this essay, to Lisa Roraback for much-needed editorial advice, and to Hank Vogler for encouragement. Most of all, I want to thank David Gauthier for years of conversation about Rousseau, for patient mentoring, and for ongoing argument and friendship.

As such, contractarian theory is deeply egalitarian (no one is asked to make concessions that will not be required of her fellows), rationalist (the appeal is to a standard of reasonable constraint guided by a view about practical rationality), and methodologically individualist (the contingently social self is the addressee of the argument, and we seek to justify the self-restraint necessary for social order in self-interested terms). Moreover, the three features of contractarian theory go together. Methodological individualism takes the self as the starting point for reflection on society. The contractarian self is characterized principally by its powers of practical reason, which allow it to set its own ends and take means to attaining them. And while some selves might be better suited than others for social success or advancement because of nature, temperament, or circumstance, all are regarded as equally rational and, to that extent, equally deserving of a good argument in support of the conditions of social cooperation. What will count as a good argument, however, will in part be determined by the overarching methodologically individualist thrust of contractarian theory: The argument must be addressed to individual selves and must present the kind of constraint on individual action prerequisite to genuine cooperation as rationally justified in self-interested terms. Society, in turn, is to be viewed as made up of individual selves who join together for the sake of mutual benefit.

My ultimate target in this essay will be methodological individualism as it shapes work on practical reason and contractarian moral and political theory. I will take as my starting point readings of David Gauthier's contractarian theory, and of Gauthier's work on Jean-Jacques Rousseau, in order to raise and consider various problems connected with contractarian thought about the self, society, and practical reason. Finally, drawing on suggestions and hints offered by Gauthier's readings of Rousseau, I will extract an argument from the first part of Rousseau's *Discours sur l'origine et les fondements de l'inégalité parmi les hommes* to the effect that adherence to strict methodological individualism in work on practical rationality, selfhood, and the well-ordered (i.e., practically reasonable and just) society is deeply untenable. This argument does not solve the problems raised in reading Gauthier, Rousseau, and Gauthier's Rousseau, but it does cast them in rather a different light.

2. Right Reason

David Gauthier is best known as the champion of secular rational individualism in moral theory, urging that we temper our enthusiasm for Humean sympathy, Kantian dignity, and Platonic harmony with sober reflection on the darker world of Hobbes in our search for an answer to the question, Why be moral? Initially, Gauthier advocated the return to Hobbes on the grounds that the requirement that morality recommend itself to self-interested rational agents as such is especially suited to our times:

I should not want to argue that radical contractarianism of a Hobbist kind has unequivocally dominated our thoughts and practices. Rather, I believe this to be the final form of the contractarian conception of society, the form toward which it develops as an ideology, gradually increasing its influence on our thoughts and leading us to abandon earlier ideas of human relationships as natural or supernatural rather than conventional.[1]

The demand that we assess all human relationships and institutions in the terms set by self-interest is rooted in the maximizing conception of practical rationality. In the terms set by this picture of practical reason, the supremely rational being "for modern Western Europeans and their descendants and offshoots" would be economic man.[2] The social contract offers mutual advantage for developing economic men and women, who increasingly strain against the remnants of a disadvantageous social order:

Neither workers, who have lacked control over the means of production, nor women, who have engaged in reproduction rather than production, have conceived themselves, or been in a position to conceive themselves, as full human beings in the sense implicit in radical contractarian ideology. Marx, mistakenly, thought religion to be the opium of the people, the real opiates, in contractarian society, have been love and patriotism.[3]

For all its liberatory potential, however, the deep structure of self-understanding at issue here has a darker aspect:

The ideology of radical contractarianism is, of course, but one among many possible ways of structuring our thought about man, society, and reason. We may see that this way of thinking is, from a practical point of view, bankrupt, and indeed that it will destroy us if we remain its adherents.[4]

Economic man is at best an icon of liberation and at worst an evil, however necessary for us. But the evil of economic man is not to be taken lightly. Haunted by the specter of this most rational of men, near the conclusion of *Morals by Agreement* Gauthier wrote that:

our belief in economic man, or in human beings as radically contractarian, runs deeper than our conscious disavowals; economic man is a caricature, or distortion, who has come more and more to shape our reality. . . . Morals by agreement would afford economic man a beneficial constraint, if only he could be constrained. Because we real human beings share some of his characteristics, morals by agreement afford us a beneficial constraint, and because we are nevertheless not economic men and women, we can be constrained. . . . But it will be well to keep in mind that here argument is not enough. In so far as the idea of economic man is part of our way of understanding ourselves, part of our idea of what it is to be human, then the rational bonds of morals by agreement may be too weak to hold us. We need exorcism in addition to argument.[5]

Rather surprising, then, to find Gauthier announcing in the Introduction to his collected papers a few years later that he had changed his mind:

> my deepest reason for endorsing a contractarian grounding of morality . . . is that no other account seems compatible with the maximizing conception of practical rationality, and I no longer find plausible the view . . . that this conception is merely part of the particular ideology of our modern, Western society. Instead, I find myself increasingly persuaded by a view of . . . reason as unifying our beliefs, desires, and feelings into the experience of a single self – an individual. And this, it now seems to me, provides the deep basis of the maximizing conception of practical rationality, transcending those aspects of our self-understanding that might be considered socially relative.[6]

To be sure, the (liberal) individual is less alarming than economic man. The individual accepts a prior constraint on its behavior that Gauthier dubs the "Lockean proviso," which forbids it from benefiting from interactions that worsen the situations of others. It wants things it could have no rational hope of getting in a Hobbist world, like the opportunity to attain a Pareto-optimal solution to a Prisoner's Dilemma, and so it abandons economic man's straightforwardly maximizing ways and "develops those dispositions, forms those intentions, and adopts those plans that afford [it] the most favorable opportunities, even though they may require [it] to act in ways that do not maximize the realization of [its] aims."[7]

Still, if maximizing rationality is the socially invariant basis of the unity of the self, one cannot but wonder if the individual isn't striking a bad bargain. An economic man who is under the impression that he has a reasonable hope of getting his most preferred outcomes by preying on his fellows may be living in a Foole's paradise, but one who faces up to the paradoxes of rationality is, at least, at one with himself. He can't count on winning, since winning will require that his fellows err on the side of constraint, but he can take his chances. The individual has no such easy choice: Its practical deliberations require that it take the measure of its fellows – to determine whether they are conditional cooperators, dupes, or predators – in order to know what to seek in any given circumstance. Economic man just goes for as much as he can get, which will be less than what he wants, but, then, no principle of choice guarantees that one will get as much as one might want.

The move from straightforward maximization to constrained maximization is a shift in the focus of maximizing practical reason, embodied in the transition from thought about economic man and thought about the liberal individual. These two figures embody contending images of right practical reason. Gauthier sets himself the task of convincing us that reason is on the side of the liberal individual. Various of his critics have found the transition from economic man to the liberal individual perplexing or frustrating, and while the thought that practical rationality brings the psychological territories of the self under common governance has been attractive to many philosophers of late, Gauthier's particular version of this view does not seem to address the concern that the transition from economic man to the liberal individual is a philosophical conjuring trick. Put bluntly, and drawing on Gauthier's bold formulation of the place of maximizing reason in human life, either maximizing practical rationality is the eternal ground of the unity of the self or it's not.

If it *is*, then the merely empirical point that we are not economic men and women would not seem to answer to the fear that the bonds of morals by agreement will be too weak to hold us. The distinction between straightforward and constrained maximization is not based upon figuring out what most of us are like. The point about economic man is *not* that he has different preferences, or makes different estimates of the future, or some such.[8] Assessments of likelihood and preferences are part of the content "unified" by practical reason. Rather, the principled "unity" of the economic self, *whatever he wants and thinks*, is the product of straightforward, rather than constrained, maximization.[9] That is, economic man is a straightforward maximizer come what may.

Now, if we are predatory to just the extent that we are rational, if, that is, maximizing reason *is* the basis for rational agency and rational selfhood, then it is hard to shake the sense that our rational imperfection is what would drive us to live as constrained, rather than straightforward, maximizers. Perhaps we haven't the heart to be ruthless with our fellows or the strength of will required to follow the dictates of maximizing reason from one act to the next. Perhaps we are too greedy to give up on those benefits of cooperation that require constraint on our part. Whatever the explanation, we fail to attain economic man's pure rational selfhood in our muddled lives, and so need another way to get what we want without falling victim to the likes of him. But we have all learned from Gauthier that no sound principle of rationality can require that some people be less rational than others.[10] And so our willingness to cooperate rather than take advantage of our liberal fellows starts to look like shared folly, if Gauthier is right about the centrality of maximizing reason to selfhood and agency. In this world, morality becomes a kind of management technique for imperfect reason, rather than reason's triumph over shortsighted self-interest.

If, on the other hand, the maximizing conception of practical reason is *not* an articulation of the eternal structure of selfhood, if it instead belongs to Eurocentric ideology, then producing moral theory that might convince people in its grip to behave decently with one another may or may not be to the point. On this view, while maximizing reason is at the core of a shared sense of self, the explanation for its centrality will go by way of history, presumably materialist history. Whatever happens next, it is at least not obvious that we should choose Hobbists over, say, Marxists as our fellow theorists of the persistent, modern state of nature.[11]

It is against this curious wobble around the unity of the self, reason, and economic man that I will read some of Gauthier's work on Jean-Jacques Rousseau. Gauthier's relation to Rousseau is exceedingly complex, but, I think, has a clear central thrust: Each time Gauthier turns to Rousseau, what emerges from the historical work is a kind of limit case for some central aspect of Gauthier's contractarian theory. In this sense, Gauthier's Rousseau emerges as Gauthier's own best critic. I will make this case in two stages: firstly by looking at how constrained maximization fares with respect to the Rousseau of Gauthier's "The Politics of Redemption,"[12] and secondly by reading the Rousseau of Gauthier's more recent essays and lectures alongside the suggestion that maximizing reason is the deep basis of the unity of the self.

Gauthier's early and later readings of Rousseau divide themselves into meditations on "the real opiates" of the masses in contractarian society: patriotism and love. Gauthier's Rousseau tries first one and then the other as a solution to a problem more serious than self-interested material acquisitiveness. While Gauthier is confident that cultivation of an especially deep form of patriotism offers us little hope, his attitude toward love is more complicated – so complicated that he carefully refrains from mentioning the ways in which Rousseau might have been offering love as a solution to the same problem that patriotism was meant to solve.

3. Rousseau's Problem and the Failed Attempt to Solve It

Gauthier's Hobbes is the first great theorist of contractarian morality. Hobbes's state of nature is a world of individuals set free in the sense derided by Marx: conceived apart from any necessary social connection to one another.[13] They are economic men and women who would be entirely content to inhabit a world of things that they could use at will, but find themselves thrust into competition with one another by scarcity.

Scarcity is not a problem in Rousseau's state of nature. Rousseauian natural men and women are, *ex hypothesi*, solitaries who, for the most part, want only those things that they can get without relying upon the powers of their fellows.[14] On the standard reading of Rousseau's state of nature (which Gauthier accepts), Rousseauian natural people do not require a social contract to keep the peace. Hobbists do. The problem Rousseau theorizes is a problem in and of society: the vicious effects of rivalry, envy, jealousy, and spite in a world where one's sense of well-being is comparative and one's office, stand-ing, and prosperity depend upon acquiring the good opinion of others through artful manipulation of appearances.

De-natured, thoroughly socialized humans are humans driven by *amour-propre*.[15] Their descent into man-made hell is traced in the second part of Rousseau's *Discours sur l'origine et les fondements de l'inégalité parmi les hommes*. At its conclusion, human beings have wound up relying upon the opinion of others for their entire sense of themselves, and so have lost all trace of independence in a social whirl conducted in the spiritual equivalent of a hall of mirrors. Appearance is everything. Substance matters not at all. Each person is alone and estranged from everyone else – superiors, inferiors, rivals – but abjectly dependent upon them for both the very prestige at issue between them and all those goods that hang in the balance. In Rousseauian society we are "always asking others what we are and never daring to question ourselves on this subject, in the midst of so much philosophy, humanity, politeness and sublime maxims, we have only a deceitful and frivolous exterior, honor without virtue, reason without wisdom, and pleasure without happiness," denizens of a world so perverse that it becomes common-place to find "that a child command an old man, an imbecile lead a wise man, and a handful of men be glutted with superfluities while the starving multitude lacks necessities."[16]

Here is Gauthier on this topic:

One is what others conceive one to be. Apart from those beliefs, one is nothing. The slave preserves his identity against his master; the social man takes his identity from his fellows; in himself, he is a void. We have reached the end point in Rousseau's story of man's fall.[17]

Gauthier points out that dependence and estrangement form the twin pillars of the Rousseauian social milieu, a scene simultaneously more glittering and less congenial than the Hobbist state of nature:

Hobbes's men compete because they recognize each other as obstacles to the attain-ment of scarce material goods required for physical preservation. Rousseau's men compete primarily because they are motivated by *amour-propre*, by the desire to be superior to their fellows. Hobbesian men seek glory because they are insecure; over-come their insecurity and most of them will forego glory, and the rest may be compelled to abandon it. Rousseauian men seek glory because their desires are no longer directed at material preservation, as in the original state of nature, but rather aim at spiritual supremacy. And the quest for glory is a zero-sum game, condemning men to the condition of universal war.[18]

Gauthier argues that Rousseau's attempt to solve the problem of vicious *amour-propre* turns on patriotism, one of the "real opiates" in contractarian society. The idea is to transform *amour-propre* into virtue by transferring the scene of the *propre* from apparent qualities of the person to the institutions, practices, and shared interests that characterize the body politic, in effect, to produce *amour de la patrie* in sufficient strength both to undo the vicious effects of *amour-propre* and to answer the citizens' demand for reputation and honor. This happens by making people into citizens with the requisite deep affection for the social order they share, "transforming each individual, who by himself is a perfect and solitary whole, into a part of a larger whole from which this individual receives, in a sense, his life and his being,"[19] through a combination of adroit legislation and excellent education guided by figures like the Legislator of *Du contrat social* and Émile's Tutor.[20] In the *Émile*, Rousseau puts the point this way:

> There are two sorts of dependence: dependence on things, which is from nature; dependence on men, which is from society. Dependence on things, since it has no morality, is in no way detrimental to freedom and engenders no vices. Dependence on [the particular wills of] men, since it is without order, engenders all the vices, and by it, master and slave are mutually corrupted. If there is any means of remedying this ill in society, it is to substitute law for man and to arm the general wills with a real strength superior to the action of every particular will. If the laws of nations could, like those of nature, have an inflexibility that no human force could ever conquer, dependence on men would then become dependence on things again; in the republic all of the advantages of the natural state would be united with those of the civil state, and freedom which keeps man exempt from vices would be joined to morality which raises him to virtue.[21]

However, Gauthier argues, if one concentrates on Émile's later misfortunes and on Julie, it becomes clear that Rousseau somehow knows better than to think that public law inscribed at the core of the person by *amour de la patrie* will save us: "Rousseau's imagination senses what his reason would deny — that there is, and can be, no politics of redemption."[22]

Gauthier offers two primary considerations in support of his thought that Rousseau senses that *amour de la patrie* cannot entirely supplant the demands of *moi individu*. First, there is the requirement that the harmonies of civil society be orchestrated and conducted by shadowy figures like Émile's Tutor, the Legislator, and, in *Julie*, Wolmar. Someone has to design the general order that supplants the chaos of dependence on particular wills. Someone has to compose the score. This creature embodies the principles he inculcates in his subjects, but is not himself produced by those principles. Just as no ratified Constitution is itself constitutional, the social engineer whose task is to make citizens or men is not himself an ordinary man or citizen. But to imagine a sound social order one has to imagine an order capable of reproducing the system of social relations in which it is realized from one generation to the next; if we imagine a social order so scripted that its members are in no position to make new members without the help of a benevolent outsider (like

Wolmar or the Tutor), then the center will not hold. This problem all on its own might be a simple failure of imagination on Rousseau's part:

> Both Julie and Émile, despite the efforts of Wolmar and the Tutor, fail to attain the liberty which seemed promised for them: The only liberty for Émile [at the conclusion of *Émile et Sophie, ou les solitaires*, in which Émile has abandoned Sophie, pregnant by another man, and winds up enslaved by Barbary pirates] is in solitude or in Stoic resignation; the only liberty for Julie is in another world. Neither is, nor can be, a truly recreated being.
>
> The lesson of imagination, it may be urged, is not the lesson of reason. The failure of Émile and Julie need not be the failure of humankind. Let the Legislator work his magic on us; let him give us a collective existence which will transform our *amour-propre* into virtue; let us be free![23]

But here the second, less tractable problem arises: The very language required to get any aspect of the solution in place invariably brings with it the possibility of conceiving one's own interests apart from the interests of the group. Citizens and men are language-users. The very medium in which we become able to imagine a world *unlike any we have inhabited* where *amour-propre* has been entirely transformed into virtuous *amour de la patrie* – language – is the precondition for a fully human sense of self, and a fully human sense of self carries with it a sense of having interests that may be, at least in principle, at odds with the interests of one's fellows. Gauthier draws upon this point (I will later suggest, from the wrong way around, however much Rousseau would appear to want things to go in this direction) in explaining why nationalism will never redeem us, even if the nation can reproduce itself from one generation to the next without the divine guidance of Tutors and Legislators:

> Our language has its origins in our individual passions. This is one of Rousseau's profoundest insights. Our first words are *aimez-moi*. But having learned such a speech, we have already acquired the conception of the *moi individu* which is fatal to the task of the Legislator.[24]

Even if we treat "the Legislator" as the name of whatever it is that lends structure, coherence, stability, and harmony to social life built upon real *liberté* and *amour de la patrie*, the possibility of harmonious social life is built of thought, and the capacity to have such a thought requires being the kind of normal, competent speaker of a natural language who can conceive his own interests apart from and in competition with the interests of his fellows.[25]

Gauthier concludes by coming very close to suggesting that Rousseau's *own* ardent wish for a better world involved a larger share of private passion than heartfelt experience of harmonious collective life:

The recreated society, the society which transforms the individuality relativized by *amour-propre* into a collective sentiment infused by *amour de la patrie*, the society which fills the void of individuals living only in the opinions of others – all this is but part of a dream, a dream of a Sparta and a Rome which history never knew, a dream in which the garden of Elysium fades into that other garden which humankind had lost before Rousseau's story began, a dream which turns to a nightmare as the liberty of the citizen becomes the liberty of the slave in the galleys of the Barbary pirates.[26]

The problem, then, is very serious. Could it be solved by conditional cooperation?

4. Constrained Maximization, the Individual and Social Man

On Gauthier's reading, Rousseauian natural humans want only what they can get without the strings of duty attached. That is why they do not require a social contract to keep the peace. Sadly, however miserable socialized humans might be, there is no return to the happy contentment of "natural" life: We cannot decide to be natural people rather than de-natured creatures of society. This would seem to leave us with something like a choice between living as economic men and living as liberal individuals. That is, it looks as though the failure of Rousseau's attempt to solve the problem of vicious *amour-propre* by the cultivation of an all-encompassing *amour de la patrie* deposits socialized humans in the world of morals by agreement. But, as Gauthier points out, Rousseauian de-natured people are poor candidates for liberal society.

Like the liberal individual, the Rousseauian socialized person seeks something that can be realized only in social life: the good opinion of her or his fellows. Unlike the liberal individual, however, on Gauthier's reading at least, the Rousseauian person is not really going to be satisfied with playing her part beautifully in the great symphony of social existence: Vicious *amour-propre* takes as its object a *necessarily* scarce good (i.e., first place in a rank-ordered social hierarchy).

To whatever extent Rousseau is right about the centrality of status in contemporary social life, "civilized" people need to feel themselves superior to other people on some grounds or other (the particular content doesn't much matter, except that the sense of superiority must be rooted in something that is collectively valued in accordance with shared standards of excellence: intelligence, wit, beauty, political or economic acumen, artistry, wealth, or what have you). While one of us might be so favored by fortune or circumstance to be the best at everything that anyone who is anyone finds worthwhile, it is structurally impossible for everyone to be so favored, and it is hard to imagine that the person who accidentally finds herself in the lead in every race will be welcomed by her fellows. Someone – or, as is more likely, *most* of us – will be lower down on at least one pecking order. It is possible that everyone might be best at something, of course, and that the citizens might prize one another for their special areas of prominence, but barring some strange quirk of fate that renders each of us well suited to win at something important, and unless each of us can content herself by repeating, "No matter what, I am the best at being me and you are the best at being you," it is hard to see why one ought to expect Rousseauian people to have easy congress with one another. Rousseau didn't. Rousseau thought that magnificent educational and political reforms were needed in order to offer some hope of a humane social order – solutions much more complex and subtle than issuing a copy of *I'm Okay, You're Okay* to each citizen.

It may seem possible that morals by agreement could provide a set of ground rules for the pursuit of status in roughly the way in which they are meant to provide ground rules for the pursuit of stuff, but in the Rousseauian world we ought to expect that some of the conditionally cooperative status-seekers are going to lose, no matter what. I take it that this rather weakens the allure of mutual constraint. There is more than one way to win status, after all: There is honest cultivation of admired traits, but should that fail (as it will for at least one of us, and probably for most of us), there is always cunning elimination of the competition. If Rousseau is right about the problem of "civilized" life, then it is hard to see why the honest-effort strategy should be preferred to the sly or backbiting approach, provided that we mediocre people can form temporary alliances with one another in order to undercut our superiors and are then clever enough to hide the traces of calumny. In the Rousseauian world, it will again be better to *appear* good than to *be* good.

This is, in a sense, the moral of *Émile et Sophie*. One could argue that our virtuous hero and heroine might have fared better as constrained maximizers, since they at least would have known *not* to cooperate with *anyone else*, but in a zero-sum game played between *individuals* (rather than between couples or tribes or nations) for the sake of supremacy there is no such thing as mutual benefit. Any fair competition between *les solitaires* for individual supremacy would have rendered their own alliance differently precarious than a marriage with no shield but the partners' virtue, but just as unlikely to survive: In the sequel, Émile and Sophie are brought to ruin by others; in a private contest for supremacy, however, they would have destroyed their own relation. Still, while their marriage might not have survived the internal workings of *amour-propre*, the two partners might otherwise have done better for themselves than they did in the novel's unfinished sequel.

Gauthier's early Rousseau emerges as providing a critical perspective on morals by agreement more daunting than anything the Foole sayeth in his heart. What is especially troubling about the Rousseauian perspective is that it introduces the possibility that a kind of good that cannot be had *except* at someone else's expense might be central to shared social life. There *could not be* reasonable acceptance of a Lockean proviso with respect to such goods, and so could not be liberal, rather than economic, pursuit of them. Status is such a good. But there are other, more intimate goods of this sort (e.g., wanting first place in the affections of one's beloved). Again, the point is formal and principled rather than substantive and empirical: The problem concerns structural features of social hierarchy rather than the detail of what any given group uses in the ranking of persons. Pursuit of goods like status can't be reliably regulated by constrained maximization. The only "empirical" question remaining is how important such goods are to a given social milieu. In his early reading of Rousseau, Gauthier effectively constructs a limit case for his own official doctrine.

5. Love and Other Illusions of the Insubstantial Self

The limit in question in Gauthier's early confrontation with Rousseau concerns a kind of good. The limit in his most recent work on Rousseau, however, concerns both this kind of good (the lover's central place in the heart of his beloved) and the self itself, the very cornerstone of moral theory on Gauthier's understanding of that enterprise. It would be possible to leave the problem of the necessarily scarce good to one side if it turned out that, in fact, the world we share is less shaped by pursuit of such things than is the Rousseauian world. It is extremely difficult to find a similar way around the kind of criticism implicit in Gauthier's more recent work on Rousseau. The lectures and essays that have begun to emerge from Gauthier's renewed fascination with Rousseau suggest not an abandonment of the confident assertions about economic man and the universality of his reason, but rather a kind of antidote to both.

Gauthier's research has lately come more and more to center on the enigmatic figure of Rousseau as he paints himself in his autobiographical writings (call the hero of these pieces "Jean-Jacques"). Jean-Jacques understands himself as first and foremost a lover, whose great sentimental attachment is to Madame de Warens, his *Maman*. Their association occasions the best happiness of his life. The relation is not, however, especially passionate. His slightly awkward but singularly successful sexual liaison with Mme de Larnage, carried out while he is pretending to be an Englishman named "Dudding," happens when he is away from Maman, seeking medical attention for an imagined heart ailment. The affair temporarily cures him. But he breaks it off rather abruptly by failing to pay a promised visit to Mme de Larnage, and races home to Maman, congratulating himself on his virtue. The decision, however, appears to have owed less to any thought of duty pure and simple (he is breaking a promise by driving on by, and the virtuous impulse never extends to telling Mme de Larnage in particular that he is not Dudding) than to fear of being unable to resist the temptation to seduce Mme de Larnage's teenage daughter, fear of the scandal that would come his way if he couldn't, or fear of being asked about the English language – of which he knows scarcely a word, – and, more generally, to cooling ardor for Mme de Larnage: "Perhaps pride played as large a part in my resolution as virtue; but if this pride is not itself a virtue, it has such similar effects that it is excusable to confuse them."[27]

He arrives home to find that Maman has installed another young man in his place (*Bref, je trouvai ma place prise*). He is crushed:

Suddenly my whole being was thrown completely upside down. To judge of it, let my reader put himself in my place. In one moment I saw the happy future I had depicted for myself vanished for ever. All the sweet dreams I had indulged with such affection disappeared; and I, who even from childhood had never contemplated my existence apart from hers, found myself for the first time alone. It was a frightful moment; and those which followed it were just as dark. I was still young, but that pleasant feeling of joy and hope that enlivens youth left me for ever. From that time, as a sensitive being, I was half dead. I could see nothing before me but the sad remains of a savourless life; and if sometimes afterwards some thought of happiness awakened my desires, it was no longer a happiness that was really my own.[28]

Gauthier writes:

The loss of Madame de Warens was, for Rousseau, the loss of his true self. And in that true self there is no trace of the independent natural man. The man who is made in the first part of the *Confessions*, and who reappears in the *Promenades* and the *Rêveries*, is no solitary but a lover. He becomes a solitary, but not by choice.[29]

Love emerges as the ground of such self-realization as the flighty, inconstant, and often tortured figure – Jean-Jacques – can manage:

The first, the greatest, the strongest, the most inextinguishable of all my needs was entirely one of the heart. It was the need for intimate companionship, for a companionship as intimate as possible, which was the chief reason I needed a woman rather than a man, a woman friend rather than a man friend. This singular need was such that the most intimate physical union could not fulfil it; only two souls in the same body would have sufficed.[30]

Notice that this need crucially involves the deepest possible dependence on another particular will. To read Rousseau on his own passions is to investigate both what makes Jean-Jacques tick and to follow the fortunes of an otherwise insubstantial self. Gauthier's recent work on this figure stresses that Jean-Jacques does not know his own mind, is not an expert witness to his own character, and is who he is only because of his relation to Maman.

Jean-Jacques is a vivid and engaging, if elusive, figure. The promise of long-term benefit, to which he is susceptible, is seldom enough to get him to stick to a single course over time. He is shortsighted ("literally" and figuratively): With the exception of gardening, writing, musical composition, and the accumulation and presentation of "evidence" concerning what he takes to be conspiracies hatched against him on all sides, very few of his undertakings show any real aptitude for carrying out a long-range plan. He moves in fits and starts, driven by sudden whims and more enduring enthusiasms, fond of grand pronouncements about himself, but rarely consistently characterized by their content. He is exceedingly defensive at friends' suggestions that he ought to behave differently with loved ones or patrons, that he is failing to do right by them, but largely shares economic man's lack of affective capacity for moral constraint: He will not ordinarily do a thing simply because he ought to do it. Instead, moment by moment, Jean-Jacques tries to get what he wants, however fickle his fancy might be. His ends shift rapidly and appear to transform themselves based upon a primary need to love and be loved.

Among other things, we see here the re-emergence of the problem of the necessarily scarce good in a more intimate environment than the one we encountered when considering *amour-propre*: A desperate search for perfect union with another person doubtless will lead to sudden changes in venue and strategy as one seeks a true mate, and if one finds oneself ill-equipped to keep first place in the heart of one's beloved, in part because one cannot figure out how to eliminate the competition, one is apt to behave erratically (especially if the next person one meets who might serve as a surrogate ideal partner, the "real" Sophie of the *Confessions*, is a married woman with a primary romantic attachment to another lover).[31]

In Gauthier's Jean-Jacques, we see little evidence of a "unified" self, in the sense of that term currently in vogue among Anglo–North American ethicists (which has very little to do with things like having perceptual experience in more than one sensory modality from a single perspective, and everything to do with emotions, thoughts, and goals). Instead, we focus on the form of self-realization that takes place through the relationship between Jean-Jacques and his Maman. It begins to appear that *intrapersonal* unity is less interesting than *interpersonal* unity: Gauthier writes about Jean-Jacques with an insight and affection unhindered by the extraordinary instability of his subject. It is neither in the naked pursuit of self-interest nor in the organic bonds of communal feeling, but rather in love that Jean-Jacques' self comes into its own: "The union of lover and beloved is precarious, fleeting, but the epiphany of love suffices to realize the self."[32] And the union of lover and beloved can be effected only if each has pride of place in the other's heart.

But Jean-Jacques' problem is not just that his self is governed by a desire for a necessarily scarce good – near-divine intimacy with the partner of his youth or the partner of his dreams – and so is destabilized by his failure to couple closely enough with either of the women he wants. All on his own, according to Gauthier, Jean-Jacques is able to produce the illusion of a stable identity only by assuming various *personae* who take courses that neither Rousseau nor Jean-Jacques could follow in his own person: Dudding, Vaussore (the name he takes when passing himself off as a musician and composer), and the Citizen of Geneva (a title Rousseau claims for himself only after he has converted to Catholicism and so forfeited all claim to Genevan citizenship).[33] In writing about *amour-propre* and *amour de la patrie*, Gauthier hints at the possibility that the thoroughly social self is "a void," but stresses the thought that the selves get into trouble because they are animated by desire for a kind of good that cannot be had except at others' expense. In reading the autobiographical Jean-Jacques, the problem isn't just a self that loses track of itself because it is too caught up with concern about how it appears to others. Rather, the problem is a self that has no proper identity: It is what it is only in moments of happy absorption with Maman; it has no clear course; it is perpetually disguised under different names, titles, and mottoes, but there is no one thing underneath the disguises. Who Jean-Jacques is, who Rousseau is – these matters are less clear than who Dudding is (an awkward amorous adventurer) or who Vaussore is (a composer and musician) or, for that matter, who the Citizen of Geneva is (the author of most of the social and political writings who is filled with the spirit of *amour de la patrie* for the Republic of Geneva and its constitution).[34] The smoke and mirrors have shifted to the interior of the autobiographical self – its identity, like the love it seeks (according to the Tutor), becomes an illusion, however harmless.

Careful as Gauthier is to refrain from any discussion of the new Rousseau readings' implications for the official doctrine – "Whether this account bears on our own ethical and political questions is, fortunately, another question"[35] – one cannot but wonder whether this careful reader of Rousseau, determined to trace the extraordinary inconsistency, the wild, contradictory self-assertions, the moments in the Rousseauian corpus where one cannot decide whether one's text is elaborately deceptive or wildly self-deceived, and so on, is entirely at ease with the view that the instrumentally rational, unified self is the source for all sound thought about value, ethics, and politics. To whatever extent the self and its interests are meant to govern moral and political thought, Gauthier's new work on Rousseau raises the possibility that, in at least some cases, the clothes have no Emperor. Because the case in question is *Jean-Jacques Rousseau* (rather than some less interesting creature), there is the further suggestion, implicit in this new work, that a being whose self could *not* play the role selves play in *Morals by Agreement* – imagine, for instance, trying to bring Jean-Jacques' considered preferences into view – might actually be a being we ought to take very seriously indeed.

6. *Les solitaires?*

I have suggested that Gauthier's work on Rousseau raises the specter of a social self lacking the substance required to serve as the starting point for liberal moral theory. But the big question mark that hangs over Gauthier's readings of Rousseau has very little to do with socialized people.

Socialized people are nothing all on their own. Even the socialized man raised to be dependent only on things, on the masterful wisdom of his Tutor, and on his "beloved" Sophie, Émile, has recourse to little beyond Stoic resignation in the end. Moreover, the troublesome *moi individu* is made possible by language, and whether language begins in *aidez-moi* or *aimez-moi* – the two starting points for language discussed in Rousseau's *Essai sur l'origine des langues* – it begins as a cry issued to another, whose response has a profound effect upon the welfare of the speaking being. After we have lost touch with nature, it is unsurprising that we have need of artifice and illusions to lend any sense of depth to the incessant nagging of *moi individu.*

The real problem is independent, solitary natural man, the thing the Tutor attempts to "preserve" through a course of education so thoroughly managed as to render Émile insecure at the prospect of having to raise his own children without the Tutor's assistance. (The work closes with our hero facing the prospect of fatherhood and telling the Tutor, "As long as I live, I shall need you. I need you more than ever now that my functions as a man begin.")[36] The fixed point in both Rousseau's rather anti-liberal social and political theory (anti-liberal in the sense that it begins from the premise that persons must be radically transformed in order to lead a just and orderly social life) and Gauthier's own liberal moral theory is the individual conceived as having no necessary social bond to its fellows. In Rousseau, this figure is *l'homme naturel, primitif et originaire.* In Gauthier, it is sometimes economic man, and sometimes the liberal individual. It is with reference to these beings that we can test real social relations for reasonableness (in Gauthier) or stability (in Rousseau). Suppose that we were to conceive *this* figure as a figment of the theorist's imagination. We have already seen that if this figure craves necessarily scarce goods, like first place in a social hierarchy or another person's affections, the calm regulation of its pursuits offered by morals by agreement will not serve its interests. Gauthier has argued that an attempt to arrange the whole of such a being's early education or public life so that it can retain by artifice the independence it has lost will necessarily fail (in politics because its very linguistic competence works against its ability to see itself as nothing but a part of a larger whole; in intimate, familial life because private virtue is no shield against public viciousness and because the passions that unite a couple have already rendered the integrity of the individual man or woman dependent upon securing love). Suppose, however, that the world of the first part of Rousseau's Second Discourse could *not* have served as a starting point for a theory of social life. Suppose that the real illusion is in the thought that you could start with *l'homme naturel* and arrive at *l'homme moral* by a series of interactions between individuals with no deep natural tie, one to another.

In a way, the failure of natural man to serve as a building block for social life is (inadvertently) suggested by Gauthier's most recent work on Rousseau. Jean-Jacques proclaims himself to be the most natural of men, even as he is busy detailing how his relation to Maman makes him who he is. Gauthier goes to great lengths to argue that in this most natural and uniquely individual of men ("My purpose [in writing these *Confessions*] is to display to my kind a portrait in every way true to nature")[37] there is *no* trace of the independent, solitary natural man, and some hint that "unified" individual selves – other than the "one" made up of Jean-Jacques-plus-Maman – are, in fact, mere disguises: products of imagination rather than expressions of the true lot of socialized people.

In the next section, I will offer a reconstructive reading of the first part of the *Discours sur l'inégalité*, drawing out a line of argument amply supported by the text, but perhaps not intended by its author, suggesting that natural man as independent, solitary, and self-sufficient is the real artifice in Rousseau's social and political thought: that, in spite of himself, he gives us good reason to suppose that the imaginary beings we meet at the beginning of the Second Discourse could not have survived, much less been the ancestors of socialized human beings. In giving this reading, I will be drawing out seeds of an argument that is, as near as I can tell, excellent and compelling and is structurally isomorphic with the curious passage at the beginning of *Contrat social* suggesting that entirely independent persons, atomistic individuals, could never come together and agree to set a common power over themselves: Barring any pre-existing form of public reason, without at least the rudiments of a general will, there could be no political order in human life. In effect, I will suggest that Rousseau (perhaps inadvertently) sets up an argument that makes natural man, like *moi individu*, a figment of a thoroughly social imagination, a fiction made possible only by the intricacy of human thought and language.

7. Paradise

Rousseau begins his discussion of natural man:

Stripping [man], so constituted, of all the supernatural gifts he could have received and of all the artificial faculties he could only have acquired by long progress – considering him, in a word, as he must have come from the hands of nature – I see an animal less strong than some, less agile than others, but all things considered, the most advantageously organized of all. I see him satisfying his hunger under an oak, quenching his thirst at the first stream, finding his bed at the foot of the same tree that furnished his meal; and therewith his needs are satisfied.[38]

The good of natural man lies in securing those things that conduce to his preservation and help him to avoid injury or pain. Lacking instinct, civilized man learns to satisfy his needs through education. How does natural man learn to satisfy his needs? Rousseau continues:

Men, dispersed among the animals, observe and imitate their industry, and thereby develop in themselves the instinct of the beasts; with the advantage that whereas each species has only its own proper instinct, man – perhaps having none that belongs to him – appropriates them all to himself, feeds himself equally well with most of the diverse foods which other animals share, and consequently finds his subsistence more easily than any of them can.[39]

The whole problem of the *Discours sur l'inégalité* is set by the attempt to make sense of human agency as the form of animal agency that is not wholly governed by instinct, and the human condition as a thing that has developed through the activity of human beings. The form that this problem takes for Rousseau is one of finding out what sort of life an isolated, asocial, sentient human animal, whose activities were neither the products of social circumstance nor straightforward functions of instinct and impulse, would lead. Could radically individual human agents invent human life *ex nihilo*?

The acts of any animal are intelligible in light of the good of its kind, and in a state of nature, the only candidates for an animal's good are its own preservation and ease, or the preservation of its species. According to Rousseau, nature equips every kind of animal with "senses in order to revitalize itself and guarantee itself, to a certain point, from all that tends to destroy or upset it."[40] Nature then guides the actions of the animals through their impulses and their sentience. The voice of nature speaks to the animal through impulse.[41] The difference between the human and other kinds of animals is that

nature alone does everything in the operations of a beast, whereas man contributes to his own operations by being a free agent. The former chooses or rejects by instinct and the latter by an act of freedom, so that a beast cannot deviate from the rule that is prescribed to it even when it would be advantageous for it to do so, and a man deviates from it often to his detriment.[42]

That is, the ends of other animals, and the means by which these ends are pursued, are set by nature. Man also feels the promptings of nature, "but he is free to acquiesce or resist."[43] Man's *liberté naturelle* consists in his power to set his own ends, here understood simply as the power to acquiesce in or resist natural impulses. This ability, all by itself, oughtn't to get natural man moving, however.

The whole shape and content of any other kind of animal's will are given by nature. When other animals are hungry, they seek food, and nature gives them not only an impulse to eat but also a partial menu of what is nourishing or edible for their kind, from which they cannot deviate – Rousseau takes it that "a pigeon would die of hunger near a basin filled with the best meats, and a cat upon heaps of fruits or grains" because "the voice of nature" will not tell the cat that it can eat grain, nor the pigeon that meat will nourish it.[44] But while some animals will starve because nature does not prompt them to try to eat different things, humans will have to figure out how to satisfy hunger for themselves. Even if natural man understands that the gnawing feeling is *hunger*, satisfying his hunger will require more than the ability to follow or resist the impulse to eat. He needs to find out what is edible.

Rousseau ascribes *perfectibilité* to natural man in order to take care of part of this problem. *Perfectibilité* helps man in the state of nature to imitate other animals in order to meet the requirements of self-preservation. It allows natural man both to adapt to his present circumstances and to learn.

But *perfectibilité* and *liberté naturelle* all on their own will not guarantee the survival of a species whose practical life is not ruled by instinct. Members of such a species also will require some sense of the kind of things they are, and some capacity to notice what they have in common with creatures of instinct, in order to "appropriate" the aims and know-how of instinctive animals. Man as we know him (but stripped of the trappings of culture and society) would perish quickly if endowed with nothing but *liberté naturelle* and *perfectibilité*. Set down in a paradise where other animals busily feed, rest, fight, and procreate, asocial man, lacking the inner drives of instinct to tell him what to do, knowing neither what manner of living thing he was, nor that he had enough in common with other animals to make imitation the means to his survival, wouldn't survive. This is why man must have some bare sense of himself, some concern for his own well-being, and some capacity to identify with other sentient creatures, in order to learn from them what to pursue or avoid.[45]

Rousseau calls the bare sense of self the *sentiment de son existence actuelle* (the sentiment of one's present existence),[46] and the attitude of concern for one's own preservation *amour de soi-même* (self-love). The capacity to identify with the suffering of others, through which man learns how to avoid suffering, is called *pitié* (pity). And so we find man in the state of nature, sharing sensations, perceptions, and some impulses with other animals, but with a will structured to compensate for lack of instinct. Nature gives man impulses that *liberté* gives him the power to follow or resist. *Perfectibilité* gives him the capacity to find means to those few ends given as impulses. *Pitié*, coupled with the *sentiment de son existence actuelle* and *amour de soi-même*, give man the capacity to recognize himself as a locus of action,

charged with securing his own good or advantage, and a capacity to learn
how to do so by imitating others. Does this take us to mature men and women
capable of looking after themselves?

While the *form* of the human will can be seen in the combination of *liberté
naturelle, perfectibilité, pitié, amour de soi-même*, and the *sentiment de son
existence actuelle*, and while the form is given by man's nature and "resides
among us as much in the species as in the individual,"[47] the *content* of the
will – the specific aims or ends adopted in the service of self-preservation,
ease, and the avoidance of suffering – cannot come from nature.

Natural man's activity begins in "purely animal functions."[48] Like other
animals, he will "perceive and feel," and "to will and not will, to desire and
fear will be the first and almost the only operations of his soul."[49] But "one
can desire or fear things only through the ideas one can have of them or by
the simple impulsion of nature,"[50] and natural man is sorely lacking in ideas:

> His imagination suggests nothing to him; his heart asks nothing of him. His modest
> needs are so easily found at hand, and he is so far from the degree of knowledge
> necessary for desiring to acquire greater knowledge, that he can have neither foresight
> nor curiosity. The spectacle of nature becomes indifferent to him by dint of becoming
> familiar. There is always the same order, there are always the same revolutions; he
> does not have the mind to wonder at the greatest marvels; and one must not seek in
> him the philosophy that man needs in order to know how to observe once what he
> has seen every day.[51]

The natural mind is diffuse, blank, and untroubled. The distinction between
natural ideas and the "ideas" that we find among language-users is so complete that the more one "meditates on this subject, the more the distance from
pure sensations [what natural man shares with other animals] to the simplest
knowledge [what men in simple societies have] increases," so that "it is
impossible to conceive how a man, by his strength alone, without the aid of
communication and without the stimulus of necessity, could have bridged so
great a gap."[52] The gap in question is, of course, the gap between natural and
social man.

By way of an example, Rousseau offers a modest catalogue of human ends,
concentrating on those associated with agriculture, and argues that even if
natural man had been "taught by the gods" to farm, and even if farming
implements "had fallen from heaven," man would have no reason to adopt
the ends of agriculture without the distinctively human institutions of property, that is, "as long as the state of nature is not annihilated."[53] The same
kind of point might be made about God-given gifts of speech. Without the
means to conduct public deliberation, with neither audience nor some common purpose to discuss with his fellows, to what end would the talking man
talk? Would he slow the progress of a pursuer with a discussion of the good
of peace? Would he negotiate or bargain with his fellow men? How *could* he

do these things without an institutional context that would make such acts and topics intelligible?

While Rousseau suggests that natural man might hunt, hunting requires foresight, and skill in the hunt is built through curiosity about the regular movements of one's prey and patient observation of their routines. Because natural man is incapable of observing once what he has seen every day, hunting as we know it is beyond the means of natural man. One might be licensed to conclude, then, that man-the-asocial-and-stupid-free-animal could not produce social life, and so could not produce civilization, and so could not adopt the sorts of ends that humans adopt.

Natural man *could* work up to human civilization if he could invent speech, however – Rousseau asks us to "consider how many ideas we owe to the use of speech; how much grammar trains and facilitates the operations of the mind."[54] If natural man could think like we do, he could adopt ends of the sort that we adopt. He could have desires and fears directed by his ideas of things, in addition to, or in place of, those given by natural impulsion. Perhaps he even could develop more interesting forms of aspiration and industry, and then design institutions to promote and protect his efforts. The indistinctness of the natural mind, given over to nothing but sensations and indeterminate urges and recoilings, could be replaced with human purposes if natural man could have ideas of the sort that language-users can have, and the argument of the first part of the *Discours sur l'inégalité* comes to rest in a discussion about whether or not natural man could invent language.

Rousseau begins by expressing doubt that natural man could have any use for speech in the first place (recall that we are considering whether or not natural man could set himself the task of inventing speech, and recall that the intelligibility of natural ends comes through their relation to man's needs, and hence his good). The humans most likely to have need of verbal expression are the young, who require the assistance of their mothers in order to survive infancy and early childhood. Could children invent conventional language? Rousseau is doubtful: "the child . . . must make the greatest efforts of invention, and . . . the language he uses must be in great part his own work, which multiplies languages as many times as there are individuals to speak them."[55] That is, while a child might work up a system of communication with its mother, the particular sounds and gestures that make up that system will be idiosyncratic, and will pass out of usage as soon as the child and mother part. But Rousseau is willing to pass over this initial difficulty.[56]

He imagines groups of mature natural men, already equipped with an impulse to communicate and minds formed so as to allow for communication – which is to say that he imagines men equipped for grasping convention – and asks next whether or not such creatures could invent conventional languages. How would they talk to one another? What sort of language would we find among them? Imagining the path by which language might develop among them, Rousseau writes:

> they multiplied inflections of the voice, and joined to it gestures which are more expressive by their nature, and whose meaning is less dependent on prior determination. They therefore expressed visible and mobile objects by gestures, and audible ones by imitative sounds.[57]

The difficulty that now arises is insurmountable. Roughly, the problem becomes one of moving from this picture of linguistic activity to one in which human speech and thought have determinate, propositional content:

> Every object received at first a particular name, without regard to genus and species, which these first institutors were incapable of distinguishing; and all individual things appeared to their minds in isolation as they are in the panorama of nature. If one oak was called A another was called B, for the first idea one infers from two things is that they are not the same; and often much time is needed to observe what they have in common. So that the more limited the knowledge, the more extensive the dictionary. The obstacle of all this nomenclature could not easily be removed, for in order to organize beings under common and generic denominations, it was necessary to know their properties and differences. Observations and definitions were necessary – that is to say, much more natural history and metaphysics than the men of those times could have had.[58]

For men, the task of identifying the relevant similarities and differences among things will have to be taken on explicitly. This is, again, because they lack the instinctive practical orientation that other animals have – nature does not sort itself into the edible and inedible, the safe and the dangerous, and so on, for natural men. But because natural men also lack natural language, they are not equipped to make the discriminations in thought and perception required to observe the similarities and differences that they *must* notice if they are to invent language: "even should we understand how the sounds of the voice were taken for conventional interpreters of our ideas, it would still remain to be seen what could have been the specific interpreters of this convention for ideas that, having no perceptible object, could be indicated neither by gesture nor by voice."[59] Rousseau explains the point this way:

> general ideas can come into the mind only with the aid of words, and the understanding grasps them only through propositions. . . . Every general idea is purely intellectual; if imagination is in the least involved, the idea immediately becomes particular. Try to draw for yourself the image of a tree in general, you will never succeed in doing it; despite yourself it must be seen small or large, sparse or leafy, light or dark; and if it were up to you to see in it only what is found in every tree, this image would no longer resemble a tree. . . . It is therefore necessary to state propositions, hence to speak, in order to have general ideas; for as soon as the imagination stops, the mind goes no further without discourse. If, then, the first inventors could give names only

to the ideas they already had, it follows that the first substantives could never have been anything but proper nouns.[60]

Human languages have propositional content and structure. Propositions express general ideas. General ideas can be had only by a thinker who already speaks a developed language. *Ex hypothesi*, natural man does not already speak a developed language. Hence, natural man does not have general ideas.

In order to develop general ideas or human language, natural man must be able to construct propositions from the content of his thought. The content of his thought does not have propositional structure. He thinks in "proper nouns." Propositions cannot be built up from proper nouns. Hence, natural man could not develop general ideas, and, by extension, could not invent language. And here Rousseau sees all hope of understanding human life as the invention of radically individual human agents dashed.

He expresses the impossibility of trying to take the project any further by way of riddles. He writes, "if men needed speech in order to learn to think, they had even greater need of knowing how to think in order to discover the art of speech."[61] The lone natural mind has nothing in it out of which to conjure language.

Next, he turns his attention to groups. Could the members of a group of animals, capable of indicating objects to one another through gesture and vocal imitation, invent speech? To do so, they would need to move from gesture and imitative sounds to a system of vocal signs. Rousseau points out that while substituting vocal signs for gestures to indicate visible and mobile objects would bring natural men much closer to language, the substitution of audible signs for gestures "cannot be made except by common consent," and it is difficult to conceive how this might occur, "since that unanimous agreement must have had a motive, and since speech seems to have been highly necessary in order to establish the use of speech."[62]

Finally, and most strongly, after having allowed men to babble and point, but having failed to find them capable of building propositions:

For myself, frightened by the multiplying difficulties, and convinced of the almost demonstrated impossibility that languages could have arisen and been established by purely human means, I leave to whomever would undertake it the discussion of the following difficult problem: Which was most necessary, previously formed society for the institution of languages; or previously invented languages for the establishment of society?[63]

Thought and language can come only from inside an already established society. From the point of view of the state of nature, conceived as populated by pre-social men and women who are somehow to try to work up to social life, the riddles are chicken-and-egg problems: The origin of any one of the three – language, general ideas, conventional social life – presupposes the other two. Natural men need to be able to think and communicate general ideas in order to invent institutions and society. Without society, however, they not only have no use for speech but also lack the modes of conventional interaction in which it might become possible for their thought and speech to develop to the point where they could participate in the establishment of new institutions.

New institutions develop from previously established modes of social interaction. Left to their own devices, natural men are incapable of joining together to participate in such modes of life because they are incapable of taking it into their heads to do so. In short, *all on his own, natural man never can leave the state of nature.* (The second part of the Second Discourse, tellingly, begins with a complex assertion of ownership, of property right, and then backpedals to show how the institution of private property developed from within simple societies; it is a vastly different place from which to start the story of humankind's fall from grace than the asocial point attempted in the first part.) All that remains to be seen is how great a distance this creates between human life as we know it and the kind of life open to natural man.

What acts are open to natural man without general ideas? I think, in fact, very few. Could natural impulses alone lead natural man into action? It's doubtful. Recall that his *liberté* consists in the ability to *resist* such impulses, often to his "detriment." One imagines the freest of natural men stubbornly starving in the shade of his oak tree, resisting impulse until death claims him. But suppose that he gives in to the gnawing feeling, and ask whether or not he could learn how to satisfy his hunger without the aid of general ideas. What would natural man imitate? Would he learn from the birds that a *kind* of berry was edible? Clearly not, since even if he thinks that he is like the birds (itself something of a stretch for an animal who calls one oak A, another B), and even if he correctly infers that the birds are also hungry and are *eating* the berries (even less likely), he lacks the capacity to discern the *kind* of a berry or its source. Would he learn that berries in a particular cluster in a particular bramble patch where a particular bird has lighted to eat are edible? Here, provided that he can get past the initial difficulty of identifying the bird as another hungry creature and as employing means that he too might employ to avoid the pain of hunger, his chance is greater. But once he has shooed away the bird, and once he has eaten all of the fruit in that particular patch, he will again be back where he started. What natural man will have to stumble upon in order to sustain himself is not food, but animals-in-the-act-of-eating. And in order to make use of this resource, he needs to see them as relevantly like himself. Here too, it seems that natural man will need general ideas. The aspects of his will that must be engaged in order to move him to action are *pitié, amour de soi-même*, and the *sentiment de son existence actuelle.*

Already in the *Discours sur l'inégalité*, *amour de soi-même* seems to have a kind of content that it could have only if natural man had general ideas – Rousseau writes that *amour de soi-même* consists in "each particular man regarding himself as the sole spectator to observe him, as the sole being in the universe to take an interest in him, and as the sole judge of his own merit," suggesting that *amour de soi-même* is already subject to general standards of judgment and comparison and involves a sense of the enduring-ness of the agent (the object of concern is *soi-même*).[64] Natural man's idea that he is one being enduring through time, responsible for his own care, and not subject to the judgments of others is a general idea – an idea not to be found among the contents of the natural mind (try to point to your responsibility for your own preservation; try to imitate its sound with your voice).

Of course, the *sentiment de son existence actuelle* does not appear to have propositional content of the sort found in *amour de soi-même*. But elsewhere in Rousseau's corpus, it seems that the *sentiment de son existence actuelle* cannot guide action for the sake of self-preservation. For example, in various passages from *Les rêveries du promeneur solitaire*, Rousseau presents himself as having fallen into states of mind that are bare of propositional content, rich in "ideas of sense." In these passages, he intimates that the *sentiment de son existence actuelle* is simply consciousness. But the description of conscious-ness is framed to show its distance from action in the service of self-preservation (deliberately? inadvertently? it is hard to say). In the *Deuxième promenade*, for instance, Rousseau recounts an accident in which he was bowled over by a large dog and fell, injuring his head. He was unconscious for quite some time. Recalling the experience of reviving, he writes:

This first sensation was a delicious moment. I still had no feeling of myself except as being 'over there'. I was born into life at that instant, and it seemed to me that I filled all the objects I perceived with my frail existence. Entirely absorbed in the present moment, I remembered nothing; I had no distinct notion of my person nor the least idea of what had happened to me; I knew neither who I was nor where I was; I felt neither injury, fear, nor worry. I watched my blood flow as I would have watched a brook flow, without even suspecting that this blood belonged to me in any way.[65]

While the description he gives of his state of mind is the closest to be found in his writings of a bare *sentiment de son existence actuelle*, one gathers that Rousseau might have died of shock, loss of blood, and exposure had no one happened along to come to his aid. Significantly, he links his state of mind to that of a helpless newborn. It is a state of mind with so little awareness of any *proprius* that he cannot even recognize his blood as his own. Dazed and hurt, he was helped home and cared for by passers-by. Consciousness does not conduce to natural man's survival without thoughts of the kind social men have.[66]

Rousseau makes the case for *pitié* even more forcefully. In the *Essai sur l'origine des langues*, he writes:

We develop social feeling only as we become enlightened. Although pity is native to the human heart, it would remain eternally quiescent unless it were activated by imagination. How are we moved to pity? By getting outside of ourselves and identifying with a being who suffers. We suffer only as much as we believe him to suffer. . . . It is clear that such transport requires a great deal of acquired knowledge. How am I to imagine ills of which I have no idea? How would I suffer in seeing another suffer, if I do not know how he is suffering, if I am ignorant of what he and I have in common. He who has never been reflective is incapable of being merciful or just or pitying. . . . He who imagines nothing is aware only of himself; he is isolated in the midst of mankind.

Reflection is born of the comparison of ideas, and it is the plurality of ideas that leads to their comparison. One who is aware of only a single object has no basis for comparison. And those whose experience remains confined to the narrow range of their childhood are also incapable of such comparisons. Long familiarity deprives them of the attention requisite for such examination.[67]

Natural man needs imaginatively to identify with other animals in order to perfect himself under their tutelage. *Pitié*, which is a natural sentiment, nevertheless cannot come to man's aid without general ideas. For man, the activation of *pitié* requires an exercise of imagination based in general ideas about commonality and difference. Again, in this passage, he makes reference to "childhood" (*enfance*) and suggests that "familiarity" deprives the man whose development has been retarded of the ability to attend to and observe what goes on around him, in a manner that cannot help but call to mind his suggestion that "the spectacle of nature becomes indifferent to [natural man] by dint of becoming familiar."

Man may not need general ideas in order to have indistinct perceptions, urges, sensations, and the like, but he does need them in order consciously to *aim* or *act*. The use of imagination required for action is reflective, and the power of reflection does not belong to natural man because he has no general ideas. Something of feeling and experience can be had without culture and society. Nothing of human action and aims can. If natural man's will has the form that ours does, then it will operate via general ideas, and natural man, deprived of these because he has neither language nor a social life in which to acquire and use it, will perish. If not, then natural man is like other animals, and his practical life is governed by nature and instinct. Natural man, insofar as he is like us, is at the stage of infancy, and has no more hope of survival than would an infant. If his chances are greater, it is because he more closely resembles the pigeon or the cat than he does the mature human being.

8. By Way of Conclusion

What happens to Gauthier's Rousseau if we extract from his subject the
suggestion that natural man either is not a man in any interesting sense, but
rather a creature of instinct like the cat or the pigeon, or else is not the lone,
self-sufficient creature familiar from the standard reading of the Second Discourse? If either of these is the case, it ought to come as no surprise that
Gauthier finds no trace of the independent, self-sufficient solitary in the
autobiographical and fictional work. *Moi individu* is, through and through, a
social being. This all by itself does not remove concern that social men find
themselves hopelessly at odds with one another, of course. But it does cast
doubt on the possibility of finding an extra-social standpoint from which to
build moral theory and, more generally, on the conviction that methodological
individualism is the best approach to work on politics and morals. The
troublesome specter of economic man's barely containable self-interested
material pursuits, the hope for an orderly liberal society, the dependence and
conflicts that plague the world of status-seekers and lovers, and the dream of
a wholly solitary life, independent and free, become various touchstones for
moral, social, and political thought about a kind of animal that is in its own
way rational *because* it is also social, political, and linguistically competent.
Not a single problem is *solved* by this reading of Gauthier and Rousseau, but
it does undercut some of the force of the suggestion that maximizing reason
is the eternal ground of the unified self. In this new Rousseau, unified selves
emerge in a social field, and are never what they are apart from that field,
even if what they are is reluctant solitaries like the mature Jean-Jacques.

Notes

1. "The Social Contract as Ideology," *Philosophy and Public Affairs*, 6(Winter
   1977); reprinted in *Moral Dealing* (Ithaca, NY: Cornell University Press, 1990),
   p. 330.
2. "The Social Contract as Ideology," pp. 326–7.
3. "The Social Contract as Ideology," p. 352.
4. "The Social Contract as Ideology," p. 354.
5. *Morals by Agreement* (Oxford University Press, 1986), pp. 316–17.
6. "Introduction," *Moral Dealing*, pp. 6–7.
7. "Rational Constraint: Some Last Words," in *Contractarianism and Rational
   Choice*, ed. Peter Vallentyne (Cambridge University Press, 1991), p. 328.
8. Although Gauthier at one point suggests that the difference between economic
   man and us is that we value participation in social life for its own sake rather
   than as a means to getting other things that we happen to want (*Morals by
   Agreement*, pp. 325–9). In effect, this way of making out the difference between
   us and him changes the payoff structure of interaction for us in favor of morality,
   as Gauthier realizes. Because he does not want to lapse into suggesting that our
   reason to be moral is that we want to be with one another anyway and morality

is the sound way of being together, he is careful to insist that morals by agreement remain the only morals economic man could accept, thereby providing a kind of heuristic device for assessing the justice of institutions and social practices even for those of us who crave the company of our fellows.

9. Some things that one might want require coordination with one's fellows. Provided that these can be had in such a way that economic man will need no real constraint on his behavior in order to get them (that is, provided they can be had contractually in circumstances where no economically rational party has to perform his part of the bargain first without any way of compelling the other parties' compliance with the terms of the agreement), economic man can pursue these goods. In a Hobbist world, people can form temporary alliances when their interests coincide and their individual powers are insufficient to bring about the desired outcome, and they can engage in crude barter. What is irrational is entering into a bargain where one Hobbist does what his fellow wants him to do, and then waits for his fellow to keep the other side of the bargain. Expecting others to do their part once they have already got what they are after from you and before there is any external force capable of hurting them if they fail to stick to the agreement is irrational in Hobbes's state of nature.

10. See "The Incompleat Egoist," in *The Tanner Lectures on Human Values*, vol. 5, ed. Sterling M. McMurrin (Salt Lake City: University of Utah Press, 1984), pp. 67–119; reprinted in *Moral Dealing*, pp. 234–73.

11. Karl Marx's account of the "state of nature" in Eurocentric ideology can be found in Part 8 of Volume 1 of *Capital*, "So-Called Primitive Accumulation." This part contains the seeds of an account of the colonial relations of production in Africa, Asia, and the Americas that pumped enough wealth into Europe to make possible the transition from feudalism to capitalism. For Marxist accounts of the ongoing importance of neo-colonial relations of production to capitalism and their significance for the production of both the individual's sense of self and economic man's sense of self, see, e.g., Gayatri Chakravorty Spivak, "Scattered Speculations on the Question of Value," in *In Other Worlds* (London: Routledge, 1987), pp. 154–75, and "Can the Subaltern Speak?" in *Marxism and the Interpretation of Culture*, ed. Cary Nelson and Lawrence Grossberg (Chicago: University of Illinois Press, 1988), pp. 271–313. For an account of these matters that radically revises Marx by writing colonial and neo-colonial relations of production into the heart of capitalism [such that the "great class divide" that marks capitalism is not the division between wage-labor and capital – both sides of which share the self-conception of interest to Gauthier – but rather the division between (1) wage-labor, capital, and others positioned to benefit from ongoing colonial, neo-colonial, and imperialist economic plunder on the one side and (2) the masses of the world's population on the other], see Omali Yeshitela, *The Road to Socialism Is Painted Black* (Oakland, CA: Burning Spear Publications, 1989).

12. Originally published in *Revue de l'Université d'Ottawa*, 49:329–56, 1979; reprinted in *Moral Dealing*, pp. 77–109.

13. See, e.g., *Grundrisse*, trans. Martin Nicolaus (London: Penguin Books, 1973), pp. 83–5.

14. The exception is heterosexual intercourse, but Rousseauian natural people manage to get this from one another without coercion and without the strings of duty attached.

Rousseau's views on the moral and political dimensions of heterosexual relations are complicated. I am inclined to side with Joel Schwartz's observation that

Rousseau's ambivalence toward masturbation owes much to his sense that the desire for sexual intercourse is one of the more reliable roots of sociability among adult human beings and requires that they conceive themselves as performing parts of a whole act rather than acting independently in ways that sum to sex. See Schwartz, *The Sexual Politics of Jean-Jacques Rousseau* (University of Chicago Press, 1985), esp. pp. 10–40, 105–7. For a deconstructive reading of Rousseau's attitudes toward masturbation and writing (the two activities that he claimed, variously, made trouble in his intimacy with Thérèse after they had married), see Jacques Derrida, *Of Grammatology*, trans. Gayatri Chakravorty Spivak (Baltimore, MD: Johns Hopkins University Press, 1976), pp. 141–64.

15. *Amour-propre*, love of [one's] own, is generally translated as *vanity*. *Vanity* is not a bad translation once the social world is such that one's material and spiritual existence is shaped by one's success at cultivating the good opinion of others by appearing to have valued qualities. The viciousness of Rousseauian social life is hard to escape to whatever extent one's means of subsistence depend upon one's reputation, that is, to whatever extent one finds oneself in the position Jean-Jacques Rousseau finds himself in again and again. The *Confessions* is, among other things, one long story about the author's misguided efforts to secure his means of subsistence through securing the good opinion of others. In the absence of any real property, the *proprius* on which *amour-propre* depends comes to center on what one can extract from one's fellows through reputation and sentimental attachment. This sows the seeds of the world in which the natural translation of *amour-propre* is, indeed, *vanity*. Nicholas Dent is one of the more stringent critics of the use of *vanity* as a translation of *amour-propre*. See, e.g., N. J. H. Dent, *A Rousseau Dictionary* (Oxford: Blackwell, 1992), pp. 33–6, where he quotes Kant's allusion to Rousseau in *Religion Within the Limits of Reason Alone* in support of an alternative reading of the term as *self-love*.

16. *Discourse on the Origin and Foundations of Inequality*, in *The First and Second Discourses*, ed. Roger D. and Judith R. Masters (New York: St. Martin's Press, 1964), pp. 180–1.

17. "The Politics of Redemption," in *Moral Dealing*, p. 88. Notice that even in this early piece, Gauthier's Rousseau rather undoes the sense that the self is a solid basis for moral theory. The selves Gauthier finds at the conclusion of the Second Discourse are practically nonexistent.

18. "The Politics of Redemption," in *Moral Dealing*, pp. 90–1.

19. *On the Social Contract*, trans. Judith Masters (New York: St. Martin's Press, 1978), Bk. II, ch. vii, p. 68.

20. The whole of which Émile is a part is not a body politic, but a marriage.

21. *Émile*, trans. Allan Bloom (New York: Basic Books, 1979), Bk. II, p. 85.

22. "The Politics of Redemption," in *Moral Dealing*, p. 108. Gauthier has himself since flirted with related "solutions" to the malaise of contemporary life in essays about virtue and the importance of cultivating a sense of justice. The attempt appears to be to deposit in character a trait that will help the rational individual keep his bargain with his fellows to constrain himself. This attempt is like Rousseau's in just this sense: By altering the character of the individual, it effectively alters its preferences sufficiently to mitigate the destructive force of maximizing behavior. One senses in this work a continuing fear over economic man's mode of being.

23. "The Politics of Redemption," in *Moral Dealing*, p. 108.

24. Ibid.

25. This may, in fact, be part of the reason why Rousseau insists that the Legislator cannot himself be an ordinary citizen. The discussion of the role of the Legislator involves various obscure allusions to language and thought, and, most especially, to the impossibility of translating the thought of the Legislator into the language of the people. See *Du contrat social*, Bk. II, ch. vii. I will take up this matter in some detail later.
26. "The Politics of Redemption," in *Moral Dealing*, pp. 108–9.
27. *The Confessions*, trans. J. M. Cohen (London: Penguin Books, 1953), Bk. VI, p. 247; translation slightly modified.
28. *The Confessions*, Bk. VI, p. 249.
29. "Making Jean-Jacques," in *Jean-Jacques Rousseau and the Sources of the Self*, ed. Timothy O'Hagan (Andershot, England: Avebury, 1997), p. 11.
30. *The Confessions*, Bk. IX, p. 386. See also, e.g., *Rousseau, Judge of Jean-Jacques*, trans. Judith Bush, Christopher Kelly, and Roger Masters (Hanover, NH: University Press of New England, 1990), pp. 124–5.
31. Jean-Jacques' next great affection arose after he had finally married his long-term mistress, Thérèse. The object of this passion was Mme d'Houdetot, whose lover, M. Saint-Lambert, was a dear friend of Jean-Jacques. See *The Confessions*, Bk. IX–X.
32. Ibid.
33. Gauthier makes this point in a series of three lectures entitled "Jean-Jacques's Last Promenade," pointing out that although Rousseau regained the right to call himself *Citoyen de Genève* in 1754, he chose not to live in Geneva and renounced Genevan citizenship in 1763. I am deeply grateful to Gauthier for letting me study the text of these lectures in manuscript.
34. Gauthier devotes the second of the lectures "Jean-Jacques's Last Promenade" to this topic. The lecture concerns the role of disguises, *personae*, in Rousseau's writings and takes as its starting point Rousseau's famous motto *Vitam impendere vero.*
35. "Making Jean-Jacques," p. 14.
36. *Émile*, Bk. V, p. 480.
37. *The Confessions*, Bk. I, p. 18.
38. *Discourse on the Origin and Foundations of Inequality*, p. 105.
39. *Discourse on the Origin and Foundations of Inequality*, pp. 105–6.
40. *Discourse on the Origin and Foundations of Inequality*, p. 113.
41. In Rousseau, the voice of nature is always prescriptive.
42. *Discourse on the Origin and Foundations of Inequality*, p. 113.
43. *Discourse on the Origin and Foundations of Inequality*, p. 114.
44. *Discourse on the Origin and Foundations of Inequality*, pp. 113–14.
45. The textual evidence for this point comes primarily from Rousseau's order of exposition. Rousseau introduces *liberté naturelle* and *perfectibilité*, then tries to fill the mind of natural man with knowledge (by getting him to invent language) in order to give him something to go on in exercising his *liberté* and perfecting himself. The attempt fails, and the three sentiments are introduced. I take it that these take the place of knowledge in the mind of natural man. I admit, however, that it is always a bit risky to rely on order of exposition in reading Rousseau.

I do not think that Rousseau believed that even the addition of the natural sentiments would give us a natural man equipped to survive in the state of nature, which is why my discussion of the work deviates from Rousseau's in order of exposition. The failure of the attempt to construct functioning human agents outside of society is foreshadowed by Rousseau's treatment of men in less tech-nologically advanced societies as "natural" men, and of other primates that appear to have social customs as proto-men.

The case of other primates is especially revealing. After going to great pains to point out that natural men can have no conception of death, in footnote 10 Rousseau considers a group of primates as candidate proto-men because, among other things, they bury their dead (which is as much as to say, because they have something that natural men lack) (*Discourse on the Origin and Foundations of Inequality*, fn. *j*, p. 205). For a nice summary of the primate debates that give the context for Rousseau's remarks, see Richard Noble's *Language, Subjectivity, and Freedom in Rousseau's Moral Philosophy* (New York: Harper, 1991), pp. 13–45.

46. *Discourse on the Origin and Foundations of Inequality*, p. 117.
47. *Discourse on the Origin and Foundations of Inequality*, p. 114.
48. *Discourse on the Origin and Foundations of Inequality*, p. 115.
49. Ibid.
50. *Discourse on the Origin and Foundations of Inequality*, p. 116.
51. *Discourse on the Origin and Foundations of Inequality*, p. 117.
52. *Discourse on the Origin and Foundations of Inequality*, pp. 117–18.
53. *Discourse on the Origin and Foundations of Inequality*, pp. 118–19.
54. *Discourse on the Origin and Foundations of Inequality*, p. 119.
55. *Discourse on the Origin and Foundations of Inequality*, p. 121.
56. Rousseau points out and passes over many difficulties, any one of which looks nearly insurmountable, en route to the most devastating objection.
57. *Discourse on the Origin and Foundations of Inequality*, pp. 122–3.
58. *Discourse on the Origin and Foundations of Inequality*, pp. 123–4.
59. *Discourse on the Origin and Foundations of Inequality*, p. 122.
60. *Discourse on the Origin and Foundations of Inequality*, pp. 123–5.
61. *Discourse on the Origin and Foundations of Inequality*, pp. 121–2.
62. *Discourse on the Origin and Foundations of Inequality*, p. 123.
63. *Discourse on the Origin and Foundations of Inequality*, p. 126.
64. *Discourse on the Origin and Foundations of Inequality*, fn. 15, p. 222.
65. *The Reveries of the Solitary Walker*, trans. Charles E. Butterworth (New York: Harper, 1979), p. 16.
66. In particular, thoughts about which things *belong* to him, and are properly his concern. The metaphoric and literal uses of terms associated with property form an especially interesting subtext in Rousseau. Among other things, they suggest that an individual's conception of his own good is framed by his participation in the institutions of his society.
67. *Essay on the Origins of Languages*, in *On the Origin of Language*, trans. John Moran and Alexander Gode (University of Chicago Press, 1966), p. 32.